AQUINAS ON ISRAEL AND THE CHURCH

"Matthew Tapie carefully analyzes the terminology of supersessionism and develops a working definition that enables us to discern the tensions in the writings of Thomas and to understand the rival assessments of his modern interpreters. Guided by his insightful commentary, we come to see a Thomas who is both a son of his own age and a rich resource for those of our own times seeking a Christian theology of Judaism that is faithful to the teaching of *Nostra Aetate*."

—**Mark S. Kinzer**
President emeritus, Messianic Jewish Theological Institute, Ann Arbor, MI

"Christians today often repudiate supersessionism, but they do not always carefully examine just what that is supposed to mean. We are in Tapie's debt for remedying this situation with special reference to the theology of Thomas Aquinas. Tapie's rich, thorough, and multi-dimensional picture of Aquinas's views on Jewish observance of the ceremonial law after Christ is destined to become a landmark."

—**R. Kendall Soulen**
Professor of Systematic Theology, Wesley Theological Seminary, Washington, DC

"Tapie has provided a definitive study on Aquinas's complex and at times contradictory reading of Paul as supersessionist or not. In the process, Tapie offers the clearest teaching I have seen on the meaning of supersessionism in modern scholarship, from Isaac to Wyschogrod, Nostra Aetate, Levering, Soulen, and much more. Without covering over ambiguities (in) Romans, Galatians, Ephesians, and Hebrews, he concludes with a sober yet hopeful account of the trajectory of Thomas's thinking—an account that should contribute significantly to contemporary discussions of Judaism and the church."

—**Peter Ochs**
Edgar M. Bronfman Professor of Modern Judaic Studies, University of Virginia, Charlottesville, VA

"The drafters of Nostra Aetate, the 1965 Vatican II document that revolutionized Catholic teaching on the Jews, felt they had to go all the way back to Scripture to find resources for rethinking theological anti-Judaism, so soundly rooted did it seem in the church's tradition. Tapie shows that they missed more proximate sources in St. Thomas Aquinas, among the most revered authorities in Catholicism. The perspectives Tapie has opened are a landmark contribution to the difficult work of reconciliation between Christians and Jews."

—**John Connelly**
Professor, University of California at Berkeley, Berkeley, CA

Aquinas on Israel and the Church

*The Question of Supersessionism in
the Theology of Thomas Aquinas*

Matthew A. Tapie

Foreword by
Pim Valkenberg

PICKWICK *Publications* · Eugene, Oregon

AQUINAS ON ISRAEL AND THE CHURCH
The Question of Supersessionism in the Theology of Thomas Aquinas

Copyright © 2014 Matthew Anthony Tapie. All rights reserved. Except for brief quotations in critical publications or reviews, no part of this book may be reproduced in any manner without prior written permission from the publisher. Write: Permissions. Wipf and Stock Publishers, 199 W. 8th Ave., Suite 3, Eugene, OR 97401.

Pickwick Publications
An Imprint of Wipf and Stock Publishers
199 W. 8th Ave., Suite 3
Eugene, OR 97401

www.wipfandstock.com

ISBN 13: 978-1-62564-602-6

Cataloguing-in-Publication Data

Tapie, Matthew Anthony.

    Aquinas on Israel and the Church : the question of supersessionism in the theology of Thomas Aquinas / Matthew Anthony Tapie, with a foreword by Pim Valkenberg.

    xiv + 198 p. ; 23 cm. Includes bibliographical references.

    ISBN 13: 978-1-62564-602-6

    1. Thomas, Aquinas, Saint, 1225?–1274. 2. Christianity and other religions—Judaism. 3. Israel (Christian theology). I. Valkenberg, Pim, 1954–. II. Title.

B765.T54 T174 2014

Manufactured in the U.S.A.   10/20/2014

To Carolyn and Diana

Then when [the Apostle Paul] says, "Do we then destroy the law?" he excludes an objection. For someone might claim that he is overthrowing the . . . law; therefore, he asks: "Do we then destroy the law through faith?" inasmuch as we say that men are justified without the works of the law? He answers: "God forbid!" in keeping with Matthew, "Not an iota, not a dot, will pass from the law" (Matt. 5:18). Rather, he adds: "we uphold the law," i.e., by faith we complete and fulfill the Law, as Matthew says, "I have come not to abolish the law but to fulfill it" (Matt. 5:17). This is true as regards the ceremonial precepts because, being figures, they were upheld and fulfilled by the fact that the truth signified by them is shown forth in the faith of Christ.

Thomas Aquinas, *Commentary on Romans* 3.4.321

What Paul sees happening in Christ and in the Christian Church, like what Jesus had said in Matthew, is the fulfillment and not the abolition of the meaning of Torah as covenant of grace. "Fulfillment" is a permanently open border between what went before and what comes next.

John Howard Yoder, *The Jewish-Christian Schism Revisited*

Contents

Foreword by Pim Valkenberg | ix
Acknowledgments | xiii

   Introduction | 1
1 The Language of Supersessionism | 9
2 Aquinas and the Question of Supersessionism | 25
3 Israel and the Church in Aquinas's Pauline Commentaries | 48
4 The Ceremonial Law as a Shadow of the Night (Hebrews) | 60
5 The Ceremonial Law as Present Spiritual Benefit for Jews (Romans) | 85
6 The Ceremonial Law as Fulfilled, Dead, and Deadly (Galatians) | 109
7 The Replacement of Israel as *Societas Sanctorum* (Ephesians) | 136
8 Rival Versions of Christ's Fulfillment of the Law: The Tension in Aquinas's Thought between Galatians 5:2 and Romans 3:1–2 | 156
9 Aquinas as Resource for Jewish-Christian Relations | 183

Bibliography | 189

Foreword

Matthew Tapie's wonderful study of Thomas Aquinas's theological approach to the significance of the Jewish religion for Christians comes as a timely reminder of both the ambiguities and the possibilities of the contribution of this Master of the Sacred Page in an era of interfaith awareness.

Now that the declaration on the relation between the Catholic Church and the other religions of humankind is approaching its fiftieth anniversary, we become more and more aware of what has been accomplished by this document of the Second Vatican Council promulgated in 1965, but we are able to see the unsolved challenges more clearly as well. The accomplishment of the document is phrased perfectly by Tapie when he remarks that his students fail to see anything remarkable in what the document says about the Jewish people. Many things that could not be said or written by Christians without severe consequences from the side of the National Socialist regime in Europe less than a century ago have now almost become platitudes. Of course Jesus was a Jew. Of course the Jews are still dear to God. In that sense, the dialogue between Jews and Christians has profited from the awareness that the atrocity of the *shoah* was made possible by centuries of Christian anti-Judaism (or, as some would prefer, anti-Semitism). Yet, apart from the fact that it took European theologians in continental Europe more than a few decennia to develop such an awareness, and that it is still a minority position in many Christian civilizations, it would be naïve to say that we are living in an era in which the dialogue between Jews and Christians has succeeded. Historians or sociologists may use categories such as "success" or even "effectiveness" to measure certain processes of interfaith communication, but theologians know that they need to talk about historical processes with an amount of eschatological reserve. While we may be thankful that theologians from the German speaking countries and from the United States have charted new territories in the landscape of

Foreword

Jewish-Christian encounters, much work still needs to be done. Following Tapie's analysis I want to single out two challenges.

The first challenge can be phrased as the relation between biblical and systematic theology. One of the great merits of Tapie's book is that he has been able to read Aquinas's systematic theology on the relation between Israel and the Church in coherence with his biblical commentaries. As he rightly argues, Aquinas has too long been read and interpreted exclusively as a systematic theologian—if he was read as a theologian at all. One of the consequences of this approach was that scholars only looked at the synthesis in Aquinas's thinking without giving enough attention to the theses and the antithesis that nourished this synthesis. If it is true that the literary genre of the *quaestio* that allows us to retrace these divergent trajectories has its origin in the scholarly reading of Scripture, as I have argued elsewhere, the consequence is that one cannot appreciate the synthetic aspects of Aquinas as a systematic theologian without paying sufficient attention to his biblical commentaries as the roots that nourished his systematic works. As Tapie confirms in his book, this approach to Aquinas as a biblical theologian is quite new and is itself a fruit of ecumenical relationships. Yet Tapie's own work shows how such an approach can be made fruitful again in interreligious conversations, starting with Jules Isaac and Michael Wyschogrod, and continuing in contemporary movements such as Scriptural Reasoning. At the same time, Tapie makes meticulously clear how appreciating Aquinas as a biblical theologian may be more fruitful in interreligious conversations: Aquinas does not have one simple supersessionist or non-supersessionist answer, but he tries to do justice to the tension created by rival narratives, such as the tension between Galatians 5:2 and Romans 3:1–2 described in chapter 8. The tension between the narratives is partly dissolved in what one may call Aquinas's "dominant" perspective, viz. that the Jewish religious ceremonies have become superfluous and even deadly after the death of Christ. Yet, at the same time, there are traces of a rival narrative, an "unofficial teaching" (Bruce Marshall) in Aquinas that argues in favor of a certain fruitfulness of these Jewish rites even for the Church. Tapie has unearthed this hidden tension in Aquinas as a heritage not only of a conflict between Augustine and Jerome, but also between Paul in his letter to the Galatians and the same Paul in his letter to the Romans. So the "perspectivist" nature of Paul's letters, implying that he emphasizes different aspects as the situation in which he writes requires, allows Aquinas to leave some of the tension intact as well, and allows us in our different

Foreword

era with different concerns to unearth what remained hidden in Aquinas's copious treasures.

Let me make clear what I mean by recurring to a famous example. In his recent work, *From Enemy to Brother*, John Connelly has shown how Karl Thieme and John Oesterreicher have paved the way towards the statements about the lasting significance of God's covenant with the Jewish people by their careful reading of Paul's letter to the Romans. In this book Tapie shows that Aquinas has done something similar in that his systematic theological works preserved the viewpoint of Paul's letter to the Romans together with the dominant voice of the Pauline tradition in Galatians and Hebrews. Now that such a viewpoint has become dominant again thanks to Thieme and Oesterreicher and *Nostra Aetate*—but not without the guidance of Jules Isaac and others—it is easier for us to re-discover it in Aquinas as Tapie has done. Yet my point here is that this breakthrough in Jewish-Christian relations has been made possible by careful attention to the Scriptures as sources of so much that we have in common in the two religious traditions. Even though this might be easier between Christians and Jews—the lack of a common religious tradition as source of authority is one of the arguments used by Aquinas to classify Islam as a kind of paganism—it might work in other forms of comparative readings as well. For example, I am convinced that careful attention to what Karl Barth has to say about the righteousness of those "outside the Church" in his commentary on chapters 9–11 of the letter to the Romans might help Christians to start understanding the Qur'anic critique of the claims to salvation brought forward by Jews and Christians. But that is material for another book.

The second challenge for future encounters between Jews and Christians can only be touched upon here, since even though it originates in Paul's analysis of the relation between Jews and gentiles in his letter to the Romans, the ramifications of this challenge seem rather dazzling to me. What is the theological consequence of the claim that God does not revoke God's covenant with the Jews, even though God enters into a new covenant with the followers of his only-begotten Son? When compared with some of his scholastic colleagues—John Duns Scotus comes to mind—Aquinas seems to be remarkably reluctant to leave the historical ground of the biblical tradition. Of course, God is free to act as God wants, but this is not an unlimited freedom because once God acts in a certain way, this makes a difference that cannot be left undone. This leads Aquinas to his famous answer to the question as to whether God would have become incarnate

Foreword

if Adam had not sinned: we could speculate about what God could have done, but the Bible gives us a certain limit for our speculations. This was in fact the point that Pope Benedict XVI wanted to make in his infamous address at Regensburg in September 2006: God can be trusted to remain true to God's initiatives in history, and therefore faith and reason cannot be in disharmony. I have always tried to explain to my students—following insights from Christian Duquoc—that the Christian faith in God as a Trinitarian God can only be explained as a combination between continuity and discontinuity. As Christians we believe that God remains true to the covenant with the people of Israel, but at the same time we believe that God took a radical new initiative, and therefore we talk about "New Testament." In the theological reflection on the dialogue between religions, this combination of continuity and discontinuity means that the two extremes of a narrow exclusivism and an unmediated pluralism cannot be true, since it would require a God who is either entirely bound or limitlessly free. As far as I can see, the great religious traditions of humankind try to steer a middle course between these extremes in their reflections on the relations between themselves and other religions. Because of its specific recognition of the covenant between God and Israel, and of the Scriptures that give witness to this covenant, Christianity needs to recognize that its relationship with the people of Israel is a divinely warranted relationship. Yet at the same time it needs to think through the consequences of such a relationship for its encounter with the other religions. This is one of the challenges of the document *Nostra Aetate* that we have barely begun to realize. As the Austrian theologian Ulrich Winkler says, Christian theology needs to learn how to balance a theology of Israel and a theology of religions. I am convinced that in this much larger project of future Christian theology, Tapie's interpretation of Thomas Aquinas's view of Israel and the Church may serve its future purpose by bringing us back to the sources on which all theology needs to be based.

Pim Valkenberg
Utrecht, the Netherlands,
July 14, 2014

Acknowledgments

This book is a thoroughly revised edition of my 2012 doctoral dissertation at The Catholic University of America, Washington, DC. My friend and colleague, the Rev. Benjamin Boswell, was instrumental in kindling my passion for some of the themes addressed here. He continues to be an invaluable dialogue partner on the Jewish people, Judaism, and the Church. I am grateful to Bruce Marshall, who provided helpful comments in the early stages of my research and emphasized the necessity of examining Aquinas's Pauline commentaries on the subject of the ceremonial law. My director, William C. Mattison, has been a crucial source of wisdom and constant support since the project began. The readers of the dissertation, R. Kendall Soulen, Fr. Frank Matera, and Joseph Capizzi, read the text with care and offered invaluable corrections and editorial suggestions. The revisions were made during my time as a Visiting Assistant Professor of Theology in the School of Theology and Religious Studies at The Catholic University of America. Teaching parts of this book to my students has been invaluable. Their questions helped me to see the importance of rewriting the chapter, "The Language of Supersessionism." I profited greatly from responses to versions of this work presented at a variety of academic meetings over the last few years, including the panel on the Interpretation of Scripture in the Middle Ages at Villanova University's Patristic, Medieval, & Renaissance Conference, in October 2013. The generous support of Catholic University's Dean of the School of Theology and Religious Studies, Fr. Mark Morozowich, and the Institute for Interreligious Study and Dialogue, allowed me to present parts of chapter 5 at the Thomas Instiuut te Utrecht, Netherlands, in December 2013. I am also grateful for the opportunity to discuss the relevance of Aquinas's thought for Jewish-Christian relations with John Connelly, whose visit to CUA was made possible because of the Department of History and the School of Theology and Religious Studies. I am indebted

Acknowledgments

to those who offered comments on portions of the manuscript, including Pim Valkenberg, Mark Nanos, Marcel Poorthuis, Mark Kinzer, John Grabowski, David Lantigua, Kevin Hughes, and Daniel McClain. I have also benefited from conversations regarding various themes in the manuscript with Michael Wyschogrod, Stanley Hauerwas, Stephen Fowl, Peter Ochs, Marc Ellis, Steven Boguslawski, David Novak, Scott Bader-Saye, and John Borelli. I am grateful to Chad Pecknold for his encouragement and guidance during the publishing process, and thankful for the proofreading work of Lionel Yaceczko and Tina Parker. I have been lucky to find in my editor, Robin Parry, an able and encouraging guide. Jim Tedrick's support and enthusiasm for the project has also been highly beneficial. My colleague James Stroud, and friend Yahnatan Lasko, have encouraged me along the way. Many others provided various forms of encouragement and support, including Our Lady Queen of Peace, Arlington, VA, the Rev. Del Glick of Washington Community Fellowship, the L'Arche communities of Washington D.C., and the prayers of Br. Ignacio González and the monks of St. Anselm's Abbey. Above all, I am thankful to my wife Carolyn Tapie, without whom this project would not have been possible. To all of you, I remain deeply grateful.

Feast of St. Benedict, 2014
Washington D.C.

Introduction

AFTER READING THE SECOND Vatican Council's declaration on the Jewish people, *Nostra Aetate* Sec. 4, my students often remark that nothing strikes them as remarkable or noteworthy. Of course the Jewish people are not under a curse or guilty of the death of Christ. Of course Jesus was Jewish. The positive language about the Jews—that Jewish people remain dear to God; that God's calling and election of these people cannot be revoked; that the Church sprang from the Jewish people—represents for them the standard Christian view of Judaism.

Few Christians realize that the core ideas behind this view of Judaism were assembled piece by piece in the shadow of the Third Reich, by a small number of theologians and activists who wrote against anti-Semitism, both before and after the horror of the *Shoah*. As John Connelly has shown, the ideas in *Nostra Aetate* emerged out of a Christian theological struggle against Nazi racial anti-Semitism in Central Europe in the years just before the Holocaust.[1] John M. Osterreicher and Karl Thieme, among others, fought to prevent the synthesis of Catholicism with Nazism during the rise of the Third Reich, and advocated for the Vatican to speak out against anti-Semitic violence. As the theologians engaged in this dangerous struggle, they were forced to question traditional Christian arguments invoked by the Nazis, such as that Jews were under a divine curse for deicide and that Judaism was an obsolete religion superseded by Christianity.

The crucial figure in the struggle was Karl Thieme, a Protestant convert to Catholicism, and the "main architect" of the new vision of the Jews.[2] Through a heated exchange with Martin Buber in 1948, Thieme came to recognize that what was needed to overcome anti-Semitism was

---

1. Connelly, *From Enemy to Brother*
2. Ibid., 212.

the rejection of its theological source, namely, the Christian perception of Jews as a carnal and degenerate people.[3] Thieme thought the root of this idea was the Christian teaching that fleshly Israel was a people "God willed only in the past but no longer; now, God willed the true spiritual Israel, the Church."[4]

Thieme challenged this traditional teaching by drawing upon the Apostle Paul's words, in the letter to the Romans, that Jews remain dear to God *despite* unbelief in Christ; that Jews retain a special dignity because God has elected this people, and given them the Law and promises. The breakthrough idea was that a Jewish person, not only as an individual but precisely *as a Jew* can be pleasing to God. "Precisely for the Jews according to the entirety of divine revelation certain promises continue to be in force, so that one can assume that even in distance from Christ the Jewish people enjoys special guidance and special grace."[5] Thieme was able to assemble these ideas about the Jews and make the argument that God, even after the passion of Christ, willed that Jews continue to exist, according to the flesh, and unto the end of time. Eventually, the "architect" of *Nostra Aetate* would appeal to this reading of Paul to uproot the traditional Christian idea that "fleshly" Israel was obsolete.[6]

Thieme's positive affirmation of the Jewish people met theological resistance. Theologians and New Testament scholars responded with appeals to Galatians and Hebrews, and claimed that the Jews' role in history as the chosen people was made obsolete and that the New Covenant had replaced the Old Covenant.[7] Jews *were* Israel according to the flesh while the Church represented the true, spiritual Israel. Nevertheless, Thieme's vision would be integrated into *Nostra Aetate* Sec. 4, and promulgated at the last session of the Second Vatican Council, in 1965.

In the decades that followed the Council, the Vatican not only developed *Nostra Aetate*'s teaching on the Jews but did so while pointing out traditional Christian teachings that must be set aside.[8] In 1985, the

---

3. Ibid., 201.
4. Ibid., 213.
5. Ibid., 205.
6. Ibid., 185.
7. Ibid., 225.
8. For an overview of the Catholic Church's implementation of *Nostra Aetate* see Cardinal Kurt Koch, "Building on Nostra Aetate." For an analysis of the development of teaching from 1965 to 1985 see Eugene Fisher, "The Evolution of a Tradition," 241.

Commission for Religious Relations with the Jews insisted that the Jewish people are a "permanent reality," and ongoing "witness" to the God of Israel.⁹ "The history of Israel did not end in 70 A.D. It continued, especially in numerous Diaspora which allowed Israel to carry to the whole world a witness—often heroic—of its fidelity to the one God."¹⁰ The Commission did not want its affirmation to be understood with reference to the Augustinian teaching that Jews unknowingly witness to the truth of Christianity by observing their religious customs.¹¹ Rather, the Commission demanded Christians set aside this doctrine: "We must in any case rid ourselves of the traditional idea of a people *punished*, preserved as a *living argument* for Christian apologetic. It remains a chosen people...."¹²

Over the last decade, scholarly comment upon Thomas Aquinas's theology of the Jewish people began to reflect the concerns expressed in *Nostra Aetate*. One way this has happened has been by means of a term, "supersessionism." Scholars now use "supersede," as well as supersessionism, as labels that identify an inadequate or problematic Christian understanding of Judaism. While the term supersessionism does not appear in *Nostra Aetate*, the question of the presence of supersessionism in Aquinas's thought can be traced directly to the systematic dialogue between Catholic and Jewish scholars that emerged in the decades after *Nostra Aetate*.

In 1982, the Orthodox Jewish theologian Michael Wyschogrod and the late Rev. Clemens Thoma (1932–2011), a priest in the Society of the Divine Word, contacted the Secretary of the Commission for Relations with the Jews, Bishop Jorge Mejía, with the intention of remedying what they perceived as a lack of attention to theological questions in Catholic-Jewish relations.¹³ Wyschogrod and Thoma shared the belief that Catholic-Jewish dialogue was too influenced by political concerns and ought to be grounded upon theological research. Their contact with Mejía resulted in a trip to

---

9. Commission for Religious Relations with the Jews, "Notes 1985." Fisher has also noted that the 1985 Vatican Notes emphasize this point. Fisher, "The Evolution of a Tradition," 6.

10. "Notes 1985," VI # 1.

11. Augustine, *Against Faustus*, 12.11; 16:21; 12: 23. See also Cohen, *Living Letters of the Law*, 59–65; Fredriksen, *Augustine and the Jews*, 276–77.

12. "Notes 1985," VI # 1. Whatever its deficiencies, Augustine's argument is arguably an improvement over the *adversus Iudaeos* tradition. See Fredriksen, *Augustine and the Jews*.

13. Thoma and Wyschogrod, *Understanding Scripture*, 4.

Rome to meet with the Vice-President of the Commission for Promoting Christian Unity, Bishop Ramon Torrella.

The meeting resulted in the formation of an academic consultation of Catholic and Jewish scholars. The consultation was sponsored by the Institute for Jewish-Christian Relations of the American Jewish Congress, and the Institute for Jewish-Christian Research of the Theological Faculty of Luzern, which acted in collaboration with the Vatican. The consultation was held from January 16 to 18, 1984, in Luzern, Switzerland, and reflects the concern of Wyschogrod and Thoma to move theological questions related to the interpretation of Scripture to the center of the dialogue. The consultation was devoted to "The Authority and Interpretation of Scripture in Judaism and Christianity"—to what Wyschogrod referred to as "topics central to the two faiths."[14]

Wyschogrod's own contribution to the consultation was entitled "A Jewish Reading of St. Thomas Aquinas on the Old Law." It was published three years later in the 1987 volume entitled, *Understanding Scripture: Explorations of Jewish and Christian Traditions of Interpretation*.[15] In this essay, Wyschogrod argues that Aquinas's teaching that Jewish observation of the "ceremonial Mosaic Law" (circumcision, Sabbath, dietary laws) after the passion of Christ is obsolete and a mortal sin (or "dead and deadly") is an obstacle for the new era of Jewish-Christian relations.[16] In Wyschogrod's view, the teaching that Jewish observances have become obsolete and sinful after the passion implies that God no longer desires for Jewish people to exist. For the existence of the Jewish people through time depends upon its obedience to Torah; if God desires that the latter cease, he must desire that the former cease as well. But if God desires that the Jews no longer exist then it follows that the Jews do not remain dear to God; that God has rescinded the promise that the Jews remain his beloved people to the end of time.[17]

Wyschogrod's essay raises a question of paramount significance concerning the relationship of Aquinas's theology to the new era of Jewish-Christian relations. Indeed, Wyschogrod's essay suggests that Aquinas's teaching on Jewish observances after the passion of Christ undermines the theological foundation of *Nostra Aetate*'s teaching on the Jews.

14. Ibid., 4.
15. Wyschogrod, "A Jewish Reading of St. Thomas Aquinas," 125–38.
16. Ibid., 138.
17. Wyschogrod, "Israel, Church, and Election."

Introduction

The question of supersessionism in Aquinas's theology has elicited deep disagreement among scholars.[18] On the one hand, scholars argue that Aquinas avoids supersessionism. On the other hand, scholars argue Aquinas is the standard-bearer of a supersessionist Church. The first and only reply to Wyschogrod's essay appeared more than a decade later, with the publication of Matthew Levering's 2002 study, *Christ's Fulfillment of Torah and Temple*.[19] Levering's book was, in part, a response to Wyschogrod's essay. In his reply, Levering claims that Aquinas "avoids supersessionism." However, as I demonstrate at length in chapter 2, Levering ultimately sidesteps Wyschogrod's claim that Aquinas's teaching on Jewish observance of the Law after Christ suggests that God desires that the Jewish people disappear from the world.

Two other limitations plague the current discussion. One limitation is the confusion of the term supersessionism with anti-Semitism, or indeed a failure to clearly define the term supersessionism at all. This confusion is due to a general lack of attention to systematic theological reflection about the term supersessionism. A second limitation stems from a lack of attention to Aquinas's biblical commentaries. Wyschogrod and other scholars who have commented upon whether Aquinas's theology is supersessionist have focused chiefly on the *Summa theologiae*. With the exception of a few studies of parts of Aquinas's commentary on Romans, scholars have overlooked his commentaries on Paul's letters to the Galatians, Hebrews, and Ephesians, which include some of Aquinas's most extended reflections on the subjects of Israel and the Church. The neglect of Aquinas's commentaries on Paul's letters represents a significant gap in the current discussion.

This study attempts to remedy these deficiencies by adjudicating conflicting claims in the discussion over whether Aquinas's theology is supersessionist. Providing an answer to Wyschogrod's critique is crucial, not only for Thomists and Catholic theologians, but for all Christians who might assume that, after Christ, Jewish religious practices are obsolete. According to Wyschogrod, the traditional teaching that Jewish observances are obsolete ultimately amounts to saying that God does not keep God's promises and, therefore, that God cannot be trusted. If this is correct, Wyschogrod's criticism of Aquinas impacts not only Thomistic studies but a whole set of

---

18. The scholars in the discussion using the term supersessionism include Mark Kinzer, Steven C. Boguslawski, Matthew Levering, and Bruce Marshall. I treat each of their views in the second chapter.

19. Levering, *Christ's Fulfillment of Torah and Temple*.

assumptions about what might be called, the standard Christian interpretation of Christ's fulfillment of Jewish Law.

* * *

In the chapters that follow, I show that the question of supersessionism in Aquinas turns on his understanding of Jewish observance of the Law after the passion of Christ, and specifically, on whether such observance can have a positive theological significance, or whether it is always and necessarily "dead and deadly." I argue that while Thomas' most commonly articulated view is that Jewish observance of the ceremonial law is discontinued after the passion of Christ, he also advanced views that set this into question, and thus represents a premodern precursor to Thieme's positive interpretation of postbiblical Judaism.

Chapters 1 and 2 are devoted to clarifying the term supersessionism. As noted, lack of clarity regarding the meaning of the term is a major problem that plagues the discussion over whether Aquinas's theology is supersessionist. In chapter 1, I examine use of the term outside the sphere of Thomistic studies per se. I recover the theological meaning by drawing upon the work of the French-Jewish historian of anti-Semitism Jules Isaac, and the Christian systematic theologian R. Kendall Soulen. I argue that Soulen's work points contemporary theological discussions on supersessionism to what is perhaps an underappreciated proposition of Isaac on the traditional Christian teaching that Christ's fulfillment of Jewish Law also entails its obsolescence or expiration.[20]

In chapter 2, I examine use of the term supersessionism among scholars who address the thought of Aquinas. I explain what Michael Wyschogrod, Matthew Levering, Mark Kinzer, Bruce Marshall, and Steven Boguslawski mean when they use the term "supersessionism," and discuss whether their use of the term is coherent. I demonstrate that the lack of precision with regard to the language of supersessionism and/or the failure to attend to Aquinas's most relevant works renders scholars' conclusions regarding Aquinas's susceptibility to the charge of supersessionism premature. I also show that the question of the status of the "ceremonial Mosaic

---

20. "Proposition 9: Jesus was born and lived 'under the Law,' did he intend or announce its abrogation? Many writers hold that he did, but their statements exaggerate, distort, or contradict the most important passages in the gospels." Jules Isaac, *Jesus and Israel*, 49.

Introduction

Law" after the passion of Christ is the crux of the matter in the debate about whether Aquinas's theology is supersessionist.

In the third chapter, I set the stage for an examination of Aquinas's view of the observance of the ceremonial law in "some of his greatest theological works," Aquinas's commentaries on Paul's letters.[21] By drawing upon Aquinas's first inaugural sermon at the University of Paris, and the Prologue he attaches to the beginning of his commentaries on Paul's letters, I demonstrate that Aquinas's commentaries contain some of the most extended reflections on Israel and Church in general, and the observance of the ceremonial law in particular.

In chapters 4 through 7 I examine Aquinas's view of the observance of the ceremonial law after the passion of Christ in the four commentaries on Paul's letters that contain the most material on this subject (Romans, Galatians, Ephesians, and Hebrews) in order to determine whether such observance can have a positive theological significance, or whether it is always and necessarily "dead and deadly." In other words, is there any sense in which these rites serve as a spiritual benefit for Jews now?

In the eighth chapter, I compare my analysis of Aquinas's views of the ceremonial law in his Pauline commentaries with his view of the theological status of the ceremonial law after the passion of Christ in the *Summa theologiae*. Scholars are increasingly attempting the task of comparing key themes in Aquinas's biblical commentaries with those same themes in the *Summa theologiae* in an effort to produce clearer pictures of Aquinas's theology. I follow this development in Thomistic studies and aim to provide a more comprehensive picture of Aquinas's thought on Jewish Law after the passion of Christ in his commentaries on Hebrews, Romans, Galatians, and Ephesians, and the *Summa theologiae*.

This study can be considered as one part of a broader trend of growing attention to the significance of Aquinas's biblical commentaries for understanding his theology.[22] The study aims to uncover Aquinas's view of the ceremonial law in these commentaries with attention to contemporary concerns of the new era of Jewish-Christian dialogue initiated, in part, by *Nostra Aetate*. The contemporary discussion indicates that a fuller picture of Aquinas's views on the ceremonial law after the passion of Christ is necessary for adjudicating claims that Aquinas's theology is or is not

---

21. Pius XII, "An Address to the Faculty and Students of the Roman Athenaeum Angelicum," in Baglow, *"Modus Et Forma,"* 26.

22. Wilhelmus G. B. M. Valkenberg, *Words of the Living God*, 2–3.

supersessionist. As Jean-Pierre Torrell has observed, "If we wish . . . to get a slightly less one-sided idea of the whole theologian and his method, it is imperative to read and use in a much deeper fashion these biblical commentaries in parallel with the great systematic works."[23]

---

23. Torrell, *Aquinas: The Person and His Work*, 55.

1

The Language of Supersessionism

ALTHOUGH THE REPUDIATION OF supersessionism is now widespread among Christians, careful use of the term is not. In an exchange in Commonweal entitled "Getting Past Supersessionism," Steven Englund referred to Christianity's "de facto supersession of Judaism," which he claimed was attested to in "a host of phrases" in *Nostra Aetate*, including Paul's teaching in Ephesians that Christ has reconciled Jews and Gentiles into one body.[1] John Connelly's response stated that *Nostra Aetate* does not "preach supersessionism."[2] Though supersessionism is mentioned throughout the exchange, and Englund even asserts that it would not be hard for Pope Francis to "reconfirm the end to supersessionism as a central presupposition of the Good News," the term is nowhere defined.

The language of supersessionism seems to dominate theological discourse about what Christians must no longer say concerning the Church's relationship to the Jewish people. Yet the word often seems to function as a term of abuse. Therefore, the aim of this opening chapter is to take a first step toward clarifying the discussion on whether Aquinas's theology is supersessionist by tracing the usage of term in order to recover its theological meaning.

---

1. Englund, "Getting Past Supersessionism," 17.
2. Ibid., 26.

Aquinas on Israel and the Church

1. THE HISTORY OF SUPERSESSIONISM

Although the term supersessionism is a relative newcomer to the parlance of Christian theology, Christians writing in English have used "supersede" and cognates for two hundred years.[3] Specifically, they have done so when describing the relation of Old and New Testaments, and specifically the idea that Christ fulfills God's purposes for Judaism and the Mosaic Law. Prior to the Second World War, such uses of the term were universally regarded as self-evident and unproblematic. Since the Second World War, however, the use of term has undergone a dramatic change. Increasingly, supersede, as well as supersession*ism*, has come to be used as labels that identify a theologically inadequate or problematic Christian understanding of Jews and Judaism.

The English term supersessionism is derived from the Latin, *supersedere*, meaning "to sit upon; to sit above."[4] The earliest usage of the term appears in contexts where scholars describe Christ superseding Jewish Law, circumcision, and "outward ceremonials." In the Oxford English Dictionary of 1790, William Paley spoke of the "supersession" of the Law that occurred with Christ.[5] The third chapter of Thelwall's 1870 translation of Tertullian's *An Answer to the Jews* is entitled, "Of Circumcision and the Supercession of the Old Law."[6] The 1873 translation of F. C. Baur's *Paulus* states that "Judaism saw itself superseded by Christianity" in the "one great idea" that "the essence of true religion did not consist in outward ceremonials, connected with a temple service confined to an appointed spot."[7]

In each of these early examples, the idea that Christianity has superseded Judaism and Jewish Law carries a positive connotation because it is used to express a complex body of ideas held to be central to the Christian faith: the positive claim that the Law of Moses is fulfilled by the grace and truth that comes through Christ.[8] Traditional interpretations of Christ's fulfillment have assumed that the primary purpose of Judaism and Jewish Law was to prefigure future things, namely Christ's birth, passion, and

---

3. By "language of supersessionism" I mean the related terms "supersessionism," "supersede," and "supersessionist."

4. Soulen, "Supersessionism."

5. Paley, *Horae Paulinae*, 167, cited in Donaldson, "Supersessionism in Early Christianity."

6. Donaldson, "Supersessionism in Early Christianity," 3.

7. Baur, *Paul the Apostle of Jesus Christ*, 181. Cited in ibid.

8. Augustine, *Against Faustus*, 19.7.

The Language of Supersessionism

resurrection.⁹ With the coming of Christ, the symbolic purpose of Jewish Law, or what Augustine referred to as the "sacraments of the Old Testament," have been fulfilled and therefore "discontinued."[10]

In the decades after the *Shoah*, Christian theologians were forced to ask how "an industry of genocide" could have been conceived and carried out in the center of Christian civilization."[11] The common suffering of Jews and Christians under the Nazis had opened channels of communication[12] between Jewish and Christian theologians. In emergency meetings of Christians and Jews, such as the International Council of Christians and Jews at Oxford (1946) and Seelisberg (1947), Christians began to consider the possibility that traditional Christian views of Judaism had "formed the deeper wellspring of contempt that made Auschwitz possible."[13] The dominant categories for this post-Holocaust examination of Christian teaching at this time were anti-Judaism[14] and anti-Semitism.[15] The term supersessionism was not yet widely used.

---

9. "Whatever observance God appointed for the former dispensation was a shadow of future things." *Against Faustus*, 6.2. "[E]verything in the law that is prophetic of the Savior's advent, whether in words or in typical actions, became truth in Jesus Christ." *Against Faustus*, 19.8.

10. Augustine, *Against Faustus*, 6.2. "The sacraments of the Old Testament, which were celebrated in obedience to the law, were types of Christ who was to come; and when Christ fulfilled them by His advent they were done away, and were done away because they were fulfilled. For Christ came not to destroy, but to fulfill. And now that the righteousness of faith is revealed, and the children of God are called into liberty, and the yoke of bondage which was required for a carnal and stiff-necked people is taken away, other sacraments are instituted, greater in efficacy, more beneficial in their use, easier in performance, and fewer in number." *Against Faustus* 19.13. A second example of how the revelation of the truth abrogates Jewish practice can be found in John Calvin's comments upon Matthew 5:17: "As regards ceremonies, if we allow that they may be reckoned somewhat incidental, it is only their practice that was abrogated: their significance was actually given more confirmation . . . the truth behind the shadows was revealed, and served to strengthen them; seeing the concrete fact, we recognize that they were not vain or useless." Calvin, *A Harmony of the Gospels*, 180.

11. Donaldson, "Supersessionism in Early Christianity," 3.

12. Connelly, *From Enemy to Brother*, 176.

13. Ibid.

14. Donaldson rightly points to Gregory Baum, *Is the New Testament Anti-Semitic?*; Rosemary R. Ruether, *Faith and Fratricide*; Samuel Sandmel, *Anti-Semitism in the New Testament?*; John G. Gager, *The Origins of Anti-Semitism*; George M. Smiga, *Pain and Polemic*; William R. Farmer, *Anti-Judaism and the Gospels*; Reimund Bieringer, *Anti-Judaism and the Fourth Gospel*.

15. Twentieth-century scholarship on Aquinas's social doctrine of the Jews mirrored

Aquinas on Israel and the Church

It appears that the first use of supersede in its post WWII sense occurs in English translations of the ground-breaking work of Holocaust survivor and French-Jewish historian, Jules Isaac (1877–1963).[16] Isaac was a high-ranking French government official, World War I veteran, and professor of history. After the Nazi occupation of France, he was removed from his post as Inspector General of Education by the Vichy government and began writing a book investigating the roots of anti-Semitism. In 1943, while away from home, his daughter, son-in-law, and several family members were seized and killed by the Nazis.[17] While on the run, hiding in farms and at the homes of priests or ministers, Isaac wrote his ground-breaking 600-page study of anti-Semitism in the Christian tradition, *Jésus et Israël*.[18] By means of meticulous historical research, the study unearthed the intellectual underpinnings supporting negative Christian views of Jews and Judaism, such as the deicide charge and the idea that Judaism was a degenerate religion.[19]

---

these concerns over the question of anti-Semitism in the Christian tradition. Scholars of Aquinas's view of the Jews have largely been concerned with Aquinas's policies concerning the Jews of his day and whether these policies can be linked to the increasing anti-Semitism of the fourteenth century. See Hanz Liebeschutz, "Judaism and Jewry in the Social Doctrine of Thomas Aquinas," 57–81. John Y. B. Hood, *Aquinas and the Jews*; Robert Chazan, *Daggers of Faith*. Aquinas's *Epistola ad ducissam Brabantiae* can be found in Aquinas, "On the Government of the Jews," 233. Commentary on Aquinas's social doctrine of the Jewish people has, for the most part, focused upon Aquinas's *Epistola ad ducissam Brabantiae* (often improperly called *De regimine Iudaeorum*), and the question of forced baptism and tolerance for Jewish worship in *Summa theologiae* Ia IIae q. 10.12 ad 4; q. 10.11. The picture of Aquinas that emerges from a survey of the secondary literature is largely an apologetic one, with the exception of the work of Jeremy Cohen. Cohen thinks Aquinas's view of the sin of Jewish unbelief in Christ in general and on Jewish complicity in the crucifixion in particular departs from what he sees as a tolerant Augustinian tradition. Jeremy Cohen, *Living Letters of the Law*, 372. Cohen extends this argument in *Christ Killers*. This older conversation about anti-Semitism in Aquinas's social doctrine pursues a different question than the more theological question of supersessionism, and can be set aside in order to take up what Pim Valkenberg and Schoot have referred to as the "theological side" of Aquinas's view of the Jews. Valkenberg and Schoot's "Thomas Aquinas and Judaism," in *Aquinas in Dialogue*.

16. Stephen Plant, "Jules Isaac," 214. See the biographical notes written by Claire Huchet Bishop in Jules Isaac, *Has Anti-Semitism Roots in Christianity?*, 27–34. Bishop's biographical notes on Isaac are also in the English translations of Isaac's most influential work on anti-Semitism in the Christian tradition, *The Teaching of Contempt*, 3–15; and *Jesus and Israel*, xi-xvii.

17. Bishop, "A Biographical Introduction to Jules Isaac," 8.

18. Isaac, *Jésus et Israël*.

19. Huchet, preface to *Jesus and Israel*, xiv; "A Biographical Introduction," 9. Huchet

The Language of Supersessionism

Remarkably, Isaac would go on to shape Jewish-Christian relations in a still more seminal way. Several years after writing *Jésus et Israël*, Isaac played a crucial role in the push for the declaration now considered the historical turning point in Jewish-Christian relations, *Nostra Aetate*. On June 13, 1960, Isaac succeeded in obtaining an audience with Pope John XXIII, presented him with a dossier that demonstrated the presence of unjust statements about Jewish people in Christian instruction, such as the idea that *diaspora* was God's punishment for Jews rejecting Christ. Isaac argued that such statements did not belong to the true tradition of the Church.[20] At the close of the historic meeting, Isaac asked whether he might "take away with him a little hope," and Pope John replied, "You have reason for more than a little hope."[21] According to John Connelly, "Isaac's appeal made the difference."[22] Despite the Pope's awareness of the need to revise Church teaching on the Jews, "he probably would not have requested a statement from the Council had Jules Isaac not made an impassioned plea . . . ."[23]

---

says Isaac completed the manuscript in 1947. Isaac explains that the work was published in 1948. Isaac, *Jesus and Israel*, xxiv. Isaac's second work was *Genese de l'antisemitisme* in 1956. It does not appear to have been translated into English. His third work would be published when he was eighty-five years old, under the title *L'Enseignement de Mépris*. It was translated into English in 1964 as *The Teaching of Contempt*. Isaac's historic rebuttal of anti-Semitic Christian ideas about Jews would become the basis for the 1947 statement now considered the "first fruit" of the new era of Jewish-Christian relations, "Ten Points of Seelisberg." Connelly, *From Enemy to Brother*, 176. "Ten Points" was published by the International Council of Christians and Jews. Aitken, "Seelisberg Conference."

20. John Oesterreicher describes the dossier as follows: "1) A brief for the correction of false and . . . unjust statements about the people of Israel in Christian instruction. 2) An example of such statements: the theological myth that the scattering of Israel was a punishment inflicted by God on the people for the crucifixion of Jesus. 3) An extract from the so-called 'Catechism of Trent' which, in its treatment of the Passion, emphasized the guilt of all sinners as the fundamental cause of Christ's death upon the cross, and thus, in Isaac's view, proved that the accusation of deicide raised against the Jews did not belong to the true tradition of the Church." "The Tridentine Catechism was published in 1566, not by the Council of Trent but as one of its fruits, under Pius V, its proper name being *Catechismus Romanus* . . . it was designed to assist preachers and catechists and to lay down guidelines for authentic instruction in Catholic faith and life." Isaac actually cited paragraphs of the *Catechismus Romanus* that emphasized that sin was the principle reason that drove Christ to the cross and that both Gentiles and Jews pushed for Christ's execution. Oesterreicher, *The New Encounter*, 105.

21. Ibid., 108.

22. Connelly, *From Enemy to Brother*, 240.

23. Connelly points out that this is not to say the Pope was uninterested in a statement on the Jews. John XXIII was instrumental in pushing the document onto the agenda of the Council. See ibid. Oesterreicher points out that it was "the measures taken

13

Aquinas on Israel and the Church

Throughout *Jésus et Israël*, Isaac is determined to identify and challenge a "special kind of exegesis"[24] that had not only portrayed Judaism as a degenerate faith but also distorted Christianity. Isaac was adamant that this tradition of exegesis was to be distinguished from true Christian faith: "It must be clearly understood, that to oppose the teaching of contempt is not to oppose a doctrine essential to the Christian faith."[25] For Isaac, it was this "teaching of contempt" that required reexamination, not normative Christian faith: "The object of our attack is a tradition, time-honored and therefore all the more powerful, influential, and destructive, but in no way normative . . . ."[26]

In his 1962 book *L'enseignement du mépris* (translated into English in 1964), Isaac is concerned to challenge the normative Christian claim that the coming of Christ entails the abrogation of Jewish Law. It is here, for the first time in English, that an author employs the term "supersede" to indicate a problematic conception of how Christ fulfills the Mosaic Law.

For Isaac, Christian views of Judaism as degenerate are deeply rooted in a tradition of apologetics that claimed the Law was obsolete after Christ and that the Jews were attached to the Law because they were "carnal beings":[27]

> This contention has its source in the earliest Judeo-Christian controversies over the Torah—the Law of Moses—and its observances. The Christian apologists maintained that with the coming of Christ, the Law had been *fulfilled and superseded* [*accomplie et dépassée*]. They taught that the Jews were attached to the letter and not the spirit of the law because they were "carnal" beings, blinded by Satan, incapable of understanding the real meaning of their own Scriptures.[28]

---

by John XXIII to remove hurtful phrases from liturgical texts that had encouraged Isaac, as he himself acknowledged, to put this requests before the Pope." Oesterreicher, *The New Encounter*, 108. The Pope's request for a statement would be shepherded by Cardinal Bea, Karl Thieme, and John Oesterreicher. See Connelly for the origins of *Nostra Aetate*, including the crucial tradition of reflection on Judaism undertaken by Catholic anti-Nazi thinkers during and after the war.

24. Simon cited in Isaac, *The Teaching of Contempt*, 34.

25. Ibid.

26. Ibid., 35.

27. Isaac, *L'enseignement du mépris*. Isaac argued the "teaching of contempt" was manifested in three main themes in the Christian tradition: 1) the dispersion of the Jews; 2) the degenerate state of Judaism; 3) the crime of deicide.

28. Isaac, *Teaching of Contempt*, 75. [Emphasis added]; *L'Enseignement de Mépris*, 67.

The Language of Supersessionism

In *Jésus et Israël*, Isaac challenges the claim that Christ's fulfillment of the Law also entails its obsolescence in three different places.[29] However, instead of *accomplie et dépassée* (fulfilled and obsolete) he uses *accomplie et périmé* (fulfilled and expired). Each time, the term *périmé* is rendered "superseded" by the English translation. Clearly, "supersede" is not a literal translation of Isaac's term, *périmé*.[30] Rather, "supersede" is used to capture what Isaac says is the *double sens* or double meaning of the traditional Christian concept of Christ's fulfillment of the symbolic aspect of Jewish Law. He uses these formulas to describe this double meaning: "fulfilled and obsolete (*dépassée*)" or "fulfilled and expired (*périmé*)."

The first occurrence of "supersede" appears in a chapter entitled "Proposition 9: Jesus was born and lived 'under the law.' Did he intend or announce its abrogation [*l'abrogation*]? Many writers hold that he did, but their statements exaggerate, distort, or contradict the most important passages in the gospels." In this chapter, Isaac critically examines modern French interpretation of Christ's fulfillment of the Law. In particular, Isaac takes issue with traditional claim that the fulfillment of the Law also means that it is *périmé* or expired:[31]

> Fulfill—what a magnificent vista this verb opens to the theological imagination! . . . "The law will be 'fulfilled' [*accomplie*] in the double meaning of raised to perfection and superseded [*double sens d'élevée à la perfection et de périmé*]," in the words of F. Ménégoz. Somewhat more cautiously (in style, that is), Father Bonsirven says, "The New Covenant and its economy do not suppress those that came before but 'fulfill' them, as does the fruit into which the flower is transformed."[32]

A second occurrence is at the end of the chapter, and he refers once again to the *double sens* of fulfillment:

> If Jesus had really been the revolutionary against the Law that he had been called; if he had presented himself as a "destroyer of Judaism"; . . . if he had let it be understood—in any way—that the whole of the Law was *"fulfilled"* [*accomplie*] *in his person and was thenceforth "superseded"* [*périmé*] in Ménégoz's phrase, . . . how is it that Jesus' most intimate disciples . . . and hundreds of thousands

---

29. Isaac, *Jésus et Israël*, 428.
30. *L'Enseignement du Mépris* was translated into English by Claire Huchet Bishop.
31. Isaac, *Jesus and Israel*, 49; *Jésus et Israël*, 96.
32. Isaac, *Jesus and Israel*, 64; *Jésus et Israël*, 118.

of converted Jews made not one allusion to it, seemed to know absolutely nothing about it?[33]

In the third and last occurrence of which I am aware, Isaac cites the Christian teaching that Jewish Law had expired as a principal cause of the widening gulf between Synagogue and Church in the first century:

> It is again an indisputable fact ... of capital importance for religion and for history that in this same period when the Gospel tradition was put down in writing, a gulf was opening between the Synagogue and its emancipated daughter, the Church. Jews rigorously faithful to the ancient Law and Christians who were breaking away from it, who declared it *superseded* [*périmé*], became adversaries, sometimes (the theologians, especially the doctors) mortal enemies.[34]

The English term supersede is used to translate Isaac's criticism of what he viewed as the *double sens* of Christ's fulfillment of the Law: "fulfilled and obsolete (*dépassée*)" or "fulfilled and expired (*périmé*)." Therefore, when "supersede" is first used to designate a problematic Christian view of Judaism in English theology it is used to name a very specific theological concept. With the coming of Christ, Jewish Law is fulfilled according to its inward spiritual intention and therefore expired according to its outer ceremonial form. It is, in short, fulfilled and therefore obsolete.

Perhaps one can only speculate that the translation of Isaac's work into English was instrumental in moving the term supersede into the conversation, but it seems a reasonable hypothesis. In the years following the translation of *L'Enseignement du Mépris* and *Jésus et Israël* into English, one finds more instances of "supersede," as well as "supersession." Rabbi Joseph B. Soloveitchik warned that a dialogue with Christians assumed acceptance of the idea of a "continuum of revealed doctrines," which means "one is ready to acquiesce to the Christian theological claim that Christianity has superseded Judaism."[35] Franklin H. Littell argued, in his 1971 publication, *The Crucifixion of the Jews*, that "the superseding or displacement myth" was the "cornerstone of Christian Anti-Semitism."[36] In 1973, a group of Christian theologians convened by the Commission on Faith and Order

---

33. Isaac, *Jesus and Israel*, 71 [Emphasis added]; Isaac, *Jésus et Israël*, 125.
34. Isaac, *Jesus and Israel*, 294. [Emphasis added]
35. Soloveitchik, "Confrontation," 5–9.
36. Littell, *The Crucifixion of the Jews*, 2.

The Language of Supersessionism

of the National Council of Churches, in collaboration with the Secretariat for Catholic-Jewish Relations of the National Conference of Catholic Bishops, published "A Statement to Our Fellow Christians" that declared: "The singular grace of Jesus Christ does not abrogate the covenantal relationship of God with Israel. In Christ the Church shares in Israel's election without superseding it."[37] The 1986 publication of the second volume of *Anti-Judaism in Early Christianity*, cites to Justin Martyr's belief that "his group and its social and cultural worlds . . . supersede" those of Trypho and the Jews as an example of anti-Judaism.[38] Numerous churches published formal documents rejecting supersessionism, such as the declaration by the Presbyterian Church (USA): "We believe and testify that [the] theory of supersessionism or replacement is harmful and in need of reconsideration as the church seeks to proclaim God's saving activity with humankind . . . ."[39] Over the last two decades of the twentieth century, the language of supersessionism has become pervasive in theological and biblical scholarship.[40] The term is now used in contemporary theology to designate problematic Christian claims about Judaism. "With respect to Judaism," writes Richard John Neuhaus, "Christians today are exhorted to reject every form of supersessionism, and so we should. To supersede means to nullify, to void, to make obsolete, to displace."[41] Reflecting on the impact of Pope John Paul II's positive contributions to Jewish-Christian relations, George Weigel commented that the Pope's teaching "challenged Catholics who had never

---

37. Statement of the 1987 General Assembly of the Presbyterian Church (USA) in Brockway, *The Theology of the Churches*.

38. See *Anti-Judaism in Early Christianity*, cited in Donaldson, "Supersessionism in Early Christianity," 5.

39. Other church statements that explicitly reject supersessionism are collected in Clark M. Williamson, *A Guest in the House of Israel*, 37; Helga B. Croner, *Stepping Stones to Further Jewish-Christian Relations; More Stepping Stones to Jewish-Christian Relations*. See Soulen, *God of Israel*, 178. Mary C. Boys has assembled a helpful chart listing statements by various Protestant denominations, Vatican statements, Papal statements, and statements by bishops. Boys, *Has God Only One Blessing?*, 252–3.

40. Donaldson references Donald G. Bloesch, "All Israel Will be Saved: Supersessionism and the Biblical Witness," 130–42; Robert R. Hann "Supersessionism, Engraftment, and Jewish-Christian Dialogue: Reflections on the Presbyterian Statement on Jewish-Christian Relations," 327–42; Ronald E. Diprose, *Israel in the Development of Christian Thought*, 31; John Howard Yoder, *The Jewish-Christian Schism Revisited*, 213–14, 278; Douglas Harink, *Paul Among the Postliberals*, 23; Eugene B. Korn and John T. Pawlikowski, eds., *Two Faiths, One Covenant?*, 3; Vlach, "The Church as a Replacement of Israel." Donaldson, "Supersessionism in Early Christianity," 7.

41. Neuhaus, *American Babylon*, 174–75.

rid themselves of the last vestiges of the belief that God's redemptive action in Christ had superseded, indeed abrogated, the covenant with Abraham."[42] The attempt to dismantle supersessionism has even been referred to by the Jewish theologian Peter Ochs as "another reformation."[43] Scholars now stress that Christ and the Church *do not* supersede Israel. They seek to affirm the ongoing role of the Jewish people in salvation history: "Christ and his Church do not supersede Judaism, but they do continue and fulfill the story which we are both part."[44]

However, increased usage of "supersede" has created a context in which confusion and ambiguity is possible. This is in part because the term is no longer clearly connected to the association with the "double sense" of fulfillment that it has in Isaac's works. The lack of careful attention to the meaning of the term tends to create a vacuum that attracts scholars' perceptions of "negative Christian views of Judaism." Mary C. Boys has suggested that the term supersessionism is "alive and well whenever we hear claims such as the following": the God of the Old Testament is a God of wrath; the God of the New Testament is a God of love; the Jews rejected Jesus as their Messiah; self-righteous and hypocritical Pharisees show how legalistic Judaism had become by Jesus' day.[45] Another scholar has also equated Christian supersessionism to demonization of the State of Israel.[46]

How can the term supersede be kept from blurring into "negative views of the Jews"? One way is to remain attentive to the fact that the word emerged in the context of Isaac's criticism of the "double sense" of Christ's fulfillment of the Law (fulfilled and thenceforth expired). Indeed, the scholar who has undertaken the most careful systematic theological treatment of the concept of supersessionism in the Christian tradition argues that a concept not unlike Isaac's "double sense" of fulfillment is *the* "heart of supersessionism."

---

42. Weigel, *Witness to Hope*, 515.
43. Ochs, *Another Reformation*.
44. Neuhaus, *American Babylon*, 175.
45. Boys, *Has God only One Blessing?* 8.
46. Levenson, "Getting Past Supersessionism," 22.

2. THE HEART OF SUPERSESSIONISM

R. Kendall Soulen is one of the first to attempt a careful definition and analysis of supersessionism.[47] Significantly, Soulen's analysis coincides with Isaac's use of the term. Like Isaac, Soulen conceives of supersessionism as entailing a double sense of fulfillment and obsolescence. In fact, this is what he calls the "heart of supersessionism."

According to Soulen, Christianity's traditional theology of the Jewish people needs to be seen in the context of its larger understanding of the narrative unity of the Christian canon as a whole. According to this larger narrative, "God chose the Jewish people after the fall of Adam in order to prepare the world for the coming of Jesus Christ, the Savior. After Christ came, however, the special role of the Jewish people came to an end and its place was taken by the church, the new Israel."[48] According to Soulen, supersessionism is most clearly manifested in this narrative framework in two forms, which he calls punitive and economic supersessionism.[49] Of these, it is the second that will concern us most directly.

Punitive supersessionism is an approach to the biblical narrative that holds that God has abrogated God's covenant with Israel on account of Israel's rejection of Christ and the gospel.[50] Because the Jews rejected Christ, God in turn angrily rejected them, and revoked their covenant. "These Christians taught that God's covenant with the Jews was over, and that henceforth the church alone stood in its place."[51] Soulen points out that supersessionism in this form speaks of God "revoking" the covenant as a punishment for sin.

Like punitive supersessionism, economic supersessionism also teaches that God has replaced Israel with the Church. But unlike it, economic supersessionism does not ascribe that to Jewish disobedience or sin.[52] Rather,

---

47. Soulen, *The God of Israel and Christian Theology*.

48. Ibid., 2.

49. Ibid., 1. A third form of supersessionism identified by Soulen is "structural." However, as I explain in a note below, structural supersessionism is more of a consequence of economic supersessionism than a form of supersessionism itself.

50. Ibid., 30.

51. Soulen, "Israel and Church," 171. This essay is perhaps the best introduction to Soulen's view of the church and its relationship to traditional supersessionist interpretations of Israel.

52. The term "economy" (Gk. οἰκονομία) refers to the traditional understanding of God's overarching redemptive work, or management, of two dispensations of the household of creation, Old and New.

the Church replaces Israel because *Christ's fulfillment of Jewish ceremonial law renders its continued observance obsolete and indeed damnable.* This approach holds that the Mosaic Law prepares humanity for redemption primarily by pointing forward to Christ in "a carnal and prophetic way," and the New Testament testifies to redemption in Christ in a "definitive and spiritual way."[53] "Circumcision, promises, law, temple, Israel's history, and so forth all point in various ways toward Christ and the church."[54] With the advent of Christ, the prefiguring function of the carnal ceremonies or sacraments (circumcision) are superseded by new sacraments (baptism): "the prophecies, types, and figures of the Old Testament are *fulfilled and superseded* by their New Testament equivalents."[55]

Both punitive and economic supersessionism are the forms of supersessionism most relevant and helpful for discussing whether Aquinas's theology is supersessionist. For this reason, it will be helpful to highlight the similarities and differences. Economic supersessionism and punitive supersessionism are similar in that they share the conclusion that the Church replaces the Jews as God's elect community. Punitive and economic supersessionism, however, do not share the "how" of the replacement. Economic supersessionism assumes the Jews are no longer God's elect because the Jewish Law is fulfilled and obsolete. Punitive supersessionism assumes the Jews are no longer God's elect because God is punishing them for rejecting Christ. Both forms of supersessionism result in the replacement of the people of Israel but arrive at this destination via different routes.[56]

Among these two forms, economic supersessionism is especially notable because it shares key features of Isaac's rejection of the traditional

---

53. Soulen, *God of Israel*, 27.
54. Ibid.
55. Ibid., 28. [Emphasis added]

56. A third form of supersessionism identified by Soulen is "structural." Structural supersessionism is an approach to the biblical narrative that renders the Old Testament largely indecisive for shaping conclusions about how God's redemptive purposes in Christ engage creation in universal and enduring ways. Israel's history is nothing more than a particular prefigurative moment sandwiched between more important, universal, and spiritual aims of God's creation and redemption of humankind. However, structural supersessionism is more a consequence of supersessionism than supersessionism itself. That Israel's narrative no longer shapes God's purposes in engaging creation in a decisive way seems to be a conclusion that follows from the economically supersessionist premise that God's only purpose for Israel was to foreshadow universal redemption in Christ. After the passion the literal meaning of the narrative of the Old Testament no longer shapes God's redemption of the world in a decisive way. Ibid., 31–32.

fulfillment concept, namely the idea of Jewish Law as "fulfilled and obsolete." Soulen's concept of economic supersessionism overlaps significantly with at least two of Isaac's insights: 1) fulfillment carries a "double sense" (fulfilled and thenceforth superseded) in the Christian tradition; 2) fulfillment understood according to this "double sense" inevitably undermines the theological rationale of Jewish existence.

First, recall that Isaac identified the double sense concept, that the Jewish Law had been "fulfilled and thenceforth expired," as the root of the Christian view that Judaism was a degenerate religion. Soulen identifies this same concept as "the heart" of economic supersessionism when he describes a "double movement" of "fulfillment and cancellation,"[57] or "fulfillment and outer obsolescence." Soulen appeals to a variety of metaphors to illustrate the point:

> The heart of economic supersessionism . . . simply affirms a double movement of inward *fulfillment and outer obsolescence*, like a butterfly that casts off its chrysalis. The chrysalis is not "revoked" or repudiated, nor is their any violation of the true organic continuity between caterpillar and butterfly. However, the chrysalis is rendered obsolete, and its retention would obviously be a serious mistake. The thought process is different from punitive supersessionism, but the destination is the same, insofar as both evacuate Israel's observance of the cultic law of positive theological significance.[58]

The double movement of fulfillment and cancellation can also be understood via the metaphor of a sculptor that sketches a figure on paper before sculpting the actual figure. Although the sculptor intends that the sketch of the figure play a crucial role in bringing about the ultimate aim of the project, the primary purpose of the sketch becomes obsolete with the appearance of the completed sculpture.[59] For both Isaac and Soulen, the traditional concept of Christ's fulfillment of Judaism and Jewish Law carries double meanings. Soulen refers to the concept as "fulfilled and cancelled," and Isaac identifies it as "fulfilled and thenceforth expired."

Second, both scholars draw attention to the fact that the traditional double sense of fulfillment inevitably undermines Jewish existence, which

---

57. Soulen, "Israel and Church," 47.
58. Personal correspondence. March 2011. [Emphasis added]
59. Paraphrase of Soulen's metaphor in "Israel and Church," 171. The image itself is used by several ancient Christian writers, including Melito of Sardis.

can only maintain itself over time through the practice of Judaism. The Christian teaching that Law is obsolete is a theological problem because it ultimately implies that the Jewish people itself is obsolete, that God no longer desires its continuation as a distinct people among the nations.[60]

However, the idea that the obsolescence of Israel's existence is a theological problem may not be immediately apparent. One might object that Jews could continue as a mere ethnic group and still be Jews. But this would be a complete misunderstanding of what is most essential and basic about Judaism.[61]

Judaism is the religion of the Jewish people, which does form a kind of ethnicity—a family descended from Abraham, Isaac, and Jacob that reproduces itself from generation to generation through the practice of ceremonial law and matrilineal descent.

However, Judaism does not form an ethnicity as this term is understood in contemporary English discourse, where it functions as a polite synonym of race and is largely a function of heredity alone. Judaism is essentially religious since it is first and foremost a covenanted people bound to God in part through God's gift of Torah.

The observance of Torah grows out of Israel's election. According to Jacob Neusner, those who observe the Torah maintain the covenant. To practice Judaism means "to act out in behavior and belief the key stories that are told in the Torah, . . . the instruction set forth by God to Israel at Mount Sinai."[62] *Significantly, the religious practices of Judaism maintain the Jewish people*: "What holds some descendants of Abraham and Sarah together as a people is the religion of Torah-observance, and this is true also of the many who do not themselves pay much attention to the *mitzvoth*."[63]

The idea that Jewish Law is obsolete because it has "done its job" by pointing to Christ's passion is a theological problem because it throws into question God's desire that Jews exist at all. Since God's election of the Jewish people is expressed through Torah-observance (including circumcision, dietary laws, and Sabbath) the traditional claim that Christ has discontinued these practices is the equivalent of saying God no longer desires the practice of Judaism. If God no longer desires Torah-observance, God no longer desires for there to be Jews in the world. This is why Isaac and Soulen

60. Soulen, *God of Israel*, 4.
61. Neusner, *Judaism: The Basics*.
62. Ibid., 11.
63. Jenson, "Toward a Christian Theology of Judaism," 9.

understand the traditional fulfillment concept (fulfilled and expired; fulfilled and cancelled) to undermine the "very existence of Jewish flesh or carnal Jewish existence."[64]

3. THE LIMITATIONS OF THE TERM

In order to prevent the term supersessionism from blurring with other concepts, such as anti-Semitism, it is important to identify its limitations. First, supersessionism should not be confused with anti-Semitism, which refers to hateful attitudes and actions directed toward the Jewish people because of their perceived ethnicity or race.[65] Rather, to supersede refers to the teaching that Jewish Law has been fulfilled and abrogated with the result that the Church replaces Israel. For example, Justin's *Dialogue with Trypho the Jew* assumes this sort of relationship between Judaism and Christianity: "the Old Law and covenant have become *obsolete* and replaced by a new law; the church has now become the *verus* Israel . . . .'"[66]

Second, supersessionism should not be confused with anti-Judaism, or "negative Christian views of Judaism," such as the idea that the God of Israel is evil or a God of wrath. This is certainly a negative view of God, and one shared by Valentinus and Marcion, but it does not amount to supersessionism since there is no claim that Christ fulfilled and cancelled the Law and subsequently replaced Israel with the Church.[67]

Third, supersessionism should not be used to refer to the idea that Judaism and Christianity are separate and distinct traditions or that they are mutually indifferent. Here, there is once again no claim about the fulfillment of the Law or any replacement of one entity with the other, but only a notion of distinct religions that avoid saying anything about the positive value of the other.

In order to prevent the term supersessionism from gradually blurring with "negative views of Judaism," on the one hand, or vague language about the differences between Judaism and Christianity, it is important to anchor the term to its origin in English theology with special attention to what Isaac and Soulen identified as the double sense of Christ's fulfillment of Jewish Law. *Supersessionism is the Christian claim that with the advent of*

64. Soulen, *God of Israel*, 31.
65. Pawlikowski, "Anti-Semitism," 22.
66. Cited in Donaldson, "Supersessionism in Early Christianity," 7. [Emphasis added]
67. Fredriksen, "The Birth of Christianity and the Origins of Anti-Judaism," 8–30.

Christ, Jewish Law is fulfilled and obsolete, with the result that God replaces Israel with the Church.

This discussion of supersessionism is in no way exhaustive but the definition I have suggested affords a way to clarify the discussion over whether Aquinas's theology is supersessionist since it recognizes the limits of the term while remaining attentive to the "double sense" of Christ's fulfillment: the teaching that Christ's fulfillment of Jewish Law also entail its obsolescence or expiration. As I hope to make clear in the next chapter, it is this concept that happens to be the central issue in the scholarly discussion over whether Aquinas's theology is supersessionist. I now turn to what Matthew Levering has referred to as a theological question of "paramount" significance: the question of supersessionism in Aquinas's theology.[68]

---

68. Levering, *Christ's Fulfillment*, 15.

2

Aquinas and the Question of Supersessionism

DURING THE LAST DECADE the discussion over whether or not Thomas Aquinas's theology is supersessionist has elicited deep disagreement among scholars. Two divergent positions have emerged, one claiming that Aquinas is the standard-bearer of a supersessionist Church and the other claiming that Aquinas avoids supersessionism. This chapter evaluates the scholarly discussion over whether Aquinas's theology is supersessionist with attention to the definition of supersessionism identified above: whether, with the advent of Christ, Jewish Law is fulfilled and obsolete, with the result that God replaces Israel with the Church. I show that the lack of precision with regard to the use of the term and/or the failure to attend to Aquinas's most relevant works, renders scholars' conclusions regarding Aquinas's susceptibility to the charge of supersessionism premature. It should become clear that the question of supersessionism in Aquinas's theology turns on whether Jewish observance of the Law can have a positive theological significance after the passion of Christ, or whether it is always and necessarily "dead and deadly." If the latter is the case then Aquinas's theology is economically supersessionist. If the former is true then Aquinas's theology avoids economic supersessionism.

Aquinas on Israel and the Church

1. "A JEWISH READING OF ST. THOMAS AQUINAS"

The question of supersessionism in the theology of Thomas Aquinas began with Wyschogrod's 1987 article, "A Jewish Reading of St. Thomas Aquinas," one of the first strictly theological treatments of Aquinas's view of the Jews.[1] Throughout the greater part of the essay, Wyschogrod is concerned to explain Aquinas's division of the Mosaic legislation into moral, ceremonial, and judicial law, as well as challenge Aquinas's claim that the ceremonial law is dead and deadly after the passion of Christ (Ia-IIae q. 103.4). Indeed, Wyschogrod challenges the same teaching that Jules Isaac challenged after the War: the idea that Christ abrogates Jewish Law after the passion of Christ. Both Jewish scholars understand this traditional Christian teaching to undermine Jewish existence.

Wyschogrod attempts to explain why Aquinas holds that the ceremonial law becomes sinful after Christ while the other two forms of law, judicial and moral, are preserved as legitimate.[2] The status of the ceremonial law after the passion of Christ is ultimately determined by what Wyschogrod refers to as the "hermeneutics of prefiguration."[3] Aquinas's reading of the Old Testament must be read in two senses and these senses correspond to the literal and spiritual meaning of the ceremonial laws: "they were

---

1. Wyschogrod, "A Jewish Reading of St. Thomas Aquinas," 125–38. Scholars had treated the topic of Aquinas and Judaism before Wyschogrod's essay, but the studies mainly discussed Aquinas's "social policy," or his teaching on toleration of Jews in Christendom. Although no one would respond to Wyschogrod's essay for well over a decade, the number of theological treatments of Aquinas's interpretation of Judaism grew substantially. For this reason, Wyschogrod's essay can be said to mark the beginning of twentieth-century scholarly attention to Aquinas's theology of the Jews. Guttmann's and Chenu's work preceded Wyschogrod's essay. Guttmann, *Das Verhältniss des Thomas von Aquino zum Judenthum*; Chenu, "La Théologie de La Loi Ancienne Selon Saint Thomas." See also Dubois, "Thomas Aquinas on the Place of the Jews in the Divine Plan," 241–66. Schenk, "Covenant Initiation," 555–93. Torrell, "Ecclesia Iudaeorum." Hofer, "The Circumcision of the Lord: Saving Mystery." Valkenberg and Schoot, "Thomas Aquinas and Judaism." Hall, "The Old Law and the New Law." The theological aspects of Jeremy Cohen and John Y. B. Hood's work should also be included in this list.

2. The judicial laws can be observed in Israel or any nation so long as they are no longer viewed as binding through enactment by God in the Old Law. Wyschogrod writes, "Thomas knows very well that the Old Law is not going to prove permanent, that there will come a time, or a time has come, when the Old Law, or at least a portion of it, will have been abolished. If this is to be made intelligible, the Old Law must be divided into sharply defined categories so that one segment of it can be considered no longer binding while another can remain in full force." Wyschogrod, "A Jewish Reading," 126.

3. Ibid., 129.

ordained for the worship of God at that time, and for prefiguring Christ."[4] Wyschogrod rightly interprets the spiritual meaning of the Law, which is the prefigurement of Christ, as primary in Aquinas. Since, for Aquinas, ceremonies are professions of faith, to observe the ceremony primarily meant to prefigure Christ after Christ has already come is tantamount to a declaration that Christ has not come. Jewish observance of the Law is, after Christ, a declaration of unbelief. Wyschogrod cites Aquinas's explanation of this teaching in Ia-IIae q. 103.4 and concludes: "It is here that the transformation from faithful obedience of the *mizvoth* to mortal sin occurs."[5] The Old Law goes from being a vehicle that pointed to Christ—who justified—to a vehicle that denies Christ and is therefore the occasion of sin.[6] In Wyschogrod's view, Aquinas "makes the prefigurement hermeneutics the foundation of his teaching of the annulment of the ceremonial law."[7]

For Wyschogrod, Aquinas's reading of the ceremonial law presents problems for the "believing Jew." Wyschogrod reads Aquinas's teaching as applying to Jews in general. When he asks whether the observance of the ceremonial aspects of the Mosaic Law ought to be interpreted more benevolently, he understands Aquinas's teaching to apply to the "Jewish reader":

> When the Christian interpreter finds in the myriad details of the Jewish ceremonial law references to the birth, passion and resurrection of Jesus, the Jewish reader cannot help feeling uncomfortable. And most of all, when Thomas makes the prefigurement hermeneutics the foundation of his teaching of the annulment of the ceremonial law, the feeling of discomfort turns into one of positive distress. For even if there is, from the point of view of Christian faith, a large element of prefigurement of Christ in the Old Testament, does it have to follow that someone who refrains from eating pork or who fasts on the Day of Atonement is committing a mortal sin? Must his action be interpreted as saying that 'Christ was to be born' (103, 4, Reply) rather than that he had been born, thereby denying Christ? Could adherence to the Mosaic Law not be interpreted much more benevolently, as love of God and his

---

4. Ibid., 129–30. Wyschogrod writes, "Whatever meaning the narratives and precepts (laws) of the Old Testament may have had at the time they were given, they also had the probably more important function of prefiguring or foreshadowing the coming of Christ." Wyschogrod's citations of the *Summa Theologiae* are all taken from the Blackfriars edition: Ia-IIae q. 103.4 in *Summa theologiae* vol. 29 ed. Thomas Gilby.

5. Ibid., 132.

6. Ibid., 133.

7. Ibid., 136.

commandments, as fidelity to a holy way of life out of which—for Christian faith—the Redeemer was born?[8]

Wyschogrod sees Aquinas' teaching as problematic for reasons that are similar to Isaac and Soulen. For Wyschogrod, the central tenet of biblical faith is that God loves and elected the people of Israel "unto the end of time."[9] Circumcision is "a searing of the covenant into the flesh of Israel and not only, or perhaps not even primarily, into its spirit."[10] This covenant is maintained through the concrete practice of circumcision and observance of Torah.

Israel and the nations have, at times, failed to accept the terms of this election.[11] The Jewish people have failed to live out their election during certain periods, forgetting that their blessing is for service of the nations. And the nations have resented the presence of carnal Israel since the existence of this people is a reminder the nations are not God's elect. Despite failures on both sides, God's love and free election of Israel is irrevocable and divinely intended for the service of the Gentile world. God's plan is to consummate creation *through* Israel's election, fulfilling God's word to Abraham that "in you shall all the families of the earth be blessed (Gen. 12:3)."[12] Therefore, for Wyschogrod, the election of Israel is about the blessing of the nations, and the distinction between Jew and Gentile is "a sign of hope, not a wall of separation."[13]

Since the covenant is maintained through the practice of circumcision, Aquinas's teaching that this custom is no longer a theologically significant act of worship entails that God has repudiated God's promise to the Jewish people.[14] Such a claim raises questions about God's trustworthiness

---

8. Ibid., 136.
9. Wyschogrod, *Abraham's Promise*, 6.
10. Wyschogrod, *The Body of Faith*, 66.
11. Ibid., 9.
12. Ibid.
13. Ibid., 13.
14. For Wyschogrod, such a problematic view of the election of the Jewish people is not only expressed in the church's attitude toward Jewish observance of Torah. Wyschogrod also thinks it is manifested in how Christians perceive the Jewish identity of baptized Jews. For Wyschogrod, if the church truly believes in "the permanence and centrality of Israel's election as central to its own identity, it will expect baptized Jews to continue to affirm their Jewish identity and continue to observe Torah." However, "if the church truly believes that it has fundamentally superseded God's covenant with Israel, it will prohibit baptized Jews from obeying Torah and maintaining a distinct identity within the church." *Abraham's Promise*, 17.

and the trustworthiness of God's promises. If God desires that circumcision become obsolete or sinful, this implies God desires that the Jews disappear from the world. Wyschogrod argues that such a low view of the Jewish people goes hand in hand with the idea that the disappearance of Jews from the world is "no theological loss":

> Were all Jews to recognize the truth, they would cease their stubborn insistence on continuing to exist as an identifiable people and become an integral part of the new Israel—the Church—which is God's new covenant partner in the world. The disappearance of the Jews from the world would be no theological loss because their place would have taken by the new people of God.[15]

For Wyschogrod, the fulfillment and obsolescence of the ceremonial law is a problem because it means God, contrary to his promise, no longer desires for Jews to exist in the world as Jews, and that, consequently, God's promises cannot be trusted.[16]

In light of Wyschogrod's understanding of the election of Israel, it becomes clear that his primary concern in addressing Aquinas is the teaching that Jewish observance of the Law is obsolete or sinful after Christ.[17] Wyschogrod's essay therefore centers the discussion on Aquinas and

---

15. Ibid.

16. David Novak explains the consequences of this point from the Christian perspective rather succinctly: "For Christians, the answer, paraphrasing Karl Barth, goes something like this: The promises God made through Jesus presuppose that God has already been keeping his promises to Israel. Indeed, for Christians, Jesus was sent to fulfill God's ultimate promise to Israel of redemption and then to extend it to the world. Nevertheless, God's initial promise to Israel is that she will not die but live, and live with duration as a covenanted people. The promises made through Jesus, which the Church accepts as normative, cannot be believed, therefore, if the Jewish people, who have a perpetual claim to be called Israel, are no longer present in the world." Novak, *Talking with Christians*, 11.

17. For a Christian description of this concern see the work of Robert Jenson: "identifiable Jewishness does not long survive within the Gentile dominated church. To be sure, identifiable continuing descent from Abraham and Sarah is perhaps more likely within the church than among those assimilated into the secular world. But even so, if God is to have a people identified by descent from Abraham and Sarah, the church as it is will not provide it. I propose to my fellow Christians that God wills the Judaism of Torah-obedience as that which alone can and does hold the lineage of Abraham and Sarah together during the time of detour. . . . By this time, the world is surely full of biological descendants of Abraham and Sarah who are not jointly part of any recognizable people. What holds some descendants of Abraham and Sarah together as a people is the religion of Torah-observance, and this is true also of the many who do not themselves pay much attention to the *mitzvoth*." Jenson, "Toward a Christian Theology of Judaism." In *Jews and Christians: People of God*, 9.

supersessionism on the problem at the "heart of supersessionism," the double sense of fulfillment of the Law.[18] From his perspective, the question of supersessionism in Aquinas turns on whether or not observance of the ceremonial law after the passion of Christ is dead and deadly for Jews, or if as he asks at the close of his challenge to Aquinas, whether Jewish observance of the ceremonial law after Christ can be interpreted more benevolently.

2. MATTHEW LEVERING'S USAGE OF THE LANGUAGE OF SUPERSESSIONISM

As Levering has observed, "A Jewish Reading of St. Thomas Aquinas" represents Wyschogrod's attempt to bring Aquinas into the contemporary Jewish-Christian dialogue.[19] Indeed, Levering's response to Wyschogrod can be considered an attempt to explain and defend the traditional interpretation of Christ's fulfillment of the ceremonial law in the new era of Jewish-Christian dialogue.

Levering's Reply to Michael Wyschogrod

Levering responds to Wyschogrod's critique by explaining the rationale behind Aquinas's view that Christ fulfills the Mosaic Law. The purpose of Divine Law, which includes the Old Law, is to direct human beings to the supernatural end of friendship with God by means of knowing and loving. Yet the Old Law only partially achieves this goal by forbidding sinful acts and by restraining disordered desires opposed to the perfection of the rational creature. Christ perfectly fulfills the Old Law in his passion and does so in order to "bring it to an end in His own self, so as to show that it was ordained to Him."[20] Christ's fulfillment of the Old Law means that the ceremonial and judicial precepts do come to an end but only in "the positive (teleological) sense of attaining their ultimate end, in which they rest or last forever."[21]

---

18. Steven Boguslawski also views the claim that the ceremonial law is useless in and of itself as part of "supersessionist logic." I will treat Boguslawski below and it should become clear that a significant convergence in the definition of supersessionism seems to appear between Wyschogrod and Boguslawski.

19. Levering, *Christ's Fulfillment*, 17.

20. Ibid., 29.

21. Ibid., 30.

Aquinas and the Question of Supersessionism

However, Christ's perfect fulfillment of the Old Law means that all members of his Body can now share in this fulfillment of the Law. Levering explains that the ceremonial aspect of the Law is indeed a covenant that lasts forever. Aquinas's fundamental answer to Wyschogrod, according to Levering, is "that the Mosaic Law, in a real sense, *is still observed by Christians*."[22] However, the ceremonial law is said to be "forever" only in regard to the "reality which the ceremonies foreshadowed," which are the sacraments of the church. Since the reality prefigured by the Law is still observed by Christians, it has not been revoked, and Levering concludes that it is unfair to associate Aquinas with supersessionism.[23] "While it would be wrong to suggest that Aquinas's thought is a model for contemporary Jewish-Christian relations," writes Levering, "it is equally unfair to tar Aquinas theologically with the 'supersessionist' brush."[24]

Levering seems to use the term supersessionism in three ways. His primary usage of the term refers to the idea that "the fulfillment of Israel's covenants means that they are now revoked."[25] A secondary usage appears to refer to the practice of forced baptism, and a third usage refers to views held by Robert Grossetesste that Jews were heretics.

Each of Levering's uses of the language of supersessionism seems to be problematic, when viewed against uses of the term in previous chapter. Regarding his second use of the term (i.e., the reference to forced baptism), Levering confuses anti-Judaism—especially as it is expressed in acts of violence—with supersessionism. As I pointed out in chapter 1, anti-Jewish violence is not supersessionism.[26]

Regarding the third usage, Levering claims that Aquinas "avoids the *kind* of supersessionism that mars Robert Grosseteste's work."[27] Here, Le-

---

22. Ibid., 28.

23. Ibid.

24. Ibid., 152. Levering appears to have changed concerning his comment that Aquinas's thought is not a model for contemporary Jewish-Christian relations. In his most recent work, *Jewish-Christian Dialogue and the Life of Wisdom*, both Levering and Novak look to Aquinas's engagement with Maimonides' theology as a model to be emulated. Levering, *Jewish-Christian Dialogue and the Life of Wisdom*.

25. Levering, *Christ's Fulfillment*, 9.

26. Although it should be noted that Jules Isaac believed the latter could be a motivating cause of the former.

27. Ibid. [Emphasis added]. Levering links Grosseteste and supersessionism in two different places: 9; 152fn. 50. In the footnote, he implies that the "supersessionism" Aquinas avoids is forced baptism of Jews and the view promoted by Grosseteste and other medieval theologians that Jews were heretics. I cannot tell if Levering meant to contrast

vering's reference to a *kind* of supersessionism hints at a view of supersessionism that seems to distinguish between various manifestations of the problem in Christian theology. However, he does not explain what type of supersessionism it is, exactly, that mars the work of Grosseteste, and this ultimately blurs similarities and differences between Aquinas and Grosseteste.[28]

Aquinas and Grosseteste on forced baptism, but if he did, the point is moot since both theologians condemned forced baptism of Jews in agreement with ecclesiastical policy. Friedman explains, "[Grosseteste] *repeats the condemnation* by his Church of the prevailing political view that the Jews were to be maltreated or exterminated as a means of forcible conversion. He lays it down that the punishment which the Almighty had ordained that the Jews suffer should neither be increased nor diminished by Christians, and recognizes that the Jews should be afforded an opportunity to gain a livelihood by honest work." Friedman, *Robert Grosseteste and the Jew*, 20 (emphasis mine). Likewise, Aquinas makes the argument that such coercion is against free will and the authority ascribed to parents by the natural law. Cf. IIa-IIae, q 10; 8; 12; III q 68 a. 10. Aside from whether the comparison between Aquinas and Grosseteste is accurate, the more serious problem is Levering's inaccurate usage of the term supersessionism to describe forced baptism. Since anti-Semitism is not supersessionism, Levering's claim that Aquinas avoids "supersessionism" does not hold.

28. The ambiguity created by the conflating of anti-Semitism and supersessionism distracts from how Aquinas's theological interpretation of the Jewish people actually shares, at least in a few places in his thought, a particular form of supersessionism also present in Grosseteste's work. This becomes clear when both theologians are viewed in light of punitive supersessionism. According to Soulen, punitive supersessionism consists of the idea that God abrogates God's covenant with the Jews on account of Israel's rejection of Christ and the gospel. It is precisely punitive supersessionism that is evidenced in Grosseteste's letter to the Countess of Winchester: "[The Jews], being guilty of murder, in cruelly killing by crucifixion the Savior of the world, our Lord Jesus Christ, lest they might through his preaching [the gospel of] salvation lose standing and caste, because of this sin they did lose their standing unhappily at the hands of Titus and Vespasian, and having themselves entered into captivity, were scattered as captives through all lands and peoples, and they shall not be restored to freedom until the very end of the world. But in the last days, when all the multitude of nations, as is written, shall enter i.e. to faith, then all Israel, namely the people of the Jews, shall attain salvation through the same belief in Christ, and shall come again out of captivity into freedom. In the meantime, however, while the same people of the Jews persisting in their unbelief blaspheme Christ the Savior of the world, and mock at his suffering, they will be held captive under the rulers of the world to the just punishment of their sin." Again, see Friedman, *Robert Grosseteste and the Jews,* 12–18. See also Robert Grosseteste, *De Cessatione Legalium,* 7. Although Aquinas is opposed to violence against Jewish people, he does adopt, in several places, a punitive supersessionist stance similar to that of Grosseteste. In his *Epistola ad ducissam Brabantiae,* Aquinas states, in his reply to the Duchess's inquiry on whether it is permissible to exact tribute of the Jews, that, "it is true, as the Law declares, that Jews *in consequence of their sin,* are or were destined to perpetual slavery; so that sovereigns of states may treat their goods as their own property; with the sole proviso that they do not

Nevertheless, the main problem with Levering's use of the term supersessionism is that he defines supersessionism only as "the revoking of the covenant." However, "revoking," implies a punishment due to a violation of a law. The form of supersessionism that has to do with God "revoking" the covenant with the Jewish people as punishment is punitive supersessionism. While Levering may be correct that Aquinas does not teach punitive supersessionism in this context, this is *not* the form of supersessionism with which Wyschogrod is concerned in his reading of Aquinas. Levering's definition of supersessionism permits him to evade or avoid Wyschogrod's main concern with Aquinas's view of the ceremonial law.

As demonstrated above, supersessionism concerns not only the punitive form that assumes a "revoking" of God's covenant with the Jews as punishment for failure to accept Christ. Supersessionism also consists of what Soulen has called the economic type, and what Isaac viewed as the *double sens* of "fulfilled and obsolete (*dépassée*)" or "fulfilled and expired (*périmé*)." Wyschogrod's critique of Aquinas's teaching on Jewish observance of the Law after Christ is concerned with economic supersessionism *not* punitive, as Levering seems to think when he defines the term only as "revoking the covenant." Nowhere in Wyschogrod's essay does he raise the issue of a punitive revoking of the covenant.

Perhaps because Levering conflates economic and punitive supersessionism, he also seems to miss Wyschogrod's concern that Aquinas's teaching contradicts the biblical claim that God has elected the Jewish people unto the end of time.[29] Wyschogrod's problem with Aquinas's teaching that

---

deprive them of all that is necessary to sustain life." As Hood has already observed, Aquinas believes that the Jews have been cast into spiritual exile for their rejection of Christ and that their social status in Christendom is proof of this. Both Aquinas and Grosseteste view the destruction of the Temple in 70 A.D. by Titus, as well as Jewish expulsion from Palestine at the hands of Vespasian, as a divine punishment for the Crucifixion. See Hood, *Aquinas and the Jews*, 75. However, such a view was not uncommon among thirteenth-century theologians. Friedman observes that the sentiment of Grosseteste and Aquinas are so strikingly repeated "that one is tempted to believe that Grosseteste's letter was known to Aquinas until [one] recalls that both are only repetitions of the authoritative Church pronouncements on the Jews." See Friedman, *Robert Grosseteste and the Jews*, 33. The Augustinian interpretation of Jewish diaspora was the standard medieval view, and the few places where punitive supersessionism does appear in Aquinas, the claim lacks the elaborate exegetical tapestry that Grosseteste attaches to it. Thomas Aquinas, "On the Government of the Jews," 233.

29. Another reason Levering misses Wyschogrod's primary concern with Aquinas's teaching may be due to the fact that he thinks Aquinas's claim that the observance of the ceremonial law is a mortal sin after Christ only applies to baptized Jews *not to Jews*

Jewish observance of the ceremonial law after Christ is a sin is that it undermines the existence and election of Israel, which is visibly maintained precisely through the observance of the Law. It is this aspect of Wyschogrod's challenge to Aquinas that Levering seems to leave unanswered by arguing only that the covenant continues because it is now fulfilled.

Yet Levering also seems aware of Wyschogrod's concern to protect the idea that God wills the corporeal existence of the Jewish people and senses a tension between this idea and his claim that the covenant continues but through the Church. This seems clear at two points in his reply. The first point is when he summarizes Wyschogrod's question to Aquinas as: "How . . . can the Church claim to recognize God's continuing covenant with Israel, which would quickly disappear as a visible reality if all Jews heeded the Church's evangelical call?"[30] The second point is when Levering qualifies his answer to Wyschogrod (which is, ultimately, that the Mosaic Law, in a real sense, is still observed by Christians through participation in Christian sacraments) by stating that Wyschogrod would not recognize the "real sense" in which the covenant continues in the form of Christian identity. He also says the claim that the covenant with the Jews is ongoing in the sense that Christians now observe it is an "apparent paradox" that requires explanation. The continuing of the covenant is a paradox because by sharing in Christ's Jewish fulfillment of Mosaic Law, Jews do not lose their identity but enter into the supernatural fullness of their identity.[31]

It is not clear though, how such a Jew, remains distinguishably Jewish in any sense of the word, i.e., how it differs from Christian identity as such. This view of Christ's fulfillment of the ceremonial law implies that authentic Jewish identity, at the end of the day, is Christian identity.[32] According to

---

generally. In a footnote, he denies that Aquinas's teaching that the observance of the ceremonial aspects of Mosaic Law after Christ is a sin applies to Jews. This claim seemed to need more attention in light of how much time Wyschogrod spends on pointing to Aquinas's teaching that the Law is dead and deadly as *the* problem.

30. Levering, *Christ's Fulfillment*, 16.

31. Ibid., 29.

32. If this is in fact Aquinas's view of the relation between Church and Israel, then his view is not unlike that of Karl Barth's. Soulen observes that Barth's theology is ultimately economically supersessionist because it holds that God's covenant with Israel is fulfilled in Jesus Christ's life, death, and resurrection. At that point Israel's distinctive role comes to an end in principle, and the church takes its place. In Barth's view, "God's work as Consummator is joined primordially not to the people of Israel as a whole but to the one Israelite Jesus Christ." Soulen, *God of Israel*, 90.

Bruce Marshall, the claim that the Mosaic Law is fulfilled in Christ is *not* the solution to the problem of supersessionism. This sort of fulfillment

> seems to suggest, that what a Jew should do in order to observe God's command regarding his eight-day-old son is take him to church and get him baptized. It seems, in other words, that on this view the way for Jews to observe the law is to become Christians. Now the notion that the law of Moses finds its complete fulfillment in Christ and the Church is, I think, indispensable for Christianity. But this ancient idea is not the solution to the problem of supersessionism. It *is* the problem.[33]

In the end, Levering embraces and defends the traditional concept that Christ fulfills and renders obsolete the ceremonial law, but he denies that this is supersessionism. Although he is right that Aquinas's teaching on the ceremonial law in Ia-IIae q. 103.4 is not punitive supersessionism, the teaching clearly amounts to economic supersessionism since such a view assumes the obsolescence of the ceremonial law. The teaching that Christ fulfills and renders obsolete Jewish Law is exactly what Isaac, Soulen, and Wyschogrod identify as supersessionism. By Levering's own account, Aquinas's teaching in Ia-IIae q. 103.4 has exactly the problematic consequences that Isaac, Soulen, and Wyschogrod foresee. It is not clear how the covenant *with* the Jews can be "ongoing" if Jewish identity is abrogated. From Wyschogrod's view, the claim that the ceremonial law is dead implies that God no longer wills the Jewish people to live as Jews but rather, to live as some other people. Therefore, Levering's interpretation of Aquinas's teaching amounts to economic supersessionism since it assumes Christ's fulfillment of the ceremonial law renders it obsolete.

Levering's Engagement with Mark Kinzer

Eight years after Levering's response to Wyschogrod, the discussion over whether Aquinas's theology is supersessionist emerges once again, this time in the context of Levering's reply to the work of Mark Kinzer.[34] According to Levering, the question of supersessionism remains a paramount theological question. He states that unless the problem is overcome, Jewish-Christian

---

33. Bruce Marshall, "*Quasi in Figura*," 480–81.
34. Mark Kinzer, *Postmissionary Messianic Judaism*, 39.

dialogue is not possible.[35] Kinzer, building on the argument of Wyschogrod, argues that Aquinas's claim that the observance of ceremonial law is a mortal sin represents the "unequivocal supersessionist theological and canonical legacy of the Church."[36] Kinzer argues that this teaching is supersessionist, which he defines as "the *ekklesia* replaces the Jewish people as the elect community in covenant with God . . . the church is the new and spiritual Israel, fulfilling the role formerly occupied by 'carnal' Israel."[37]

Kinzer argues that the New Testament does not support the claim that the ceremonial aspect of Mosaic Law is dead for Jewish Christ-followers—a claim articulated by Augustine in his correspondence with Jerome, and later adopted by Aquinas.[38] For Kinzer, this teaching is a tradition that forces Aquinas to adopt the claim that the Law causes spiritual death for Jews. Kinzer concludes that, "Only a preexisting theological commitment to supersessionism could lead one to be satisfied with the explanation of the relevant biblical texts offered by Augustine and accepted by Aquinas."[39]

Levering takes issue with Kinzer's claim about Aquinas's "preexisting theological commitment" to supersessionism. He rejects Kinzer's exegesis on the basis of a thorough review of several New Testament texts and argues that Aquinas's claim that the ceremonial Mosaic Law is deadly after

---

35. See the excursus at the end of the chapter.

36. Kinzer does say that Aquinas cannot be held responsible for creating the Christian consensus on the *mortifera* character of the Mosaic Law since he is interpreting ecclesiastical tradition whose roots go back to the early second century and which became official at the second council of Nicaea in 787. Such a view seems to underestimate Aquinas's understanding of the relationship between Scripture and *sacra doctrina*, not to mention overlook the possibility that original insights on relevant texts regarding the Law may exist in Aquinas's works, especially his neglected biblical commentaries on the Pauline epistles. Both Kinzer and Wyschogrod employ a selective reading of Aquinas, a point I will return to below.

37. Kinzer, *Postmissionary Messianic Judaism*, 12.

38. See also Carolinne White, *The Correspondence (394–419) between Jerome and Augustine of Hippo*.

39. Kinzer, *Postmissionary Messianic Judaism*, 39. Kinzer's view of Aquinas's preexisting commitment does not take into account the fact that Aquinas thinks that Paul teaches (in Gal 5:2) that observance of the ceremonial law after Christ makes Christ no profit and thus must mean it is a mortal sin. Aquinas does not commit to theological positions first and then look for support in Scripture. Aquinas's biblical commentaries represent a critical engagement with the text that accords with his official title of "Master of the Sacred Page." His adoption of the Augustinian view of the Law as dead and deadly is determinatively shaped by his reading of Hebrews and Galatians, as I demonstrate in chapter 8.

the Passion of Christ is an accurate expression of New Testament theology. In short, Levering argues that Christ has fulfilled and "reconfigured" Torah and Temple around himself and that Scripture supports this view.

It is interesting that Levering does not claim Aquinas avoids supersessionism as he did in his original response to Wyschogrod. In his reply to Kinzer's argument that Aquinas is the standard-bearer of a supersessionist Church, he steps away from the language of supersessionism. Instead, he argues that Aquinas's fulfillment theology expresses the view of the New Testament.

However, though Levering shifts away from the language of supersessionism, he does use the language of "replacement," which may indicate he may be more comfortable with the equivalent term, "replacement theology." After stating that Aquinas's fulfillment theology expresses the New Testament view, he attempts to describe a positive ongoing role for Jews in the present. He argues that the Jews in fact, do have "a place" in the world, and explains how Aquinas's view does not "negate" Judaism:

> God gave his covenantal people the Torah, as the "place" in which they would be formed in true worship of the one God, and Judaism and Jews continue to possess this covenantal "place" even as Christians invite the Jewish people to discover the messianic fulfillment of this "place." The fact that in the new covenant Jews fulfill their covenantal obligations (Torah observance) sacramentally, in union with Gentiles in the Body of the Messiah, does not take away the "place" of Judaism and Jews, because this "place" participates in the saving work of the Messiah.[40]

Here, Levering essentially restates the position outlined in his reply to Wyschogrod.[41] The difference is that in his encounter with Kinzer, he states his position in terms of "place" and argues more explicitly that Jewish observances are now practiced in another place: the Church.

Overall, Levering's approach seems to sidestep the paramount question of supersessionism. In his reply to Wyschogrod the term is conflated with anti-Judaism. In his engagement with Kinzer he seems to drop the language of supersessionism altogether.[42] By addressing Kinzer's exege-

---

40. Levering, *Jewish-Christian Dialogue*, 39.
41. Levering, *Christ's Fulfillment*, 29.
42. In his engagement with Novak, his emphasis on teleological fulfillment seems only to pay lip service to the call for the renunciation of harsh Christian supersessionism. Levering's argument against Kinzer (that the Church and sacraments are the new place for the Jewish people) sits in direct tension with his approval of Novak's renunciation

sis instead of the question of whether Aquinas's theology consists of supersessionism, Levering begs the paramount question put to Aquinas by Wyschogrod: "How... can the Church claim to recognize God's continuing covenant with Israel, which would quickly disappear *as a visible reality* if all Jews heeded the Church's evangelical call?"[43]

3. BRUCE MARSHALL AND STEVEN BOGUSLAWSKI ON THE LANGUAGE OF SUPERSESSIONISM

Bruce Marshall and Steven Boguslawski acknowledge that the traditional concept of Christ fulfilling and rendering obsolete the ceremonial law amounts to supersessionism. In fact, these Thomists understand the term "supersessionism" to refer to the idea that Jewish Law after Christ is obsolete or cancelled. Their usage of the term overlaps greatly with how the word functions in the thought of Isaac, Soulen, and Wyschogrod.

Bruce Marshall on the Supersessionism of the *Summa theologiae*

For Marshall, supersessionism involves "the thought that the gifts God gave and the promises God made to the Jews now apply to us, the Church, *instead* of to the Jews. They have been taken away from the Jews and given to us."[44]

Marshall rightly understands that the affirmation of God's ongoing election of Israel, such as the one in *Nostra Aetate*, raises the question of the status of observance of the ceremonial law, since it is through the observance

---

of harsh Christian supersessionism, since Novak rejects precisely this form of replacement theology. Ironically, Novak uses the language of "replacement" as synonymous with supersessionism in the works that Levering draws upon for his appropriation of Novak's views of supersessionism. Indeed, Novak believes it is the sort of replacement theology articulated by Levering that must be overcome: "Christian supersessionism lends itself to an easy way to proselytize Jews. It simply tells Jews that they are living in an irretrievable past. It thus tells Jews to become 'full Jews,' that is, to become Christians and leave Judaism behind." Novak, *Talking with Christians*, 24. The harsh Christian supersessionism that Novak requires Christians to reject is precisely the argument that invites Jews to become "full Jews" by fulfilling, in Levering's words, "their covenantal obligations (Torah observance) sacramentally, in union with Gentiles in the Body of the Messiah." Levering, *Jewish-Christian Dialogue*, 40.

43. Levering, *Christ's Fulfillment*, 16. [Emphasis added]
44. Marshall, *Quasi in Figura*, 477.

Aquinas and the Question of Supersessionism

of the Torah that God's covenant with the Jews remains a covenant with the Jews: "The Jewish people," writes Marshall, "cannot be permanently elect unless they can be distinguished at all times from the nations, and the observance of traditional Jewish Law seems to be the one mark by which this distinction can be sustained *post Christum*."[45]

For this reason, Marshall thinks the traditional views of fulfillment, such as the one in the thought of Levering, which claims Torah is fulfilled by observing the sacraments of the church, are supersessionist. Marshall, like Wyschogrod, thinks Aquinas's teaching that the observance of the ceremonial law after Christ is a mortal sin represents supersessionism. He writes,

> Thomas clearly regards the continued observance of the Torah after Christ as fatal. That is, the vast bulk of Mosaic legislation, everything in the "Old Law" which Aquinas considers distinctively Jewish (everything, that is, except the ten commandments), has been set aside by the coming of Christ. More than that: everything which pertains to the worship of God in Israel . . . —what Aquinas calls the "ceremonial law"—is now not only useless, but destructive. After Christ these laws are not simply dead (*mortua*), but deadly (*mortifera*); those who continue to observe them "now sin mortally."[46]

An important aspect of Marshall's handling of this teaching in Aquinas is his attentiveness to possible tensions in Aquinas's position on the matter. Marshall suggests there is a positive view of Israel in the Romans commentary and that Aquinas affirms the election of Israel in a way that repudiates supersessionism.[47] The possibility of such a tension suggests that contemporary Thomistic scholarship lacks a complete picture of Aquinas's thought on the subject of the ceremonial law after the passion of Christ.[48]

---

45. Ibid., 92. Marshall elaborates on this point in another essay: "the Jewish people cannot continue to exist in the long run without Judaism. . . . The irrevocable election of the Jewish people evidently requires the permanence of their religion[;] . . . without a substantial core of faithful Jews, who practice Judaism well and teach their children to do the same, it seems impossible that the Jewish people could endure in the long run. Without Judaism, the Jewish people would surely, if slowly, disappear form the earth, as other ancient people have done. They would cease to be a distinct people, and vanish into *gentilitas*, as medieval Christian theologians called the mass of us not descended from Abraham, Isaac, and Jacob." Marshall, "Elder Brothers," 122.

46. Marshall, "*Quasi in Figura*," 479. Marshall has in mind Ia-IIae q. 103.4; q. 104.3.

47. Marshall, "Postscript and Prospect," 523–4.

48. In his reply to Marshall, Emmanuel Perrier commented, "If it happens that Aquinas does not achieve a homogeneous doctrine on a given subject, it is always a good

For this reason, Marshall's work points to the necessity for filling-out the complexity of Aquinas's thought, especially in the Pauline commentaries.

Steven Boguslawski on How Aquinas Avoids Supersessionism

Boguslawski argues at length that there is a positive view of Israel in the Romans commentary but, unlike Wyschogrod and Marshall, he argues that Aquinas's view of the Jews in the *Summa theologiae* avoids supersessionism.

The term supersessionism features prominently in Boguslawski's main argument that Aquinas's commentary on Romans represents a correction and development of Augustine.[49] Boguslawski views supersessionism as synonymous with what he refers to as a "problematic Augustinian supersessionism,"[50] that relegates "Israel's divinely ordained prerogatives to prefigurements of the Christian dispensation."[51] By "Israel's divinely ordained prerogatives," Boguslawski means the covenant and Law[52] where "covenant" corresponds to "the pact of circumcision given to Abraham" and Law means the Mosaic legislation.[53] In particular, supersessionism is "relegating Israel's divinely ordained prerogatives to prefigurements of the Christian dispensation."[54]

For Boguslawski, Aquinas avoids supersessionism by maintaining the historical *realia* of Israel's prerogatives of Law and covenant. Aquinas is unlike Augustine because he does not resort to "deconstructing the Jews' historical, covenantal privileges." Rather, Aquinas advances "his own distinctive exegetical contribution to the commentary tradition without

---

method to verify beforehand that one is truly faced with such a situation." Perrier, "The Election of Israel Today," 485–503. Perrier does not seem to recognize why supersessionism is a theological problem. He asserts only that fulfillment is the way to understand the election. But this leaves the Jews, once again, in an ambiguous role that fails to attend to Wyschogrod's challenge to Thomistic studies that God wills there to be Jews in the world.

49. Boguslawski, *Thomas Aquinas on the Jews*.

50. Ibid., 4.

51. Ibid., xv.

52. Ibid., xvi; 108, fn8.

53. Ibid., 108, fn8. Novak also uses the language of "prerogatives" of Israel to describe that which is relegated and therefore marks a significant convergence of language between a contemporary Jewish theologian and Aquinas. As I shall demonstrate, Boguslawski's view of supersessionism also shares much with Wyschogrod's view of the problem.

54. Ibid., xv.

deconstructing the Jewish people's historical prerogatives or resorting to theological supersessionism."[55]

In another place, Boguslawski equates supersessionism with the idea that "Christian believers supersede Jews as the *verus Israel*."[56] Taken together, these two components of Boguslawski's view of supersessionism overlap with Soulen's term, economic supersessionism. Boguslawski seems to identify the "deconstruction" of Israel's prerogatives and their status as God's elect people, with supersessionism, which is essentially the same move that Isaac, Soulen, Wyschogrod, Kinzer, and Marshall all make.

Yet unlike Wyschogrod, Kinzer, and Marshall, Boguslawski argues Aquinas avoids supersessionism. He claims that Aquinas differs from Augustine in that Aquinas avoids teaching that the ceremonial is obsolete. Boguslawski explains that, for Augustine, Jewish prerogatives are only allegorical "foreshadowings" of Christian realities. Aquinas, however, strives to preserve Jewish prerogatives as grounded in literal, historical *realia*. Therefore, Aquinas, "corrects and develops Augustine."

It is not at all clear, based on Boguslawski's analysis, that Aquinas avoids this move. The main problem with Boguslawski's argument is that nowhere does he address Aquinas's teaching in the *Summa theologiae* that the observance of the Mosaic Law is a mortal sin because it amounts to a declaration of unbelief in Christ's passion. For this reason, his claim that Aquinas avoids deconstructing the literal meaning of circumcision and Mosaic Law to Christological prefigurements does not hold.

4. THE CEREMONIAL LAW IN AQUINAS'S PAULINE COMMENTARIES

All the scholars in the discussion over whether Aquinas's theology is supersessionist agree that the question turns on what Aquinas teaches about ceremonial law. Levering says that Aquinas teaches exactly what Wyschogrod is concerned to address: that Jewish observances becomes obsolete after Christ and that Jews can now only enter into the fullness of their Jewish identity by participating in Christian sacraments. Levering claimed this teaching was not supersessionism, but his usage is idiosyncratic and also confuses the term with anti-Judaism. In his most recent engagement with

---

55. Ibid., 29.
56. Ibid., 127.

Kinzer, Levering drops the term, but restates his position that the place for Jews to maintain the "ongoing" covenant is the Church.

Marshall and Boguslawski, on the other hand, understand the term supersessionism in a way that substantially coincides with Isaac and Soulen's critique of the Christian claim that with the advent of Christ, Jewish Law is "fulfilled and expired" or "fulfilled and obsolete." Both scholars view the Christian claim that the Jewish Law is obsolete as a problematic idea and therefore provide significant agreement upon the question raised by Wyschogrod's "Jewish Reading of St. Thomas Aquinas."

However, these scholars disagree about where Aquinas stands in relation to the question of supersessionism: Boguslawski argues Aquinas's teaching in the Romans commentary and *Summa theologiae* avoid supersessionism. Marshall thinks Aquinas's teaching in the *Summa theologiae* is supersessionist, while the Romans commentary is not supersessionist.

What can we conclude? The discussion over the question of supersessionism in Aquinas's theology contains a substantial overlap and consensus in the use of the term supersessionism, with the exception of Levering. This consensus over the meaning of the term coincides with the work of Isaac and Soulen. Therefore, my analysis of the discussion indicates that there is a rather straightforward way to pose the question that guides the rest of the study: the question of supersessionism in Aquinas's theology turns on whether Jewish observance of the Law can have a positive theological significance, or whether it is always and necessarily "dead and deadly."

In order to tackle question of supersessionism in Aquinas's theology, a more thorough analysis of Aquinas's teaching on the ceremonial law in the commentaries on Paul's letters is necessary. Although Marshall and Boguslawski's work broadens the discussion on whether Aquinas's theology is supersessionist to include Aquinas's Romans commentary, all scholars in the discussion over whether Aquinas's theology is supersessionist have overlooked Aquinas's extended reflections on some of the most relevant texts on the subject of the Jewish people: his commentaries on Paul's letters to the Galatians, Hebrews, and Ephesians.

As I show in the next chapter, Aquinas comments extensively on Jewish observance of the ceremonial law before and after Christ's passion in these commentaries. What sort of theological status does Aquinas attribute to the ceremonial law in the Pauline commentaries and how does this teaching relate to the teaching in the *Summa theologiae*? Does Aquinas teach that the ceremonial law is "fulfilled and expired," in the words of Jules

Isaac, or do these practices retain a positive theological significance after the passion of Christ?

EXCURSUS

Levering's engagement of Kinzer appears in *Jewish-Christian Dialogue*. The larger aim of the project is to engage the work of Jewish theologian David Novak. In the context of Levering's engagement with Novak, the language of supersessionism becomes rather complex and more idiosyncratic than in his engagement with Wyschogrod. "Jewish-Christian dialogue," Levering writes, "begins with the question of 'supersessionism'" and he offers his own definition of the term: Supersessionism is "what happens when Christian theologies leave no theological space for Judaism or Jewish theologies leave no theological space for Christianity—due to the Christian proclamation that Jesus of Nazareth is the Son of God incarnate who fulfills God's covenant with Israel and reconfigures Israel around himself."[57] It is not clear what Levering means here by the phrase "no theological space." The definition of supersessionism seems odd for several reasons. For one thing, it seems unrelated to previous uses of the term by Soulen, and others. For another, the definition seems to define supersessionism so narrowly that it is hard to imagine how any theologian could manage to be supersessionist. Apparently, any theologian who provided "theological space" of some sort for Judaism avoids supersessionism. On this definition, Justin Martyr or Melito of Sardis could be said to avoid supersessionism. Even Marcion could be said to avoid supersessionism, since he provided a theological space for Judaism, albeit an entirely negative one, completely opposite the church. Such a definition evacuates the term of its meaning.

More important than this definition of supersessionism is Levering's view that Jewish-Christian dialogue still "begins with the question of supersessionism." In order to overcome the problem of supersessionism, Levering draws upon David Novak's understanding of supersessionism, which he argues points the way forward for Jewish-Christian dialogue. In Novak's view, supersessionism consists of two forms: mild and harsh. The mild form holds the promise for moving forward in Jewish-Christian dialogue while the harsh prevents dialogue. The mild form of Christian supersessionism is characterized by two positive affirmations: 1) Jesus Christ is the Messiah and 2) the covenant with the Jews has not been revoked. Mild

---

57. Levering, *Jewish-Christian Dialogue*, 12.

supersessionism, explains Levering, is the view that Christianity "solves the problems of Judaism better than Judaism can do without Christianity because Christianity provides the savior to whom Judaism has always looked."[58] Because of this particular Messiah, Jesus of Nazareth, "Christianity 'supersedes' Judaism in the sense of 'going beyond it.'" As an example, Novak offers Edith Stein as one who "goes beyond" Judaism in her conversion to Christianity. According to both Novak and Levering, mild supersessionism is unavoidable for Christians because it involves the claim that Jesus Christ "goes beyond" Judaism. And yet, this mild form does not need to be "anti-Jewish" and does not require "condemnation of Judaism."

It is not at all clear, based on even the most basic definition of "supersede," how these two claims—(1) Jesus Christ is the Messiah and (2) the covenant with the Jews has not been revoked—are supersessionist in any way, since though the claims are in tension, Christ is not at all described as fulfilling and making obsolete Jewish Law and then replacing Israel with Church. Novak's language of a "mild" supersessionism as "going beyond" is too ambiguous to be helpful. His second term, harsh Christian supersessionism, is a more precise definition. Harsh supersessionism is more problematic than mild, in Novak's view, because it has the Church replacing the Jewish people.[59] Harsh supersessionism is the view that "the Jewish people are no longer special people in the eyes of God; they lose their covenantal prerogatives altogether, and fall back to the status of all other peoples." Novak is concerned here to protect the elect status of carnal Israel, as is Wyschogrod. In particular, Novak rejects what he refers to as the use of "teleological logic" of harsh supersessionism, which is used in the Christian interpretation of the relationship between Israel's covenants (the Old Testament) and Christ (the New Testament). Here, Novak's concern clearly correlates with the "heart of supersessionism" as defined in chapter 1. The Old, for Novak, should not be seen as the earlier "potential" to the New or as prior "cause." In contrast to such logic, Novak proposes a "parallel relation" between Jews and Christians that avoids "teleological" arguments of one entity replacing the other."

Levering quotes approvingly of Novak's rejection of harsh Christian supersessionism but backpedals when he speculates about what *sort* of teleological logic Novak actually rejects. "Viewed in light of Christ, biblical Israel—and Judaism—find teleological fulfillment in Christ, but not

---

58. Ibid., 14.
59. Novak, *Talking with Christians*, 41.

the kind of fulfillment that can be seen to emerge necessarily from the operation of the mechanism, nor the kind of teleology that brings about its own fulfillment from within its own resources and that has value only in its end or goal. God's Word includes his good gifts to Israel. *That these gifts are ordered to a further fulfillment is indeed teleological, but the gifts cannot be reduced to an immanent and mechanical teleology.*" [60]

Novak does not mention "types" of teleological logic or specify any distinction in relation to the term whatsoever. Yet Levering attempts to create a distinction where Novak offers none. Here, Levering proposes one form of teleology that is legitimate and another that is illegitimate, which he calls "mechanical." The mechanical is identified as problematic because it somehow reduces God's "good gifts to Israel." "I take it that [Novak] means to exclude a *mechanical teleology*, stripped of real final causality that treats biblical Israel as a mere mechanism by which God brings about Jesus, and which has no value once Jesus arrives."[61] He implies that a non-mechanical teleology that provides "real final causality" and that leaves the opposite of "no value" (some value?) for Israel would be acceptable to Novak.

It is important to unravel this terminology in order to try and understand what problem Levering understands the language of harsh supersessionism to identify. "Real final causality" is the form of teleological logic that is acceptable (to Levering) so long as it does not deny "realities" that Jews and Christians affirm together. Levering asks: "Once one allows for teleology, does one bring in supersessionism . . . through the back door? Assuming an appropriate time and setting, cannot Jews tell Christians to 'come home'? Yes, but neither Christians nor Jews can do so *in a manner that denies or discards the realities that Christians and Jews affirm together.*"[62]

This qualification about an "acceptable form of teleology" that does not discard "realities" Christians and Jews affirm together seems as if it is a way of sidestepping Novak's harsh Christian supersessionism. Levering seems to say that teleological logic is acceptable to Novak so long is it does not discard or deny "the realities that Christians and Jews affirm together." Yet Levering does not say what Jewish "realities" must not be denied. He mentions "good gifts to Israel," and "Sinai." Based on these terms, I take "realities" that Jews and Christians affirm and cannot be denied to mean God's gift of the Law and covenant with the Jews. If this definition is accepted,

---

60. Levering, *Jewish-Christian Dialogue*, 21.
61. Ibid., 25 (emphasis mine).
62. Ibid., 22 (emphasis mine).

the form of teleological logic of harsh Christian supersessionism (a distinction created by Levering and not Novak) that is "acceptable" must therefore positively "affirm" Jewish realities in a way that affirms Israel as somehow valuable. But if this is the case, why not refer to this form of acceptable teleological logic as mild supersessionism, since the mild form already positively affirms Israel's covenant? Again, "mild supersessionism" is defined as the idea that the Jews are not rejected as God's covenant people and the covenant is affirmed as an 'ongoing reality' that possesses positive meaning. Levering's category of acceptable teleology, which he also refers to as "real final causality" ultimately says nothing positive about Israel. "Mechanical teleology" only identifies, in ambiguous terms, what cannot be said about biblical Israel: e.g., one may not reduce biblical Israel's realities; one may not say that biblical Israel has no value. Nothing is said about what exactly must be affirmed about Israel. The distinction between acceptable (real final causality) and unacceptable (mechanical) teleology ultimately seems like a way of stepping around Novak's rejection of harsh Christian supersessionism, which Novak defines as, "the Jewish people are no longer special people in the eyes of God; they lose their covenantal prerogatives altogether, and fall back to the status of all other peoples." The distinction between an unacceptable and acceptable teleology essentially takes the teeth out of Novak's definition of harsh Christian supersessionism.

Novak is explicit that the mark of Christian supersessionist logic is the teleological logic that assumes the replacement of the Jews as God's elect people with the Church. He writes, "Christian supersessionists assert that God has rejected the Jews *and replaced them with the Church*...."[63] In Novak's view "the heart" of supersessionism is the teleological logic that requires that the "Church replaces the Jewish people as Israel."[64] He writes, "if the New Testament replaces the Old Testament and the Church replaces the Jewish people as Israel, then the old has been overcome—that is, has been superseded—by the new." Novak's whole purpose in calling for the renunciation of harsh Christian supersessionism is that the replacement of one entity by another prevents the sort of parallelism that he points toward as a solution for Jewish-Christian dialogue. Moving beyond harsh Christian supersessionism, especially its teleology that requires that the Church replace carnal Israel as God's elect, is Novak's aim, as the title of his article indicates: "From

---

63. Novak, *Talking with Christians*, 9.
64. Ibid.

Supersessionism to Parallelism in Jewish-Christian Dialogue."⁶⁵ Thus when Levering claims "Novak's way of handling the loaded term of 'supersessionism' identifies a path for Jewish-Christian dialogue" he seems only to pay lip service to Novak's understanding of the term.

For both Novak and Wyschogrod, Christian supersessionism refers to something far more precise. For Wyschogrod and Novak, *the* problem with supersessionism is the idea that the advent of Christ also entails that Jewish Law is obsolete and results in the Church replacing the Jews as God's elect community. In both of Levering's engagements with these Jewish theologians, the main concern of the Jewish thinkers regarding the paramount question of supersessionism is bypassed—whether God intends carnal Israel to exist or be replaced by the Church.

---

65. Ibid., 8.

3

Israel and the Church in Aquinas's Pauline Commentaries

THE QUESTION OF SUPERSESSIONISM in Aquinas's theology turns on whether Aquinas teaches that such observances are "fulfilled and expired." Although scholars such as Wyschogrod have commented upon texts in the *Summa theologiae* in relation to this question, the Pauline commentaries have largely been overlooked. This chapter sets the stage for an examination of Aquinas's view of the observance of the ceremonial law in "some of his greatest theological works," the commentaries on Paul's letters.[1] Aquinas viewed Paul's letters as a distinct unit of the New Testament that treated how the power of grace exists in the Church, and he considered the Apostle Paul to be first and foremost among theologians.[2] However, the Pauline commentaries also contain some of Aquinas's most extended theological reflections on the subject of Israel in general and the observance of the ceremonial law after Christ in particular.

---

1. Pius XII, "An Address to the Faculty and Students of the Roman Athenaeum Angelicum," cited in Baglow, *Modus Et Forma*.

2. *Prologus* 6. As Torrell has pointed out, "Despite the heterogeneity of these [fourteen letters], it is nonetheless certain that Thomas thought of his [Pauline] commentary as a whole. The proof of this is given in the Prologue that he placed at the head of this whole."

Israel and the Church in Aquinas's Pauline Commentaries

1. MASTER OF THE SACRED PAGE

For the majority of his academic career, Thomas Aquinas was *magister in sacra pagina*, or "Master of the Sacred Page."[3] Of the functions of the master, reading and commenting upon Scripture verse by verse was the primary duty.[4] Jean-Pierre Torrell remarks that although Aquinas's teaching on Scripture has been long overlooked in favor of the *Sentences* or the *Summa*, this kind of biblical teaching was nevertheless "Thomas's ordinary labor." "[I]t was in this way," writes Torrell, "that he commented on a little more than half of the New Testament and several books of the Old."[5] Aquinas wrote commentaries on five Old Testament books: Psalms, Job, Isaiah, Jeremiah, and Lamentations. He wrote two on the Gospels: Matthew and John. And he wrote fourteen commentaries on all the Pauline letters: Romans, 1 and 2 Corinthians, Galatians, Ephesians, Philippians, Colossians, 1 and 2 Thessalonians, 1 and 2 Timothy, Titus, Philemon, and Hebrews.[6]

---

3. The office of the *magister in sacra pagina* in the twelfth century consisted of a threefold function: *legere* (to read Scripture and comment on it verse by verse); *disputare* (to teach through objections and responses on a given theme); and *praedicare* (to preach). These three tasks correspond directly to three qualities Aquinas says doctors in sacred Scripture must possess in order to carry out the triple function of the office. Aquinas lists these qualities in his *principium,* or first inaugural lecture, which he presented as part of the ceremony for his installment as *magister in sacra pagina* at the university of Paris. The title of the lecture is *Rigans montes de superioribus*, taken from the verse which Aquinas puts at the beginning of the lecture: "Thou waterest the hills from thy upper rooms," a quotation of Psalm 103:13. For *Rigans montes* see S. Thomae Aquinatis, *Opuscula theologica*, 441–43. Torrell, *Saint Thomas Aquinas*, 54.

4. Ibid., 55.

5. Ibid.

6. Eleonore Stump observes that the early catalogues of Aquinas's works also list a commentary on the Song of Songs, but no such commentary has been found. As I explain below, my study will focus only on the commentaries on Paul's letters that treat the theme of the ceremonial law. This will include sections from: Romans, Galatians, Ephesians, and Hebrews. Aquinas, of course, thinks Paul wrote Hebrews. See Stump, "Biblical Commentary and Philosophy." Critical editions of two of the commentaries have been published: *Expositio super Iob ad litteram* in 1965, and *Expositio super Isaiam ad litteram* in 1974. See Thomas Aquinas, *Expositio super Iob ad litteram*, vol. 26. Aside from Isaiah and Job, the rest of the biblical commentaries are, unfortunately, among the last works to receive critical revision by the Leonine commission. Nevertheless, the lack of critical editions for most of the commentaries has not prevented a number of scholars from beginning to mine the commentaries for insights into what are increasingly viewed as some of Aquinas's greatest theological works. Until the Leonine edition of all the biblical commentaries is published, however, the best complete resource of Aquinas's works is Roberto Busa's edition designed as a supplement to his computer-generated lexical

Aquinas on Israel and the Church

In order to grasp the advanced level from which Aquinas engaged the Pauline letters it is necessary to briefly survey the stages in Aquinas's teaching career that led up to his inauguration as master of the sacred page. The first stage of his academic career consisted of his discipleship under the Aristotelian master Albertus Magnus, which lasted from 1245 to 1252, in Cologne.[7] During these years, Aquinas produced the first of his biblical commentaries—known as "cursory lectures"—on Scripture. A cursory lecture runs lightly over the text by reading and paraphrasing difficult passages as well as rendering superficial glosses on the text.[8] In a cursory lecture, a biblical bachelor did not "enter into the details of all the different interpretations."[9] Rather, the aim of the cursory lecture is to "make the literal sense of the text understood." The cursory lectures, often referred to as "literal expositions" include commentaries on Isaiah, Jeremiah, and Lamentations.[10] Although scholars are certain Aquinas commented upon these books during his time in Cologne, determining the dating of the other biblical commentaries becomes increasingly difficult as one moves away from the commentaries on Isaiah, Jeremiah, and Lamentations.

The second stage of his academic career came in September of 1252, when Aquinas was appointed to the university of Paris at the recommendation of Albert, and tasked with commenting upon the *Sentences* of Peter Lombard.[11] Although it is clear that Aquinas's time in this period was devoted to teaching as bachelor of the *Sentences*, it is not clear whether he

---

analysis and concordance, the *Index Thomisticus*. See Busa, ed., *Busa Opera Omnia*. For the Latin texts of the Pauline commentaries I rely upon the Marietti edition, which Busa lists as the best edition of the text published thus far. The Marietti edition adds a system of helpful paragraph numbers, known as "Marietti numbers." This study mostly relies upon the updated and corrected text of English translations of the Marietti version of the Pauline commentaries published by the Aquinas Institute for the Study of Sacred Doctrine. I indicate my changes to the Aquinas Institute translations with [emended]. Following the Aquinas Institute, I cite the Marietti chapter number, lectio number in that chapter, and the Marietti paragraph number (for example, *Ad Ephesios* 1.1.3). Aquinas, *Commentaries on the Letters of Saint Paul*. Vol. 37–4.

7. In Cologne, Aquinas served as an assistant to Albert, and was tasked with ordering his notes from courses taught by Albert on Dionysius's *Divine Names* and Aristotle's *Nichomachean Ethics*. Torrell, *Saint Thomas Aquinas* 27.

8. "The basic purpose of the cursor," writes Weisheipl, "was to familiarize himself and the students with the text of Scripture." James A. Weisheipl, *Friar Thomas D'Aquino*, 45.

9. Torrell, *Saint Thomas Aquinas*, 27.

10. The most well-known and best example of Aquinas's cursory lectures is the *Expositio super Isaiam ad litteram*. Ibid., 337.

11. Ibid., 96.

would continue to lecture upon Scripture.[12] As Torrell observes, "scholars find themselves in difficulties when they try to identify the biblical books that relate to this first period of teaching in Paris."[13]

Aquinas's duties as bachelor of *Sentences* were transitional, and in 1256, he was ordered to prepare his inaugural lecture for the ceremony in which he would become *magister in sacra pagina*.[14] A master was "allowed ... to give a much more searching commentary" than the cursory style exemplified in the exposition on Isaiah. The master of the sacred page was required to not only offer a detailed exposition of the biblical text, but also to engage the various problems and questions that emerge from the text, especially as these problems are identified by "the mediating exegetical and scholarly traditions."[15] These inaugural lectures therefore mark milestones in Aquinas's teaching of Scripture, and especially for his teaching of Paul's letters. Most scholars believe Aquinas lectured on Paul after his installation as master. Aquinas is thought to have taught twice on Paul sometime after 1256. From the seventeen-year period beginning with these inaugural lectures of 1256, to his regencies in Orvieto, Rome, Paris, and then to Naples in 1273, it is certain that Aquinas's ordinary labor is to teach Scripture at the advanced level of the *magister*. Aquinas's biblical commentaries are products of his classroom lectures.[16] And it is in this advanced

---

12. Tugwell, *Albert and Thomas*, 247.

13. Torrell, *Saint Thomas Aquinas*, 55.

14. I will return to the content of the first inaugural lecture below since it serves as a resource for understanding how Aquinas views the structure of the commentaries on Paul's letters. According to Torrell, there were, up until recently, two texts claiming to be Thomas's inaugural lecture. One is the *Rigans montes de superioribus suis* and the other is transmitted under the title *Hic est liber*. See Marietti, *Opuscula theologica*, vol. 1, 435–43. Weisheipl suggests, however, that the second is not the inaugural lecture but the text of Thomas's presentation on the day of his *resumptio* or reprise. The *resumptio* was a session that took place on the second day of the installation ceremony. Torrell, *Saint Thomas Aquinas*, 50–53. Therefore, the inaugural lecture was actually followed by a second lecture on the second day of a two-day installation ceremony for the new master. Both of these presentations treated the subject of Scripture and demonstrate Aquinas's abilities as an exegete. Torrell, *Saint Thomas Aquinas*, 53. For the inaugural sermons see McInerny's notes in *Thomas Aquinas: Selected Writings*.

15. Wawrykow, "Aquinas on Isaiah," in *Aquinas on Scripture*, 44.

16. Most of Aquinas's "commentaries" on Paul's letters are recorded lectures, usually referred to as *reportationes*. These classroom lectures come to us in two forms: *lectura* in the form of *expositio*, and *lectura* in the form of *reportationes*. All of Aquinas's lectures on the books of the Old and New Testaments fall into either of these two categories. An *expositio* refers to a lecture written by Aquinas or dictated *directly* to a scribe. See

stage of his academic career that scholars situate both the composition of the *Summa theologiae* and the production of his lectures on Paul's letters.

However, identifying the precise dates within this stage of his career that Aquinas commented upon the Pauline letters will remain difficult "for a long time until the critical edition of the texts will have allowed us to replace hypotheses, if not always with certitude, then at least with more certain data."[17] Although the exact dating of the commentaries on the letters is inconclusive, it is clear that the commentaries are authentic works produced during the most mature period of Aquinas's academic career.[18]

Torrell, *Saint Thomas Aquinas*, 337. 1 Corinthians 1–7:14 and the first eight chapters of the lecture on Romans are considered expositio since it is in these texts that Aquinas's hand is, as Torrell remarks, "rather directly perceptible." Ibid., 340; Keating, "1 and 2 Corinthians: The Sacraments and their Ministers," in *Aquinas on Scripture*, 128. A *lectura* in the form of a *reportatio*, on the other hand, is a report of the live lecture taken down by a student or scribe. *Reportationes* are notes taken down by persons in the audience and later filled out from memory or other sources to look more like the actual transcript of a letter." Jeremy Holmes, "Aquinas' *Lectura in Matthaeum*," in *Aquinas on Scripture*, 74. Weisheipl and Torrell identify the following lectures of Aquinas as *reportationes*: the lectures on Matthew and John; the lectures on 1 Corinthians 11 to 2 Corinthians; Galatians; Ephesians; Philippians; Colossians 1 and 2 Thessalonians; 1 and 2 Timothy, Titus and Philemon; and Hebrews. The text of 1 Corinthians 7:15–10:33 is missing. See Keating, "1 and 2 Corinthians," 127. A *reportatio* does not, according to Weisheipl, purport to be an official redaction. However, this should not impugn the reliability of these texts as accurate copies of Aquinas's lectures. Indeed, as Baglow has observed, "if this were the criterion for reliability, many if not most of Thomas' works would have to be set aside. . . ." This includes the commentary on John, which is also a *reporatio* and considered among contemporary scholars as reliable record of Aquinas's actual *lectura*. See Baglow, *Modus et Forma*, 120. A *reportatio* is, according to Torrell, a "carefully corrected clean copy of a course of lectures heard by a student, or taken in shorthand by a secretary." See Torrell, *Saint Thomas Aquinas* 29. The productions of Aquinas's works were well supported by secretaries. "In order to cope with his prodigious output," observes Baglow, "an entire team of secretaries was at his disposal from the first Parisian regency through the end of his life. . . ." Aquinas's lectures were not simply taken down by any willing secretary or student. The *reportationes* would be taken down *only* by a cleric who Aquinas thought would be capable of the work. The secretary during Aquinas's first stay in Paris was the cleric Peter of Andria, a Dominican, and a secular cleric whose name is unknown. See Baglow, *Modus et* Forma, 120. From 1259 until his death, which is the range of dates proposed by most scholars for the lectures on Paul's letters, Aquinas's secretary was Reginald of Piperno. Based on the best available scholarly dates for the Pauline commentaries, it seems Reginald of Piperno recorded all of Aquinas's lectures on Paul's letters. Yocum and Keating, *Aquinas On Scripture*, 21.

17. Torrell, *Saint Thomas Aquinas*, 340.

18. In order to avoid a rather imbalanced picture of Aquinas as mostly producing works on Scripture it is necessary to briefly address one more genre of text. Although the lecture was the primary form of university teaching, it could *not* satisfactorily meet an

2. THE THEME OF GRACE AND THE PREROGATIVES OF ISRAEL IN THE PAULINE COMMENTARIES

Aquinas's comments upon the ceremonial law in the Pauline commentaries do not take place apart from the overarching theme of grace. Aquinas views Paul as the exemplary teacher of grace, and he organizes each commentary in relation to the theme of grace. Aquinas's view of the connection between the theme of grace in the New Testament and the theme of grace in Paul's letters becomes clear only when one reads Aquinas's inaugural lecture, *Hic est liber*, alongside the preface he attaches to his commentaries on Paul's letters.

Aquinas's View of Grace as the Primary Theme of Paul's Letters

In 1912, two previously lost lectures of Aquinas were discovered at the Santa Maria Novella, in Florence.[19] Aquinas presented these lectures at his installation ceremony at the university of Paris. The first lecture,

---

essential requirement of theological education: the concise presentation of the whole of sacred wisdom that made clear the relationships of the objects under consideration. Only the disputed question could enable the *magister* to accomplish this task. It was out of insufficiency that Aquinas set out to write a *summa* or summary of the teaching of theology, conformed to the study of its object, which is God, and adapted to the questioning of the beginner. Chenu has observed that Aquinas's speculative theology is the fruit of submitting the Word of God to rational investigation not for the reason's sake alone, but for growth in one's knowledge and love of God. Such rational investigation of the sacred page was conducted "in a way that makes its questioning a profound homage to faith and its awareness of its divine object." Chenu, *Aquinas and His Role in Theology*, 133. See also Per Erik Persson, *Sacra Doctrina; Reason and Revelation in Aquinas*, 8. Scripture was "very much the basis and ongoing centre of Thomas's work as a university theologian."

19. The Latin titles are 1) *Hic est liber mandatorum Dei* and 2) *Rigans montes de superioribus*. These two works were discovered among the writings of Remigio dei Girolami, a student of Aquinas. The title *Hic est liber mandatorum Dei* is taken from the verse which Aquinas puts at the beginning of his lecture: "This is the book of the commandments of God," Baruch 4:1. It is sometimes referred to in English as *Commendation of and Division of Sacred Scripture*. Following Torrell, I refer to it as *Hic est Liber*. The Latin text can be found in the Marietti edition of the *opuscula*: S. Thomae Aquinatis, *Opuscula theologica*, t. 1, 435–39. The title of the second lecture, *Rigans montes de superioribus* is taken from the verse from Psalm 103:13, which Aquinas puts at the beginning of the lecture: "Thou waterest the hills from thy upper rooms...." It is sometimes referred to as *On the Commendation of Sacred Scripture*. For the Latin text of *Rigans montes* see the same volume, pp. 441–43. Below, I rely on Ralph McInerny's translation and commentary. I cite Marietti numbers to facilitate ease of reference.

"Commendation and Division of Sacred Scripture," also referred to as *Hic est liber*, is of particular interest because it contains Aquinas's view of the theological theme of grace in the New Testament and the relationship of this theme to the Pauline letters.

For Aquinas, Scripture leads humankind to life and away from death in two ways, which correspond to the function of the Old Law and the New Law. The Old Law brings to life by "commanding through the mandates which it proposes."[20] And, the New Law brings to life by "helping, through the gift of grace which the lawgiver dispenses."[21] Aquinas understands John 1:17 to summarize these two important functions: "Both of these," writes Aquinas, "are touched on in John 1:17: 'For the Law was given through Moses; grace and truth came through Jesus Christ.'"[22]

For Aquinas, the twofold origin (Moses and Christ) and function ("commanding" in the Old Testament, and "helping" in the New) represents the primary distinction for understanding the whole order of sacred Scripture. This division does not remain as a static principle mentioned in the inaugural sermon and then forgotten. Aquinas consistently relies upon this division throughout his commentaries on Paul's letters.

Aquinas says the New Law, which is given in the New Testament, is organized according to three parts of grace: In the first the *origin of grace* is treated, in the Gospels. In the second the *power of grace*, and this in the letters of Paul. In the third, the *execution of the aforesaid virtues* is treated, and this in the rest of the books of the New Testament.[23]

Paul's letters concern the "power of grace" and represents the second part of the New Testament.[24] *Hic est liber* makes clear that Aquinas sees the

---

20. *Hic est liber* 2.

21. *Hic est liber* 2.

22. Specifically, Aquinas sees both the Old Law and the New Law directing humankind toward its proper end, which is beatitude. *Hic est liber* 2.

23. *Hic est liber* 2.

24. Aquinas says that the first part of the New Testament, which concerns the origin of grace, is constituted by the Gospels. The Gospels are then divided again according to Christ's twofold nature, where John concerns the divine nature, and Matthew, Mark, and Luke concern the human nature. These latter three are then further divided according to the "threefold dignity that belongs to the man Christ:" Matthew speaks of Christ's royal honor; Mark speaks of Christ's prophetic honor; and Luke speaks of Christ's priestly dignity. See *Hic est liber*. The third section of the New Testament treats the execution or progress of the origin and power of grace in the Church. This "progress" of grace then receives a threefold division: 1) the beginning of the Church in the Acts of the apostles; 2) the progress of the Church in the canonical letters (James, 1 and 2 Peter, the letters

Israel and the Church in Aquinas's Pauline Commentaries

Pauline letters as a distinct unit embedded in a teaching on grace and distinguished from all the other books of the New Testament by its content.[25]

However, the part of *Hic est liber* that deals with *how* the power of grace functions in the individual Pauline letters is actually missing. Therefore, the particular relationship between the individual Pauline letters and the primary theme of grace is unclear solely from a reading of the sermon. Another text of Aquinas is required: the prologue that Aquinas attaches to the beginning of the commentaries on the Pauline letters serves to fill in the rest of the picture.[26]

Aquinas uses Acts 9:15 to structure the Pauline corpus: "This man is to me a chosen vessel to carry my name before the *Gentiles* and *kings* and the sons of *Israel*."[27] It was necessary for God to use Paul to carry "precious liquid"—the divine name of Christ because God's name was far from men due to sin and the darkness of human understanding.[28] For this reason, Aquinas understands Paul to bring the name of Christ to the Gentiles in "disclosing Christ's grace and mercy."[29] Yet this is not the only group to

---

of John, and Jude); and 3) the end of the Church in the Apocalypse, in which the whole content of Scripture concludes.

25. The letters are also distinguished because of their authorship, which is attributed to "the Apostle," whom Aquinas views as "first and foremost of all theologians." Aquinas sees Paul as a systematic theologian who above all is the teacher of the grace and mercy of Christ to the Gentile Church as well as to the sons of Israel. More will be said in the next section about Aquinas's view of Paul's identity and mission to preach the mercy of the gospel to these two groups. Valkenberg has identified how Aquinas sees Paul as the teacher of systematic theological insights. Aquinas uses the Pauline letters not as sources of testimonial data but, rather, as purely systematic theological insights. For example, Valkenberg argues that "Paul is the main source for Aquinas when considering the soteriological value of the resurrection of Christ. He considers Paul as the first and foremost of all theologians, someone who indicates the significance of the salvation Christ brought to us...." Valkenberg, *Words of the Living God*, 41.

26. The prologue to the Pauline commentaries is placed first, before the commentary on Romans. Additionally, each commentary contains its own prologue. Hereafter cited as *Prologus*. The section numbers follow the Marietti edition.

27. *Prologus* 1. [emphasis added]

28. *Prologus* 4. Aquinas also explains that because of this human darkness, the angels bestowed God's light, the apostles brought the gospel teaching from Christ, and Moses and the prophets were read to instruct people in the teaching of the Law. There is a clear unity in function of the old and New Law as a remedy to the darkness of human understanding that mirrors the treatise on law in the *Summa Theologiae*. *Hic est liber*. Cf. Ia-IIae q. 99.

29. *Prologus* 6.

whom Aquinas understands Paul to deliver the teaching on the grace of Christ.

Aquinas views Paul as one who carried Christ's teaching to the "sons of Israel."

> Hence the usefulness or fruit of this vessel is expressed by the words, *before the Gentiles*, whose teacher he was: "A teacher of the Gentiles in faith and truth" (1 Tim 2:7), *and kings*, to whom he preached the faith of Christ, for example, to Agrippa (Acts 16) and even to Nero and his princes. . . . *And the sons of Israel*, against whom he argued about Christ: "But Saul increased all the more in strength, and confounded the Jews who lived in Damascus by proving that Jesus was the Christ" (Acts 9:22).[30]

This is the second mention of Israel in the prologue and signals that Aquinas may return to the theme in the individual commentaries.[31]

After listing these three groups (Gentiles, kings, sons of Israel), Aquinas presents the threefold division of the Pauline corpus. It becomes immediately clear that the division of the fourteen letters corresponds rather directly to the three groups just mentioned:

> The Apostle wrote fourteen letters: *nine* of them instruct the *Church of the Gentiles; four* the *prelates and princes* of the Church, as well as kings; *the last* is addressed to the Hebrews, *the sons of Israel*. The teaching bears entirely on Christ's grace, which we can consider under a triple modality.[32]

Paul's instruction on the grace of Christ to each group provides the ordering principle for all three divisions of the fourteen letters.

Each letter corresponds to one of three ways Christ's grace is present in the Mystical Body. The first way in which the grace of Christ is present is 1) the existence of grace in "the Head himself, Christ, and it is thus that we find it in the Letter to the Hebrews."[33]

The second way in which the grace of Christ is present, explains Aquinas, is 2) the existence of grace in the "principle members of the mystical

---

30. Fabian Larcher's translation of *Prologus* 9. See Aquinas, *Commentary on Romans*, trans. Fabian Larcher.

31. The first mention of Israel is from the Acts 9:15 text Aquinas attaches to the beginning of the prologue.

32. Torrell's translation of the Prologue 11. The translation can be found in Torrell, *Aquinas: The Person and His Work*, 255. [Emphasis added].

33. *Prologus* 11.

body, and it is thus that we find it in the letters addressed to the prelates and kings."[34] Letters to the prelates include 1 Timothy and 2 Timothy, Titus, and Philemon.

The third way in which the grace of Christ is present is 3) the existence of grace "according as it is in the mystical body itself, which is the Church, and it is thus that we find it in the letters addressed to the Gentiles."[35] Aquinas devotes the largest amount of material to this third group, the Gentile *ecclesia*, which includes nine letters: Romans, 1 and 2 Corinthians, Galatians, Ephesians, Philippians, Colossians, and 1 and 2 Thessalonians.

The division of the letters in the prologue indicates that Israel and Church are major themes in the commentaries on Paul's letters. The two sections of the Pauline corpus to which Aquinas devotes the most material are the first and third divisions: *the sons of Israel and the Gentile ecclesia*. Therefore, based on Aquinas's own division of the corpus and the amount of material he devotes to the first and third divisions, the commentaries on Paul's letters provide some of the largest amounts of material on Aquinas's view of grace as it relates to Israel and Church. Next, I outline which of the individual commentaries of the Pauline corpus directly treat of the observance of the Mosaic Law.

The Prerogatives of Israel in Aquinas's Commentaries on Paul's Letters

The structure of the prologue indicates that relevant texts on Israel and the Church may be found in the first and third divisions of the Pauline corpus. The actual content of the individual letters in these divisions confirms this view. Both divisions, including the division devoted to the Gentile ecclesia, contains crucial material on Aquinas's view of the prerogatives of Israel.

In the prologue to the Pauline commentaries Aquinas explicitly states the letter to the Hebrews is a teaching directed to the sons of Israel. Moreover, in the prologue to the Hebrews commentary, Aquinas explains that the letter concerns Christ's grace as it is "in the Head, namely, Christ." It is as priest that Christ is head of the Mystical Body. This letter deals with Christ's priesthood, which is explained to be higher than the angels and the Mosaic priesthood. Paul's purpose in writing the letter, as Aquinas understands it, is also relevant to this study: "The Apostle wrote this letter

34. *Prologus* 11.
35. *Prologus* 11.

against the errors of some who, having converted from Judaism to the faith of Christ, wanted to keep the legal observances along with the Gospel, as if the grace of Christ did not suffice unto salvation."[36] Hebrews is divided into two parts, with the first treating this error of "converts" from Judaism. I investigate Aquinas's view of the ceremonial law in the Hebrews commentary in chapter 4 of this study.

It might seem that Aquinas's comments upon Israel are limited only to the commentary on Hebrews. However, the topic of Israel recurs throughout the third division on the Gentile *ecclesia*. As I show below, Paul's argument against the sons of Israel is a theme that runs throughout the commentaries in this third division. In particular, Aquinas comments at length upon Israel, the Old Law, and the ceremonial law, in the following three commentaries in the third division on the Gentile *ecclesia*: Romans, Galatians, Ephesians.

As stated above, Aquinas understands this third division of the Pauline corpus to possess a threefold structure. The third division of the Pauline corpus (addressed to the Gentile *ecclesia*) includes nine letters total, each of which treat how the grace of Christ exists in the Mystical Body itself. Aquinas writes that these nine letters "are distinguished from one another according to the three ways the grace of Christ can be considered."[37]

The first way that the grace of Christ can be considered is "in itself," and this way is set out in the letter to the Romans. The prerogatives of Israel are treated in detail in chapters 2 through 4 of the Romans commentary and Aquinas also discusses the prerogatives of Israel in chapter 9. The commentary on the Romans mentions the Jews more than any other commentary in the Pauline corpus.

The second way the grace of Christ can be considered is in the nature of the sacraments, and this way is set out in the letters to the Corinthians and Galatians.[38] The material in 1 and 2 Corinthians is relatively sparse. However, in the letter to the Galatians, Aquinas addresses what he refers to as "superfluous sacraments," by which he seems to mean the ceremonial law. In this letter, writes Aquinas, the "Apostle reproves the Galatians who

---

36. *Ad Hebraeos* 1.1.6.
37. *Prologus* 11.
38. In 1 Corinthians, Aquinas briefly mentions the sacraments of the "old people" and the "new people," and the paschal lamb as a figure of Christ. In 2 Corinthians Aquinas comments upon another figure of Christ, which he states is the veil over the face of Moses. Nevertheless, for Aquinas, Galatians is the letter that deals particularly with the "old" sacraments.

had been so deceived by false teachers as to observe at once the rites of the Law and those of the Gospel."[39] Here, Aquinas understands Paul to once again address the error of certain believers in Christ observing the ceremonial law along with the gospel, as he did in Hebrews. Aquinas also comments on divine providence as it relates to the destruction of the Temple in 70 AD; the Antioch incident between Paul and Peter; and the controversy between Jerome and Augustine on the Jewish apostles' observance of the ceremonial law in Acts. The number of references to the Jews in the Galatians commentary is second only to the commentary on Romans.

The third and final way Christ's grace can be considered is in regard to the unity it produces in the Gentile *ecclesia*. In Aquinas's view, Paul addresses the third way that Christ's grace can be considered in the letters to the Ephesians, Philippians, Colossians, and 1 and 2 Thessalonians.[40] I do not examine Philippians, Colossians, and the letters to the Thessalonians because these texts do not treat the ceremonial law or the Jewish people. Ephesians, however, contains some of the most profound comments of Aquinas on ceremonial law, including the joining of both Jews and Gentiles into unity. Aquinas comments at length on the unity shared between these two peoples and how they are now "incorporated" and built together like living stones by Christ.[41] The third division, addressed to the Gentile *ecclesia*, clearly contains a considerable amount of relevant material on Israel and the Law.

This study of Aquinas on Israel and the Church will therefore focus on the following commentaries in this order: Hebrews, Romans, Galatians, and Ephesians. My aim in each treatment of the commentaries is to uncover Aquinas's view of the ceremonial law with attention to what Soulen refers to as the "heart of supersessionism."

What theological status does Aquinas attribute to the observance of the ceremonial law after the passion of Christ in his commentaries on Paul's letters? Are Jewish observances interpreted as fulfilled and cancelled for all? Or do the rites retain a theological value after the passion?

39. *Ad Galatas, Prologus* 1.

40. There is a reference to the duration of the ceremonial law after the passion of Christ. *In Thess.* 2.2. I treat this concept in my discussion of the Galatians commentary. The relevant material on the ceremonial law in Philippians and Colossians is sparse, and will also be considered but only as it relates to the larger theme of unity between Jew and Gentile treated at length in Ephesians. Therefore, the brief material from these commentaries will be incorporated into the chapter on Ephesians.

41. *Ad Ephesios* 2.5.111.

4

The Ceremonial Law as a Shadow of the Night (Hebrews)

MORE THAN ANY OTHER of Paul's letters, Aquinas understands Hebrews to demonstrate the preeminence of Christ over the Old Law.[1] Indeed, the letter addresses a subject at the crux of the matter in the discussion over whether or not his theology is supersessionist: the observance of the ceremonial law after the passion of Christ.[2] For Aquinas, Paul's letter teaches the Hebrews that Christ's priesthood and Law bring about the voiding of the ceremonial law, which is likened to a shadow of the night. For this reason, the commen-

---

1. In Ia-IIae q. 98.3, Aquinas states that letter to the Hebrews is especially important in showing how the New Law transcends the old. Aquinas states that "Paul—especially in Hebrews—proves that the new law transcends the old...."

2. Each citation will include the chapter, lecture, and paragraph numbers from the Marietti edition of the commentary. For example, *Ad Hebraeos* (hereafter *Ad Heb.*) 3.2.173. As explained above, English translations are from the Aquinas Institute edition of Aquinas's commentary on Hebrews. However, I also draw upon Chrysostom Baer's 2006 translation as well. Thomas Aquinas, *Commentary on the Epistle to the Hebrews*, trans. Chrysostom Baer. I indicate my changes to the Aquinas Institute's text with "[emended]." According to the Aquinas Institute editors, Aquinas appears to be familiar with more than one translation of Scripture, often quotes from memory, and paraphrases. The closest available version of Scripture to Aquinas's text is the Clementine Vulgate of 1598, and the closest translation of the Clementine Vulgate in English is the Douay-Rheims version. Therefore Scripture citations are of the Douay-Rheims.

The Ceremonial Law as a Shadow of the Night (Hebrews)

tary on Hebrews represents a rather concise statement on a commonplace medieval teaching: the cessation and obsolescence of the Law.

1. THE PRIMARY THEME AND DIVISIONS OF THE HEBREWS COMMENTARY

At the close of the prologue Aquinas raises the ancient question of Pauline authorship of the letter to the Hebrews, states two objections to the idea of his authorship offered at the Council of Nicaea, and presents a *respondeo*.[3] His reply to one of the objections reveals three features of his view of the observance of the ceremonial law after the passion of Christ: that there exists a Pauline teaching on the subject; that the teaching is tied to the dispute at the Jerusalem council chronicled in Acts 15; and that the teaching is addressed to a particular group.[4]

First, Aquinas thinks Paul taught directly on the ceremonial law, and that his teaching created great controversy among the Jews. Indeed, from Aquinas's view, the Apostle did not claim authorship because of the controversial teaching that the "legal observances," or the practices of circumcision, Passover, and dietary laws, can no longer be followed.[5] "[Paul's]

3. *Ad Heb., Prologus* 5.

4. Aquinas views the letter to address the subject as it relates to "Jewish converts" to Christianity *as well as Jews*. He understands the teaching to apply to those that followed the Law.

5. Following Boguslawski, I also refer to these particular rites of the ceremonial law as the prerogatives of Israel. Aquinas does not make a clear distinction between these three rites (or what I am referring to as prerogatives of Israel) in this commentary but he does in the *Summa theologiae* and in the commentary on Romans. In general, Aquinas uses *legalis* to refer to law in general, human law, or the Law of the Old Testament. Here, the context is of course the Law of the Old Testament. See Deferrari, *A Latin-English Dictionary of St. Thomas Aquinas*. According to Deferrari, Aquinas's use of the phrase *observatio legalis* refers to the "observance of the prescriptions of the Old Testament." Although it is not exactly clear in this section of the commentary which laws Aquinas is referring to, his mentioning of *legalia* in relation to Acts 15:2 reveals he is more than likely referring to three specific rites or "legal observances" that can be considered under the broader category of *caeremoniae veteris legis* (or ceremonies of the Old Law): these rites include the sacraments of circumcision and Passover, and observance of dietary regulations. Additionally, associating "legal observances" with these rites in particular seems justified by a reading of *Ad Galatas*. 2.1 In this text, Aquinas refers to Acts 15:2 as a discussion among the apostles that resulted in the handing down of a decree on not observing the rites of the Law: *legalibus non observandis*. In Ia-IIae q. 101.4, "observances" *are only one category of caeremoniae veteris legis* or ceremonies of the Old Law. Aquinas divides the ceremonies of the Old Law into four categories: 1) *sacrificia* or

name was odious to the Jews, since he taught that the observances of the Law were no longer to be kept, as is clear from Acts 15:2. Consequently, he concealed his name, lest the salutary doctrine of this epistle go for naught."[6] Second, Aquinas interprets the idea that the ceremonial law is no longer to be kept as a teaching approved by the council.[7] Third, Aquinas explains

---

sacrifices; 2) *sacra* or sacred things; 3) *sacramenta* or sacraments; and 4) *observantiae* or observances. All of these categories are referred to together as *caeremoniae veteris legis*. The 1) *sacrificia* include sacrificial animals offered by the Levite priesthood. 2) *Sacra* include instruments such as the temple, tabernacle and the vessels. 3) *Sacramenta* include circumcision, "without which no one was admitted to the legal observances" (102.5) and the eating of the paschal banquet. Aquinas actually refers to the paschal banquet as an observance but it is treated in the same article on sacraments, indicating that the Passover, for him, may fit into both *sacramenta* and *observantiae* categories. 4) *Observantiae* mostly refers to dietary regulations, which include the prohibition of blood and fat of animals. According to Aquinas, the latter two precepts, which are the 3) sacrament of circumcision and 4) observances both function together to consecrate the Jewish people to the worship of God. Indeed, in Ia-IIae q. 102.6 Aquinas affirms the literal, rational cause for the *observantiae* of the Law as "a special prerogative of that people." All of these precepts are ceremonial in character in the sense that they give public expression to divine worship. Replacement of the Jewish people as God's elect people has more to do with the third and forth categories than the first two. Replacement is brought about by the teaching that the latter two categories of ceremonial law are now useless (3) *sacramenta* and 4) *observantiae*) and *not* that the former two categories (1) *sacrificia* or 2) *sacra*) are useless. This is because Jews can remain Jews without *sacrificia* of the Temple and without *sacra*. However, they cannot remain Jews without *sacramenta* and *observantiae*. Interestingly, even Aquinas recognizes the importance of ceremonial law categories 3 & 4 for the distinctiveness of the Jewish people. On his own terms temple sacrifice (or *sacrificia*) and sacred things (or *sacra*), such as the tabernacle, are *not* tied to the "special prerogative of that people." The "special prerogative of that people" is tied to category 3 and 4 of the ceremonial law: *sacramenta* and *observantiae* or circumcision, Passover, and dietary laws. In *Ad Heb.* 7.3.359 he seems to employ the term *mandatum carnale* or carnal commands in order to refer to two of these prerogatives when he explains that the Old Testament is a carnal commandment "because it had certain carnal observances such as circumcision and carnal purifications." But the distinction is not as explicit as it is in the *Summa theologiae*. That Aquinas recognizes the special dignity of these markers of Jewish identity as "prerogatives" (in the *Summa theologiae*) rather than collapsing all rites into ceremonial law in general seems as if it is a nuanced achievement in its own right that might be a fruit of his engagement with Maimonides.

6. *Ad Heb.*, Prologus 5.

7. Acts 15:1–2 reads as follows: "And some, coming down from Judea, taught the brethren: That, except you be circumcised after the manner of Moses, you cannot be saved. And when Paul and Barnabas had no small contest with them, they determined that Paul and Barnabas and certain others of the other side should go up to the apostles and priests to Jerusalem, about this question." Aquinas's interpretation of the Jerusalem council of Acts 15 becomes clearer in *Ad Galatas*. He discusses the controversy over the observance of the Law between Paul and Peter (referred to as the "Antioch incident"),

The Ceremonial Law as a Shadow of the Night (Hebrews)

that Paul's teaching in this letter is directed to "converted" Jews: "He wrote this letter against the errors of those converts from Judaism who wanted to preserve the legal observances along with the gospel, as though Christ's grace was not sufficient for salvation."[8] For Aquinas, Hebrews is therefore an argument to "converted Jews" on why the salvific efficacy of Christ's grace is more excellent than the observances of the Law—a Law that has passed away. "The time of the New Testament is called the day," Aquinas states, "because it repels the shadow of night of the law."[9]

As was customary in scholastic exegesis, Aquinas begins his Hebrews commentary with a citation of a Scripture, which he understands as an interpretive key to the *divisio textus*.[10] "There is none among the gods

---

and refers to the teaching as a "decree" that the Law ought not be kept in *Ad Galatas* 2.1; 6.3.

8. *Ad Heb.* 1.1.6: Although it might appear that the intended audience is Jewish Christians or what Aquinas refers to as "Jewish converts" the argument he understands Paul to make applies to Jews who observe the rites after the passion of Christ. Near the end of the commentary, in *Ad Heb.* 13.3.774, Aquinas comments once again upon the audience of the message and it seems to include anyone who followed the observances of the Law. Although Paul's letter contains a salutation to the saints and other disciples, he explains that the letter is not written to them but to those that followed the Law: "He does not write to them since he had no intention to write except against those who followed the observances of the Law."

9. *Ad Heb.* 3.2.173.

10. Such scholastic practice is referred to as "division of the text." Boyle's explanation of the practice is worth quoting in full: "In a division of the text, a commentator states some theme that serves an interpretive key for his commentary. . . . With the theme stated, the commentator begins to divide the text, dividing each division in turn into smaller and smaller parts down to the verse or even smaller. Thus, St. Albert divides the Gospel according to St. Mark into seven initial parts according to seven properties of [a] lion. The division of the text provides a sustained structural analysis by which the parts of the Gospel stand in relation both to the whole and to each other. No verse stands in isolation, but rather each stands in a rich and organic set of relations to the rest of the Gospel. The division maintains the integrity of the Gospel in the midst of careful, detailed, and often word for word interpretation. In the *De Potentia*, Thomas stated that one of the criteria for considering the legitimacy of a given interpretation of Scripture is that 'the circumstance of the letter' is preserved. By providing a context that reaches not only to the surrounding verses or even chapters, but to the Gospel as a whole, the division of the text articulates in a highly formal way the circumstance of the letter." Though Boyle is speaking of the commentary on the Gospel of John, his analysis of the *divisio textus* applies to all Aquinas's scholastic exegesis, which include the commentaries on Paul's letters. Indeed, Aquinas's method of division routinely slices down sentences to the smallest of phrases, often devoting entire paragraphs to explicating only two words, such as "hold fast." See Boyle, "Authorial Intention and the Divisio Textus," 7–8; "'Division of the Text' with Particular Reference to the Commentaries of Saint Thomas Aquinas," 276–83.

like unto you, O Lord: and there is none according to your works [Psalm 85:8]."[11] In Aquinas's view, the spiritual meaning[12] of this verse expresses the two main subjects of the book of Hebrews: 1) the excellence of Christ in regard to sacred persons such as angels, prophets, and priests,[13] and 2) the effects of Christ, which refers to the faith that joins members to his body.[14] Aquinas understands Paul to divide the letter according to these two subjects, where he first (chs. 1–10) "extols Christ's grandeur in order to show the superiority of the New Testament over the Old," and in division two (chs. 11–13) he discusses "what unites the members to the head, namely, faith."[15]

More than two thirds of the commentary is devoted to division one, which contains the most relevant material on the subject of the ceremonial law.[16] These chapters compare Christ to angles, prophets, and priests, which Aquinas also calls the "three sacred persons" contained in the Old Testament.[17] In general, chs. 1–6 of the commentary reveals Aquinas's view of the authority of the Old Testament as it relates to the authority of Christ. In chs. 7–10, Aquinas comments on the ceremonial law at length. Since these chapters in division one contain the bulk of the relevant material on the ceremonial law they receive the most attention.

---

11. *Ad Heb., Prologus* 1.

12. By "spiritual meaning" I refer to the broader definition of the term, which means "the Christian interpretation of the Old Testament in light of Christ and the New Testament." Henri de Lubac, *Medieval Exegesis*, ix.

13. *Ad Heb., Prologus* 2. Citing the *Shema* in Deut. 6:4 (Hear, O Israel, the Lord your God is one Lord), Aquinas explains that though God is only one in nature, there are many gods in heaven and on earth. These gods though, are not like the one God. They are only sometimes called gods on account of some excellence, such as shining with the glory of God as in the case of angels, or possessing knowledge of the word of God as in the case of prophets.

14. *Ad Heb., Prologus* 1.

15. *Ad Heb.* 1.1.6.

16. Division two consists of chapters 11 through 13, which Aquinas considers as the works or "effects" of Christ. The little relevant material from these chapters is incorporated into subsection three.

17. *Ad Heb., Prologus* 2.

The Ceremonial Law as a Shadow of the Night (Hebrews)

2. THE AUTHORITY OF THE NEW TESTAMENT OVER THE OLD TESTAMENT

Aquinas's commentary is an elaborate and theologically rich Christological treatise worthy of study in its own right. To give adequate attention to its Christology would require an entire study. I therefore limit my overview of the argument in the first six chapters to how this section relates to the Mosaic Law in general. The treatment of this first part of the first division is meant to provide context for the examination of chapters 7 through 10, which directly treat of the ceremonial observances of the Law. I argue here that, initially, Aquinas emphasizes continuity between the New and Old Testaments and then moves into an exploration of the differences between the two testaments via a contrast of Christ and the "sacred persons" of the Old Testament.

Continuity between the New and Old Testaments

As explained above, Aquinas understands the occasion of the letter as a misunderstanding on behalf of Jewish converts who wanted to keep the legal observances along with the gospel. According to Aquinas, in order to convince these Jewish converts that the grace of Christ is sufficient for salvation Paul argues that the New Testament transcends the Old Testament in its authority.

However, Aquinas attempts to maintain continuity between the two testaments. Though he does not use the term "continuity," the theme appears as early as the first lecture and recurs at several points in the first division. The first example is evident when Aquinas explains how the Apostle Paul "removes the Manichaean error." Paul removes the error in two ways: "First, by calling God the author of the Old Testament; second, in saying that he made temporal things."[18] That God spoke in "times past" rules out the view of the Manicheans.[19]

The continuity is further maintained when Aquinas explains several positive attributes concerning the goodness of the Old Testament, inspired again by the first verse of Hebrews: "God, Who, in many ways and in diverse manners, speaking in times past to the fathers in the prophets. . . ."[20]

18. *Ad Heb.* 1.1.23.
19. *Ad Heb.* 1.1.19.
20. *Ad Heb.* 1.1.

Here, explains Aquinas, Paul praises the Old Testament for its "authorship, because it is from God; second, subtlety and sublimity, because *in many ways and in diverse manners*; third, duration, because *in times past*."[21] The Old Testament was promulgated among many persons, such as Abraham and Noah, and it contains the revelation of *divina* or divine things.[22]

Another example of continuity between the testaments appears in lecture three where Aquinas briefly discusses the unity created by Christ between Jews and Gentiles.[23] Aquinas comments upon the contrast between Christ as the builder of the house that is the communion of the faithful and Moses the servant.[24] Although Moses is very honorable, explains Aquinas, Christ is more honorable as the maker of the house of the faithful and its principal lawgiver. Paul proves that Christ is the builder of the house because Christ unifies diverse parts in the same way a builder unites wood and stones.[25] These diverse parts include both Jews and Gentiles: "The assembly of the faithful, which is the Church and the house of God, is composed of various elements, namely, Jews and Gentiles, slaves and free. Therefore, the Church as any other house, is put together by someone."[26] Aquinas then cites 1 Peter 2:5 and Ephesians 2:20, which he understands to strengthen Paul's argument.

In another place, Aquinas stresses that the new covenant brings justice to the house of Israel. He teaches that the new covenant is for *both* Jews and Gentiles. "They . . . who have obtained God's grace are Israel by faith, and Judah by confession."[27] Here, Aquinas strikes a strong chord of continuity, emphasizing that Gentiles who obtain grace are "of Israel" and "of Judah." Gentiles are of Israel through faith and with Israel rather than in the place of

---

21. *Ad Heb.* 1.1.11. [Emended]. Baer translates *commendat vetus testamentum* as "he commends the Old Testament" yet the context suggests "commendation" may be too reserved for describing the laudatory character of all the praises of the Old Testament in *Ad Heb* 1.1.11.

22. *Ad Heb.* 1.1.9.

23. This is a theme Aquinas will expound upon greatly in the commentary on Ephesians.

24. *Ad Heb.* 3.1.155. Aquinas comments upon Heb. 3:1–4: "the apostle and high priest of our confession, Jesus . . . was counted worthy of greater glory than Moses, by so much as he that hath built the house, hath greater honor than the house. For every house is built by some man: but He that created all things, is God."

25. *Ad Heb.* 3.1.163.

26. *Ad Heb.* 3.1.163.

27. *Ad Heb.* 8.2.397.

Israel. Here, Aquinas also draws upon Paul's words in Romans 11 to strike an even stronger chord of continuity. Aquinas states that the new covenant is a shared covenant: "Gentiles are made partakers (*participes*) of the New Testament as the wild olive tree is grafted into the good olive tree and *shares* (*participat*) of its fatness, as is said in Romans 11:24.[28] Here, Aquinas does not say that the Gentiles are grafted on top of the good olive tree or in the place of, but, rather, Gentiles are grafted into and share and participate in Israel, the good olive tree. In these texts, Aquinas sees the Church as a sharer of Israel's faith and the grafting of Gentiles into Israel does not seem to entail a replacement or passing away of the good olive tree.

Christ More Excellent than Angels, Moses, and Aaron

The greater part of the commentary is devoted to explicating the differences between the two testaments. Aquinas comments upon differences between the two testaments beginning in the fifteenth section of the first lecture, and in the context of this discussion on God's dual authorship of the testaments.[29] Though God speaks through both testaments, it is more

---

28. *Ad Heb.* 8.2.397. This translation is from Chrysostom Baer's. [Emphasis added]

29. In Ia-IIae q. 98.3, Aquinas compares the difference between God's relationship to the Old Law and the New Law to the difference in relationship between a shipbuilder to the materials produced or prepared for his use by subordinates. He comments on the difference as it relates to 1) the two types of mediators (angels and Christ) and 2) the two effects which the Law produces. These two differences, both treated in the *Summa theologiae* seem to operate as a summation of the entire first division of the Hebrews commentary. Both reflect the content of the Hebrews commentary since chapters 1 through 6 pertain to Christ the more perfect mediator and chapters 7 through 10 demonstrate that the Old Law was imperfect (or accomplished different effects than the New Law). This mirrors the twofold difference between the testaments in 98.3: "it was right for the Old Law to be given by angels. For, as we have already said, the Old Law, while itself imperfect, nevertheless prepared the way for the perfect salvation of the human race which was to be achieved through Christ." He then goes on to explain the difference between the testaments by employing the ship-building analogy: "Now the following general rule may be taken to apply whenever we find a series of causes of this sort ranged in order according to the degree of their potency and the effects which they produce. With regard to the principal and perfect effect the agent who is above all the rest acts of himself in person to produce this. But with regard to those factors which merely induce the right dispositions for the ultimate perfection to be achieved, he operates these through his subordinates. Thus for instance, a shipbuilder puts the parts of the ship together himself in person, but makes use of subordinate assistant builders to prepare the materials. For this reason then, it is appropriate that the perfect Law of the New Testament should have been given directly by God made Man in person, and that the Old Law, on the contrary,

important that God speaks through them in different ways "according to the degree of their potency and the effects they produce."[30] Aquinas's comments emphasize varying degrees of discontinuity between Israel and the Church through a comparison of Christ's superiority over the Levitical priesthood. Metaphors of discontinuity are also employed, such as night and day, and new regime and old regime.

In Aquinas's view, the two testaments receive their authority directly from the mediators of the respective covenants. The greatness of the New Testament over the Old is, therefore, first and foremost grounded in the authority of its mediator, Jesus Christ the Incarnate Word of God. From section fifteen of the first lecture, and all the way to the end of the first division, Aquinas comments upon Christ's excellence over Old Testament mediators. The speech of God in the New Testament is mediated through Christ, whereas, in the Old Testament, God spoke through the prophets "by revelations in the minds of men." The Old Law, explains Aquinas, "derived its authority from three things, namely, from the angels, from Moses, and from Aaron the high priest."[31] Christ, on the other hand, does not mediate the speech of God in the same way as these mediators. This is because Christ does not simply mediate God's speech, but rather, Christ *is* God's speech. Christ, "the incarnate Word is related to the uncreated Word as the [word of the voice] is related to the [word of the heart]."[32] In this way, the Apostle, according to Aquinas, shows the "excellence of Christ as regards the peculiarity of His origin."[33] The first argument that Aquinas offers for the superiority of the New over the Old Testament is therefore Christological.

Aquinas then applies this Christological argument to angels, Moses, and Aaron, from the second chapter of the commentary all the way to the sixth, and with exhaustive detail. Because Christ is greater than angels, it is more necessary to obey [his] commandments rather than the Old Law.[34]

---

should have been given to men through the ministers of God, in other word the angels." Aquinas then concludes: "This is the way in which St. Paul—especially in Hebrews—proves that the New Law transcends the Old." Ia-IIae q. 98.3 seems as if it is a concise summation of the major points of the Hebrews commentary.

30. Ia Iae 98.3. Aquinas returns to the notion that Scripture is the speech of God delivered through mediators. This is an idea he first employed in his inaugural sermon, *Hic est liber*, 5.

31. *Ad Heb.* 3.1.155.

32. *Ad Heb.* 1.1.15.

33. *Ad Heb.* 1.1.7.

34. *Ad Heb.* 2.1.90.

The Ceremonial Law as a Shadow of the Night (Hebrews)

Christ is more excellent than Moses because, although Moses was "very honorable" and a faithful servant, he was only one who proclaimed.[35] Moreover, Moses was a servant in the house of the Lord but Christ is as the Lord in his own house.[36]

Lastly, Christ is more excellent than a priest of the Old Law, such as Aaron. Two things pertained to the high priest, and, according to Aquinas, Christ exceeds both of these. One was the priestly office, which required him to enter once a year into the holy of holies with blood. The other is that he was to be of a certain tribe. Christ exceeds the high priest since he entered through his own blood into the holy of holies, the sacred heavens. He is without sin, perfect in obedience, and the priest of a nobler tribe than Aaron because of his origin as Son of God.[37]

Christ is also a high priest of temporal as well as future and eternal goods: "For the [priesthood of the Old Law] was temporary and passed away with the coming of the One prefigured." But the priesthood of Christ is eternal since it is of truth, which is eternal.[38] Although Aquinas explains figures in the Old Testament several times throughout chapter 1 through 4, this text is the first occurrence of the concept applied to the Old Law.[39] Aquinas returns to the subject of the prefiguring function of the Old Law in greater detail in chapter 7 through 10.

The Conclusion of the Argument that Christ is More Excellent than the Old Law

The conclusion that follows from the comparison of Christ with the mediators of the Old Law is that the New Law is to be obeyed rather than the old.[40] The commandments of the New Law in particular are to be followed

---

35. *Ad Heb.* 3.1.165.
36. *Ad Heb.* 3.1.168.
37. *Ad Heb.* 4.3.234.
38. *Ad Heb.* 5.1.252.
39. References to figures in the Old Testament appears in *Ad Heb.* 1.3.51; 4.1.202. The first time Aquinas elaborates on the prefiguring aspect of the Old Law is in his explanation of the sense in which the Levitical priesthood is described as "perpetual" in Exodus 27:21. The most explicit treatment of the prefiguring function of the ceremonial law seems to be in 7.3.352, which I discuss in section three of this chapter.
40. *Ad Heb.* 2.1.89.

with more diligence than the commandments of the old,[41] because of the "usefulness of the things said," since the commandments of Christ are "the words of eternal life, as it says in Jn. 6:69, *Lord, to whom shall we go? You have the words of eternal life*, etc."[42] Christ's commands provide salvation while the Old Testament does not. This is because the Old Testament does not provide grace: "[the Old Testament] did not confer grace, for grace is conferred in the New Testament." Aquinas then cites John 1:17: "Grace and truth came by Jesus Christ."[43] The commandments of the Old Testament are only *bonorum temporalium* or temporal goods. The temporal nature of the commandments is due to the end for which the "word spoken by angels" is ordered: the commandments only provided knowledge of sin and knowledge of God.[44]

Regarding knowledge of sin, the Old Law is described as subjecting man in servitude because of what Aquinas understands the apostles to say about this Law. Once again, Aquinas's interpretation of the apostolic decree in Acts 15 is key. "In Acts 15:10, the Law is called a 'yoke ... which neither our fathers nor we have been able to bear.'"[45] Likewise, Aquinas understands the Old Law as revealing a crucial knowledge of God but only in a temporal way. The Old Law was a time of expectation and shadows in comparison to the New Law: "[God] spoke first in a time of expectation and shadows, but the latter in these days, that is, in the time of grace. Rom. 13:12: Night is passed, and the day is at hand, etc. The Old Law 'was called night.'"[46] The promises of the Old Testament are to be understood spiritually: "It should be noted that the things promised in the Old Testament should be understood spiritually."[47]

Aquinas then explains that everything that was foretold in the Old Law has been fulfilled. Here, Aquinas strikes another strong chord of continuity with Israel and Church when he says, citing Matthew 5:18 ("not one dot or one iota of the Law shall pass away until all be fulfilled"), that this

---

41. Aquinas gives a total of three reasons. The first reason has already been discussed at length: Christ's authority as the Creator and Son of God gives his commandments a status far above that of an angel, which is only a creature. I only include the second and third reasons here. *Ad Heb.* 2.1.90

42. *Ad Heb.* 2.1.90.

43. *Ad Heb.* 2.1.97.

44. *Ad Heb.* 2.1.97.

45. This twofold servitude includes a subjection to sin and the Law.

46. *Ad Heb.* 1.1.14.

47. *Ad Heb.* 4.1.198.

fulfillment does not mean that the Old Law was made void (*non fuit irritatus*) in these latter days. Rather, Aquinas explains that in the fulfillment through Christ, the Old Law "became steadfast (*firmus*)."[48]

Another reason that the commandments of the New are to be more diligently followed than the Old is that the latter are *gravia* or heavy. Aquinas again cites the words of Peter at the Jerusalem council in Acts 15:10 as evidence of the *gravia* of the Old Law: "This is a yoke which neither we nor our fathers have been able to bear."[49] The commandments of the New Law, on the other hand, "are not burdensome," since, as Aquinas explains, Jesus taught "For my yoke is sweet" in Matthew 11:30. Acts 15:10 is read not only as a judgment by the apostles that the Old Law is burdensome, but that it should no longer be observed now that the New Law has come. Aquinas's comment on the heaviness of the Law illuminates his reference to the same verse in the *Prologue* and reveals what he views as the rationale behind an apostolic decision to end observances of the Law.[50]

In summary, Aquinas argues in the first division that Christ holds more authority than angels, Moses, and Aaron, because of his diverse excellence. Because he possesses more authority than these sacred persons, his commandments in the New Testament are more to be followed than the commandments of the Old Testament.

---

48. *Ad Heb.* 2.1.94: "Factus est ergo firmus, quia *non fuit irritatus*" [emphasis added]. Chrysostom Baer also translates *irritatus* as "void." Deferrari defines the term as "void" and lists other meanings "vain, useless, without effect, ineffectual." The Marietti text points the reader to 1.1.15, which explains the way in which the Old Testament spoke in the past. The note seems to imply that the Old Testament is not void or useless because God spoke divine things through it. Both Larcher and Baer translate the term as "void." In chapter seven, Aquinas will say, using a different term, that the Law is rendered void—the opposite of his statement in *Ad Heb.* 2.1.94.

49. *Ad Heb.* 2.1.90.

50. Aquinas also refers to the Law as a heavy yoke and refers to Acts 15:10 in *Ad Heb* 2.4.145 and 12.4.704.

See also 12.4.704, when commenting upon Hebrews 12:21. The Old Law is a law of fear, while the New Law is viewed as a law of grace. As the study progresses, it should become clear that for Aquinas, Acts 15:10 is an official apostolic decision that the ceremonial law no longer be observed by all.

3. THE CHANGE IN THE MODE AND ORDER OF THE DIVINE REGIME

The impact of the new priesthood of Christ upon the prerogatives of Israel becomes clearer in chapters 7 through 10. Aquinas understands the perfect priesthood of Christ to render the Levitical priesthood void. This change affects what Aquinas refers to as the "whole mode and order" of the regime, including the observances of the carnal ceremonial law.

The Perfect Priesthood of Christ Renders the Levitical Priesthood Void

Aquinas unfolds a detailed comparison between Christ and the Levitical priesthood beginning in lecture one of chapter 7. Despite having been born after Melchizedek in time, Aquinas explains that Christ is more excellent because "Christ ... as God and as the Son of God ... exists from eternity."[51] Christ's priesthood is eternal because "no mention is made of the end of his priesthood or of his successor."[52]

Aquinas then contrasts the perpetuity of Christ's priesthood with the perpetuity of the Levitical priesthood since he is aware of the Old Testament texts that state the priesthood and the Law is forever. "Even in Scripture it is frequently referred to as perpetual. Ex. 27:21: 'It shall be a perpetual observance throughout their successions among the children of Israel.' Lev. 24:3; 'By a perpetual service and rite.'"[53] Aquinas explains the sense in which the latter are perpetual by drawing once more upon the prefiguring function of the ceremonial law. The priesthood is described as perpetual in so far as it functioned as a symbol since "that which was symbolized by it was perpetual." Melchizedek is "a priest forever" because "that which is prefigured, namely Christ's priesthood, lasts forever."[54] Lecture one of chapter 7 is the second appearance of the concept of the prefiguring function of the Old Law.[55] The theme appears again in lecture two of chapter 8: "There

---

51. *Ad Heb.* 7.1.334.
52. *Ad Heb.* 7.1.334.
53. *Ad Heb.* 7.1.334.
54. *Ad Heb.* 7.1.334.
55. Aquinas uses the perfect passive participle *figuratum* and then the imperfect passive *figurabatur* in this paragraph to describe the priesthood's function of prefiguring. The tense emphasizes that the prefiguring *was* and is now no longer functioning. He does

they were a figure, but here the truth expressed by the figure. Therefore, this testament is better throughout."[56] And again, "In the Old Testament, there were only figures, but in the New, the truth of the figures; so the New completes and perfects the Old."[57]

Because the imperfect priesthood of the Old Testament is recognized as "perpetual" only in its prefiguring function, it is changed by the arrival of that which it prefigured. The perfect priesthood of Christ renders the mode and order of the Levitical priesthood changed since "the perfect voids (*evacuat*) the imperfect."[58] Aquinas then interprets 1 Corinthians 13:10 to express this change in the priesthood: "when that which is perfect is come, that which is in part shall be done away." For Aquinas, Paul's teaching proves that "the priesthood of Christ renders the Levitical priesthood void."[59]

A Complete Change in the Entire Mode and Order of the Imperfect Regime

The change in the priesthood brings about a change of the Law.[60] Aquinas explains the nature of the change by drawing upon the analogy of how the law of a polity is affected by regime change, as understood by Aristotle:

> And the reason for this is that the end being changed, it is necessary that the means be changed, just as he who changes the intent of traveling by water, changes the intent of searching for a ship. For every law is ordained to human behavior according to some regime [or polity]. Hence, according to the Philosopher in the *Politics,* to change behavior it is necessary that the law be changed. Moreover, just as human law is ordered to a human regime, so is spiritual and divine law ordered to the divine regime [*regimen divinum*]. But this regime is designated through the priesthood.

---

not refer to the priesthood as *figura*. This lecture may also be unique for its treatment of the idea of the perpetuity of the Old Law. I investigate this further when I correlate my findings with that of the *Summa theologiae*.

56. *Ad Heb.* 8.2.392.

57. *Ad Heb.* 8.2.396.

58. *Ad Heb.* 7.3.349.

59. *Ad Heb.* 7.3.349. Aquinas cites 1 Cor 13:10 again in 9.3.437 to explain how Christ's entering of the holy of holies is the coming of the perfect tabernacle and the cessation of the imperfect tabernacle.

60. *Ad Heb.* 7.3.350.

> Therefore, the priesthood being translated, it is necessary that the law be transferred.[61]

The change is not a slight one brought about by *a* new priest. Aquinas explains that the Law would not be changed if one priest dies. Rather, the change in the regime, or polity, is more dramatic. Drawing upon Aristotle's explanation of how a city's law is affected by a complete regime change, Aquinas explains that because the *entire* priesthood has changed, a proportional change occurs in the regime's laws.[62] Therefore, "the whole mode and order of the regime is changed" (*totus modus et ordo regiminis*).[63] The change this metaphor implies should not be overlooked. Aquinas thinks such a sweeping change in the order of an old regime does not leave the identity of the citizens intact, but rather destroys it.[64] If the order of the regime is changed, the city and citizens do not remain the same.

Aquinas then explains the nature of the change in the regime throughout chapters 7 through 10, using a series of contrasts between the old and new priesthoods.[65] The old is characterized by a carnal command while the new is a spiritual command. The promise to Abraham, Isaac, and Jacob is a carnal and temporal promise, while the promise in the new concerns heavenly and eternal things. The Old Law is ordained to an imperfect end while the new is ordained to the perfect. The Old Testament was a time of shadow while the New is a time of grace. I examine each contrast below.

The Coming of the Eternal Priesthood Renders the Old Testament Void

From Aquinas's view, the reason for the change of the divine regime is due not only to the divine institution of the perfect priesthood. The priesthood

---

61. *Ad Heb.* 7.3.350. [Emended.] I am aware that *regimen* could be translated "rule." Nevertheless, it can also mean "regime" or "polity" (*politia*), as indicated by Aquinas's reflections on *Politiae et legislatio* in *Sententia libri Politicorum* 3.1.348–50. Chrysostom Baer's translation is therefore to be preferred over the Aquinas Institute's since it carries a stronger political context of *regimen* as the rule of some polity as it relates to human behavior, which is how *regimen* is used in the *Sententia libri Politicorum*, 1.1.13–15; 29. Aquinas relies upon Aristotle to help describe the process of the change of the Old Law in the Ephesians commentary as well. See chapter 7.

62. *Sententia libri Politicorum* 3.2.359.

63. *Ad Heb.* 7.3.351.

64. *Sententia libri Politicorum* 3.2.364.

65. *Ad Heb.* 7.3.351.

is brought about in connection with a twofold *ratio* for the new priesthood. The new priesthood is brought about because of the 1) imperfection of the Law and 2) what Aquinas refers to as a "change of time." The imperfection of the Law consists of its carnal nature and its inability to lead to beatitude.[66]

For Aquinas, the Levitical priesthood is inseparable from the ceremonial law, which was only a temporal and carnal commandment as opposed to the perfect priesthood of Christ, which is spiritual and eternal. The Old Testament is a carnal commandment because it had certain "carnal observances, as circumcision and purifications of the flesh and because it promised carnal punishments and rewards."[67] The New Testament, on the other hand, is "not dispensed by carnal things, but consists of spiritual things." And that which is spiritual is perpetual, and the New Testament dispenses perpetual goods and punishments. The Old Law was only a shadow of these good things to come.[68] "In the Old Testament there were only figures, but in the New, the truth of the figures; so the New completes and perfects the Old."[69]

This consummation and perfection also involves the making void of the "carnal commands" of the Old Testament. According to Aquinas the introduction of the New brings about "the voiding of the Old Testament."[70] This voiding is an *evacuatio*.[71] Again, the reason is due to the change in the priesthood:

> If a new priest arises, this will not be according to the law of a carnal commandment, but according to the law of an eternal and indissoluble life; the reason being that the first was according to that law. It is proper, therefore, to say that the new one be according

---

66. The ratio behind the institution of the new priesthood, which administers the new covenant seems due to both the inadequacy of the imperfect Old Law as well as the change of time orchestrated by divine providence. Despite the space attributed to the inadequacy of the Old Law, Aquinas repeatedly returns to the change of time. He does this when he considers the objection that the Law is not evil but only fitting for a time (*Ad Heb.* 7.3.362); and when he considers the objection that God's Law cannot change because God is also immutable (*Ad Heb.* 7.3.352).

67. *Ad Heb.* 7.3.359.

68. *Ad Heb.* 8.1.388.

69. *Ad Heb.* 8.2.396.

70. *Ad Heb.* 7.3.361.

71. *Ad Heb.* 7.3.361. *Evacuo* means to make void.

to another law, if a new [priest] does actually arise. But a new one does arise.[72]

The carnal commands of circumcision and purifications were not perpetual because they did not consist in eternal and spiritual things that Christ establishes.[73] The new priesthood therefore requires a spiritual law and renders the carnal commandment void.

The Temporal Promise

Aquinas also understands the promise to Abraham, Isaac, and Jacob, as a promise of carnal things. He is keenly aware of Old Testament witnesses that indicate the covenant is to endure forever: "He says moreover, to their fathers, namely to Abraham, Isaac, and Jacob, with whom He had initiated a special covenant. Ps. 104:8: 'He hath remembered his covenant forever: the word which He commanded to a thousand generations. Which He made to Abraham, etc.'" Yet, this promise, explains Aquinas, was regarding *only* carnal things, such as the deliverance from slavery in Egypt: "But he promised carnal things to those who came out of Egypt."[74] While discussing how Christ is the mediator of a better covenant, he writes of the Old Testament that "Then, temporal things were promised. Is 1:19: 'If you be willing, and harken to Me, you shall eat the good things of the land.'" Now, however, "heavenly things are promised." Aquinas concludes that the content of the promises of the New Testament are not transitory and therefore they are better: "Therefore, this one is better in regard to what it promises men."[75]

Imperfect But Not Evil

In addition to the carnal nature of its commandments and promises, the former priesthood was imperfect because it did not lead to perfection. Aquinas explains that the priesthood was not perfected.[76] This is because

---

72. *Ad Heb.* 7.3.359.

73. The carnal command is contrasted with what is genuinely perpetual, that of spiritual virtue. It is only through spiritual virtue that there "is generated in us a perpetual life." See *Ad Heb.* 7.3.359.

74. *Ad Heb.* 8.2.401.

75. *Ad Heb.* 8.2.392.

76. *Ad Heb.* 7.2.348.

the Old Law only provided knowledge of sin and knowledge of God. But it failed to bring the perfection of justice.[77] Aquinas then cites Matthew 5:20 in support the idea of the Law's imperfection: "For I tell you, that unless your justice abound more than that of the scribes and Pharisees, you shall not enter into the kingdom of heaven." Christ's command to let justice abound more than Pharisees is taken to mean that the Old Law was imperfect. The Law administered by this priestly office did not give the helping grace to avoid sin, but only to know it.[78] Christ's priesthood is perfect because it brings a justice that abounds more than that of the scribes and Pharisees. The institution of the new covenant is necessary because only the sacraments of the new covenant bring perfect justice. The voiding of the Old Law is therefore followed by a transfer to a New Law.

In Aquinas's view, this transfer is indicated in Scripture by two verses. The first is Jeremiah 31:31, which, Aquinas cites as: "I will make a new covenant with the house of Israel, and with house of Judah, not according to the covenant which I made with their fathers, etc." The second is Romans 8:2, which states "For the Law of the spirit of life, in Christ Jesus, hath delivered me from the Law of sin and of death." Here, Aquinas takes the "Law of sin and death" mentioned in this Romans 8:2 to refer to the Old Law: "For the Old Law is called the law of sin and death, because it did not confer grace *ex opere operato,* as the sacraments of the new law do."[79] The New Law joins man to God through divine grace and provides perfect cognition of God and the remission of sins.[80] The Old Law contained "no grace in itself."[81] This was true even for the fathers of the Old Testament who Aquinas admits are described in the Old Testament as holy. Abraham and Moses were holy *only* because of faith in Christ, not the observances.[82]

Aquinas is quite aware of how the imperfection of the old priesthood and Law might be taken to mean that these were evil. He is again concerned

---

77. *Ad Heb.* 7.3.348.

78. *Ad Heb.* 8.2.393.

79. *Ad Heb.* 7.3.352. Aquinas's view here represents his mature view on circumcision where grace is mediated only through faith in Christ *not* through the Law itself. Aquinas adopts the same position in the Galatians commentary and the Romans commentary, as well as in the *Tertia Pars* of the *Summa theologiae* where he rejects his earlier position on circumcision (that the rite saves in and of itself) in the *Sentences*. See Schenk, "Views of the Two Covenants in Medieval Theology."

80. *Ad Heb.* 8.3.405.

81. *Ad Heb.* 9.1.415.

82. *Ad Heb.* 9.2.431.

to guard against the Manicheans who "condemn the Old Testament, saying that it was formed by an evil principle, namely, the devil."[83] Citing Romans 7:1, Aquinas replies to the objection by explaining that the Law is holy and just and not evil." It was "not evil in itself but . . .unsuited to the time,"[84] meaning the time of the New Testament: "For the things of the Old Testament are not to be kept in the New Testament."[85] Both the Law and the priesthood are rejected, not because these are evil, but because of imperfection: "for that is said to be weak which cannot produce its effect; but the proper effect of the Law and of the priesthood is to justify."[86] The Law could not justify but it was nevertheless useful in its own time, inasmuch as it disposed to faith.[87]

When Aquinas considers the question why God would institute such a weak and imperfect law, he offers the argument that a change of time occurred:

> It is true that they would have been uselessly instituted if they were to remain always. But just as one ought to give a teacher to a child, but when he arrives at the perfect age he is given the manner of comporting himself according to the judgment of the ruler of the republic: so in the Old Law those things which were instituted until the perfect time arrived, and then those things which lead to perfection had to be instituted. And so he says, "Until the time of correction," that is, the time in which it is corrected, not as something evil, but imperfect: "For the law is good," as it says in 1 Tim. 1:8.[88]

Here, Aquinas states for the first time in the commentary that the ceremonial law possessed a literal *ratio*: it disposed the Jewish people to faith in God though only for a time.[89] He affirms this again in an explicit way

---

83. *Ad Heb.* 11.2.566.

84. *Ad Heb.* 7.3.362.

85. *Ad Heb.* 7.3.362.

86. *Ad Heb.* 7.3.362.

87. *Ad Heb.* 7.3.362.

88. *Ad Heb.* 9.2.434. Aquinas thinks that there is a twofold cleansing: one from the stain of the guilt of sin, and "regarding this the Law could not do anything." The other cleansing is in regard to "worship, namely, so that they would be allowed to minister at these sacrifices; and thus the Law did cleanse." *Ad Heb.* 9.2.430. Cf. 9.3.443; 9.4.449; 9.4.460.

89. Here, the commentary comes into full agreement with Aquinas's view of the twofold ratio for the ceremonial law in the *Summa theologiae*: it served to prefigure the

when he says that the "ceremonies of the law were ordained to one thing according to that state; but to something else, insofar as they were figurative, namely, inasmuch as they represented Christ."[90] I return to the idea of the concept of the change of time at the end of this section.

The Renunciation of the Ceremonial Law

As stated above, because the Law has been made void, to practice the laws of the old regime is now considered a sin. While commenting upon Paul's statement that the priesthood was obligated to take the tithes of the people according of the Law, he explains that the ceremonial laws are no longer to be followed.[91] The commandment to tithe provides Aquinas with the opportunity to explain why it is acceptable to tithe even though tithing is a commandment of the Old Law, which has passed away. When Aquinas introduces his comment on the problem he summarizes this objection to tithing and mentions that observing the ceremonial law is now a sin: "*since the observance of a commandment of the law is now a sin*, it seems unlawful to give or receive tithes now."[92] Aquinas then responds to this objection by presenting the famous distinction between moral and ceremonial law:

> I answer that there were in the law some precepts purely ceremonial, such as circumcision, the offering of the lamb, and son on. *Such laws, since they were only figurative, it is no longer licit to observe,* for they were a figure of something to come; hence, anyone who observes them now would be signifying that Christ is still to come. But others were purely moral, and these must be observed now. Among these was the giving of tithes . . . but the determination of such a portion is now made by the Church, just as in the Old Testament it was determined by the law.[93]

---

perfect priesthood of the One who was to come; and it enclosed the Jewish people in proper worship of God.

90. *Ad Heb.* 9.1.422. [Emphasis added]

91. Heb. 7:5 in the Douay-Rheims reads: "And indeed they that are of the sons of Levi, who receive the priesthood, have a commandment to take tithes of the people according to the law, that is to say, of their brethren: though they themselves also came out of the loins of Abraham."

92. *Ad Heb.* 7.2.339. [Emphasis added]

93. *Ad Heb.* 7.2.339. In lecture two of chapter 8, Aquinas makes the distinction between moral and ceremonial law once more: "in the Old Law there were precepts pertaining to the worship of God, namely the ceremonial precepts, and some that pertained to correct conduct, namely, the moral precepts, which continue; but the others do not."

The observance of the ceremonial law has been made illicit in what Aquinas refers to as "the time of grace." Later, Aquinas asks why God would command sacrifices if he did not desire them, and states once more that observance of the ceremonial law after Christ is a sin.[94] God does not want these observances "for that time in which the shadows cease with the advent of truth, and hence *a person would sin by offering them now*."[95] These ceremonies have never been pleasing to God but were accepted because "they were figures of Christ whose passion was accepted by God" and they restrained the Jews from idolatry.[96] To observe ceremonies after the passion "would be an insult (*iniuria*) to the sacrifice of Christ."[97] After the passion, all those who observed the ceremonies must go "outside the general community of carnal things, or outside the observances of the Law, or outside the senses of the body."[98] Again, he writes, "Let us renounce [*renuntiemus*] the ceremonies of the law, now that the truth has come, on account of which we are a reproach among the Jews, that is, on account of the signs of penance which are a reproach to carnal things."[99] Both Christ and the apostles are examples in this renunciation of the Law: "For just as Christ was accused of subverting the law, so the apostles were reproached for preaching that the ceremonies of the law should not be observed."[100] After the passion of Christ the ceremonies are void and must be renounced.

The Change of Time

Aquinas anticipates an objection to the idea that divine providence would change an immutable law. The objection actually contains a premise similar to Wyschogrod's argument that the Law is perpetual and cannot be declared dead or deadly, because to say so implies that God has lied to the people of

---

Ad Heb. 8.2.392.

94. Heb. 10:5–6, in the Vulgate reads: "Wherefore when He cometh into the world, He saith: Sacrifice and oblation Thou wouldest not: but a body Thou hast fitted to Me: Holocausts for sin did not please Thee."

95. *Ad Heb.* 10.1.488. It seems clear here that Aquinas is describing how the observing the ceremonial law, in this case, the sacrifices, is a sin for anyone who offers such things, not only Jewish believers in Christ.

96. *Ad Heb.* 10.1.488.

97. *Ad Heb.* 10.1.500.

98. *Ad Heb.* 13.2.749.

99. *Ad Heb.* 13.2.749.

100. *Ad Heb.* 13.2.749.

The Ceremonial Law as a Shadow of the Night (Hebrews)

Israel and no longer desires for them to exist as his distinct people.[101] One might think that divine providence implies immutable law:

> But the Manicheans raise an objection here: if the Old Law was given by divine providence, which is immutable, the law itself should be immutable; consequently, it should not be changed. Therefore, since it was changed, it was not given by divine providence.[102]

In his reply, Aquinas marshals Augustine's *Against Faustus* and appeals again to the change of time that comes with the advent of Christ. In so doing he makes clear that he understands the ceremonial law to have exhausted its figuring function:

> I answer, as Augustine says in *Against Faustus*, that just as a wise dispenser by one and the same arrangement and providence gives different laws according as times and persons differ, one law for summer and another for winter, one for children and one for adults, one for perfect and another for imperfect, and yet is the same providence; so with divine providence remains unchanged, the law was changed to fit the times; because before the coming of Christ precepts were given to prefigure his coming, but after his coming precepts were given to signify that he had come. Furthermore, the precepts were given to them as to children, but in the new law as to the perfect. Hence, the law is called a pedagogue, which is strictly for children. Therefore, if something in the law suggests perpetuity, this is by reason of the one prefigured.[103]

Aquinas already introduced the concept of the prefigurement of the Law above. Here, he explicitly explains why the prefiguring function ceases after the coming of Christ. The Old Testament's language of perpetuity refers only to that which is truly perpetual: the future coming of the new

---

101. Of course the conclusion that Wyschogrod comes to is all together different than the Manichean, since he understands the change in the immutable Law not to indicate that the Law was not given through divine providence but that this providence is somehow lacking in goodness: that God lied about the promise to Abraham to create a people and tie the identity of the people to the perpetuity of the Law. Here, however, Aquinas defines both the promise to Israel and the ceremonial law as temporal as well as separates the two concepts. While the Old Law ordained Israel to knowledge of God and knowledge of sin, the promise to Abraham is reduced to the deliverance out of Egypt and other temporal goods. The dividing of the Law from the irrevocable and perpetual promise to the people seems to provide the occasion for viewing the Law as a temporal manifestation.

102. *Ad Heb.* 7.3.352.

103. *Ad Heb.* 7.3.352. [Emphasis added]

priesthood of Christ. After the coming of Christ, the precepts are replaced by precepts of the New Law. The ceremonial law was good but imperfect and it is now changed and rendered void by the time of Christ's advent. To observe the carnal ceremonies after Christ would be a serious mistake.

4. ISRAEL AND THE CHURCH IN THE HEBREWS COMMENTARY

It seems rather clear that the Hebrews commentary represents a sophisticated and concise statement of Aquinas's teaching on the ceremonial law after the passion of Christ that is quite similar to his teaching in Ia-IIae q. 103.4. In the Hebrews commentary, Aquinas teaches that observing the ceremonial law after the passion of Christ is a sin because its observance is understood as a profession that Christ has yet to come despite his already coming. The eternal priesthood of Christ, the advent of the truth, fulfills the Old Law in its totality. Aquinas frequently states that the Law is rendered void; that the coming of the New is likened to a day that repels the shadow of the Law's night. The shadow of the Law's night is comprised of a matrix of the Law's attributes: its prefiguring function; its temporal and carnal characteristics; and its inability to lead to beatitude. Although the legal observances of the ceremonial law *were* figures of the eternal and perfect priesthood of Christ, these ceremonies are no longer to be kept because the change of time manifested in the coming of Christ, which renders them void. Moreover, to observe the ceremonies after the institution of the New commandment is not only a sin but an offense to the sacrifice of Christ. It seems there is no theological value in the prerogatives of Israel after the passion. Indeed, the ceremonies are harmful, and must be renounced.

It is this rendering void of the carnal command that Isaac and Soulen challenged. Moreover, the same concern drives Wyschogrod's critique of Aquinas. It is also what Matthew Levering seems to miss when he interprets Aquinas's teaching on the ceremonial law to apply only to Jewish Christians (or what Aquinas would refer to as "Jewish converts") and *not* to Jews.[104] To the contrary, the rendering void of the *mandatum carnale* is, for Aquinas, similar to how light repels shadow. "The time of the New Testament is called

---

104. "Aquinas does not condemn the observance of Torah by Jews who do not believe in Jesus Christ, but neither does he condone not believing in Jesus Christ." Levering, *Christ's Fulfillment*, fn. 64, 161.

the day," Aquinas states, "because it repels the shadow of the Law's night."[105] The shadow is the temporal nature of the ceremonial law and the coming of the light of the New Testament does not leave it intact. The Old Law is replaced by the new in the way that the ruler or a new political order might replace the laws of the old order. God no longer desires these sacrifices "for that time in which the shadows cease with the advent of truth." It seems safe to conclude that Aquinas's view of the relationship between Israel and the Church in the Hebrews commentary is economically supersessionist.

My examination also reveals a tension in Aquinas's thought on the Law. Early in the Hebrews commentary Aquinas states that the fulfillment of the Old Law by Christ *does not* render the Old Law void.[106] Aquinas is concerned to avoid Manichean interpretations of the Old Law as evil and argues that the ceremonial law was good for a time. He preserves the literal reason for Jewish worship *before* the coming of Christ. His view therefore overlaps with the *Prima Secundae* where the ceremonial law is described as having a twofold ratio of prefiguring Christ and enclosing the Jewish people in the worship of the one God. However, in 7.3.361, and at other places in the text, Aquinas contradicts his earlier statement that the Old Testament is not void when he says that the introduction of the new priesthood and testament brings about "the rendering void of the Old Testament."[107]

The economic supersessionism in the commentary sits in tension with two important points in Aquinas's thought. The tension exists between the Aristotelian regime change analogy and two metaphors Aquinas draws directly from Scripture: the olive tree metaphor of Romans 11 and the household metaphor of Ephesians 2. The regime analogy seems to point to the complete replacement of the temporal priesthood and the Old Law with the eternal priesthood and New Law. The transfer from one regime to another brings about a total change in the mode and order of the former regime, which includes the complete voiding and renunciation of the carnal commandments.

However, Aquinas also draws upon the olive tree metaphor of Romans 11 to describe the Gentile *ecclesia* as grafted into Israel or existing with and *alongside* of Israel in faith. He states that the Gentiles "were made partakers" of the New Testament. The wild olive tree is grafted into the

---

105. *Ad Heb.* 3.2.173.
106. *Ad Heb.* 2.1.94.
107. *Ad Heb.* 7.3.361.

good olive tree and "shares of its fatness."[108] Additionally, Aquinas brilliantly synthesizes the olive tree metaphor with the Ephesians metaphor to describe Christ as a builder of a house uniting Jews and Gentiles. The Ephesians household metaphor and the Romans olive tree metaphor do not emphasize replacement of Israel with Church and seem to sit in tension with the Aristotelian regime change metaphor. Aquinas's use of the olive tree metaphor as well as his argument that the Church is a union of Jews and Gentiles can be seen as echoes of more positive descriptions of Israel's promises in the commentaries on Romans and Ephesians. Next, I attempt to answer whether a similar view of the ceremonial law can be found in the Romans commentary.

---

108. The "sharing" relationship between Israel and the Church which Aquinas builds using these metaphors is not unlike the one described by George Lindbeck, "Critical Exegesis and Theological Interpretation," 166.

5

The Ceremonial Law as Present Spiritual Benefit for Jews (Romans)

AQUINAS'S LECTURES ON HEBREWS and Romans provide a rich theological picture of his view of Israel and the Church. Whereas the letter to the Hebrews concerned Paul's teaching on grace for the "sons of Israel,"[1] Aquinas understands the letter to the Romans as Paul's instruction on grace for the "church of the Gentiles."[2] However, Aquinas's Romans commentary contains an affirmation of the Jewish observance of circumcision as a spiritual benefit *even after* the passion that undermines the argument in the Hebrews commentary that Christ's priesthood completely voided the Law.[3] Indeed, the teaching of Aquinas's Romans commentary represents a premodern precursor to Karl Thieme's breakthrough idea: that the Jew can be pleasing before God *as a Jew*, despite unbelief in Christ.

---

1. *Prologus* 9.

2. *Prologus* 11.

3. I am not the first to point out Aquinas's positive view of the Jews in the Romans commentary. Steven Boguslawski and Bruce Marshall have both treated the topic. See Boguslawski, *Thomas Aquinas on the Jews*; Bruce Marshall, "*Quasi in Figura*." I view this chapter as building on Marshall and Boguslawski's work by drawing upon Soulen's reading of the significance of Paul's present tense descriptions of Israel, especially as these relate to the ceremonial law.

Aquinas on Israel and the Church

1. THE PRIMARY THEME AND DIVISION OF THE ROMANS COMMENTARY

Although Aquinas understands the letter to the Romans to treat the grace of Christ and grace in the Church,[4] themes related to the Jews, the Old Testament, and the ceremonial law appear in each division of the text, the greeting and the body.[5] In the greeting, themes related to Israel and the ceremonial law surface in Aquinas's comment upon the "errors" of the Manicheans and Galatians. Aquinas teaches that Paul's words in the greeting contradict the Manichean assertion that the God of the Old Testament and the Father of our Lord Jesus Christ are not the same. This is "excluded," when Paul says, "that which God had promised before, through his prophets, in the Holy Scriptures."[6] The Apostle also excludes the Manichean condemnation of the Old Testament when he identifies this testament as the only holy writing before the Gospel.[7]

The theme of the Law appears in the greeting when Aquinas contrasts the faith of the Romans to the Galatian believers who struggled because of a particular teaching on the ceremonial law.[8] The Galatians' faith "was not yet perfect" due to the same error he understands to have plagued the Hebrews: "some of them had been reached by false apostles, who taught that the rites of the Law must be joined to the Gospel."[9] Aquinas has now mentioned this false teaching in the Hebrews commentary, and the Romans commentary.[10] He will also discuss the problem in the commentary on Galatians.

---

4. *Ad Rom.* 1.1.15.

5. *Ad Rom.* 1.1.15.

6. *Ad Rom.* 1.2.41.

7. *Ad Rom.* 1.2.41. I do not mean to imply that in the greeting Aquinas is solely concerned with the errors of the Manicheans. Aquinas also understands Paul to exclude errors of Arius, Apollinaris, Nestorius, and Sabellius.

8. *Ad Rom.* 1.5.77.

9. *Ad Rom.* 1.5.77.

10. *Ad Rom.* 1.5.77; *Ad Hebraeos* 1.1.6. As I show in the next chapter, Aquinas discusses this problem directly and at length in his *Super Epistolam ad Galatas*. The theme of the observance of the ceremonial law along with the gospel as a teaching of pseudo apostles runs through the commentaries. See *Ad Galatas, Prologus* 1; and lectio 1: "The Apostle therefore writes the Galatians this epistle in which he shows that with the coming of the grace of the New Testament, the Old Testament should be cast out, so that with the fulfillment of the truth, the figure may be abandoned, and with the attainment of these two, namely, grace and truth, one may arrive at the truth of justice and glory. And these two are acquired, if, abandoning the observance of the *legalia* [i.e. the ceremonial

The Ceremonial Law as Present Spiritual Benefit for Jews (Romans)

Nevertheless, the great majority of Aquinas's commentary consists of his interpretation of the body of Paul's letter, which he divides into two parts.[11] The subject of "Jews and Gentiles" is prominently featured throughout the first division, and can be said to function as a secondary theme, alongside the primary theme of the gospel of grace.[12] Aquinas explains that chapters 1 through 11 consider three things in relation to the power of Christ's grace: to what the gospel of grace extends, which is salvation; how the gospel confers salvation, which is through faith; and finally, "the people for whom the gospel works salvation, namely, both Jews and the Gentiles."[13]

Throughout these chapters, Aquinas takes care to treat the precepts of the ceremonial law under the category of "prerogative of the Jews" (*praerogativa Iudaeorum*) in the "era after grace" three different times.[14] My examination of the commentary focuses rather narrowly on Aquinas's view of the ceremonial precepts in the era after grace. A word about this term "prerogative of the Jews" is in order.

My use of "prerogative of the Jews" includes but is not limited to the particular rites of the ceremonial law, namely the practices of circumcision, Passover, and dietary laws.[15] In the Romans commentary, Aquinas uses the term frequently and more broadly. In addition to Law and circumcision he includes the term "race" (*gens*) as a prerogative.[16] He uses the term prerogatives of the Jews (in the singular or plural) at least eight times. Each of these occurrences refers to the prerogatives of the Jews in regard to the Law. Aquinas uses "advantage" (*amplius*) of the Jews several times and interchangeably with prerogative.[17] He also refers to the Jew's "dignity"

---

precepts of the Old Law], we concentrate fervently on observing the Gospel of Christ."

11. *Ad Rom.* 1.6.97.

12. *Ad Rom.* 1.5.74; 1.5.97.

13. *Ad Rom.* 1.6.98–101.

14. Aquinas refers to the ceremonial precepts nine times. In one place he refers to these as ceremonial works. Jews' prerogative or Judaism's prerogative appears six times. Boguslawski points out that Aquinas uses Israel and Jews interchangeably throughout his commentary. I therefore refer to the Jews' prerogatives or Israel's prerogatives interchangeably. The phrase "era after grace" appears in the commentary in 2.4.238; 4.2.357.

15. Therefore, my use of the term here is similar to the usage in chapter 4, on the Hebrews commentary, as well as my view of Aquinas's handling of the term in the *Summa theologiae*. See the footnote on the term "prerogatives of Israel" in chapter 4 of this study for a brief treatment of how this term relates to the ceremonial law in the *Summa theologiae*.

16. *Gentis* can also be interpreted as "tribe" or "people."

17. *Ad Rom.* 3.1.249.

or "greatness" (*dignitas*).¹⁸ The term "prerogative" is used interchangeably with both "advantage" and "dignity." The term prerogative always includes the Mosaic Law in general, and the ceremonial law in particular. I therefore use the term "prerogatives of Israel" to refer the matrix of advantages Aquinas ascribes to Judaism. The chapters that contain material directly related to the prerogatives of Israel include 2 through 4, and 9.¹⁹

2. THE "SHOCK" OF PRESENT TENSE PREROGATIVES

Below I treat five of Aquinas's extended remarks upon the prerogatives of Israel in the Romans commentary: 1) The first reflection is on the privileged state of the Jews as a light to the nations, and occurs as a comment upon the present tense of the phrase "But if you call yourself a Jew" of Romans 2:17; 2) The second reflection on the prerogatives of Israel occurs as a comment upon Paul's present tense answer to his own rhetorical question, "What advantage has the Jew?" in Romans 3:2, which is, "Much in everyway!"; 3) The third reflection includes Aquinas's defense of Jewish prerogatives despite the vice of unbelief. Aquinas considers an objection he understands Paul to raise regarding the advantage of the Jew: The objection is represented by another rhetorical question in Romans 3:3, "What if some of them have not believed? Shall their unbelief make the faith of God without effect?" and his answer: "God forbid!"²⁰ 4) The fourth reflection includes an affirmation of the ceremonial law as "a figure of a spiritual benefit" for Jews, even after Christ, and unfolds as a comment upon Paul's present tense statement "They are Israel," in Romans 9:4–5. The fifth reflection includes an affirmation of the prerogatives of the Jews as promises that cannot be revoked in Romans 11:28–9: "They are most dear for the sake of their fathers . . . the gifts and the call of God are without repentance."²¹

In each case, a present tense Pauline phrase about the Jews provides Aquinas the opportunity to comment at length on the prerogatives of Israel. Soulen's work suggests this connection between the prerogatives and

---

18. *Ad Rom.* 9.1.743–47.

19. Although the content of the chapters overlaps at points, especially on the subject of circumcision, my examination of the prerogatives is organized thematically in order to include relevant but isolated texts from chapters that discuss the prerogatives of Israel indirectly.

20. *Ad Rom.* 3.1.251.

21. *Ad Rom.* 11.4.912–26.

the three phrases is not a coincidence.²² For Soulen, Paul's present tense descriptions of Israel—that they "are Israelites"; that they "are beloved"—problematizes the traditional characterization of carnal Israel as a transitory phenomenon. Soulen writes, "The single most important element of Romans 9–11 for Jewish-Christian relations is its use of the present tense to characterize the Jewish people—Paul's kinsmen 'according to the flesh'—as the heirs of God's covenant promises."²³ Soulen warns that when Paul's present tense descriptions of the Jews are ignored it leads to a reading of the election of the Jewish people as a phenomenon of the past:

> When Christians do not attend in a serious way to "the shock of the present tense" in Romans 9–11, they are prone to read their Scriptures in ways that lead them to conclude that God's election of the Jewish people was a phenomenon of the *ancient past.* Perhaps if they pay a little attention to Rom 11, they will also think of Israel's election as a phenomenon of the *eschatological future,* when "all Israel will be saved" 11:26. This traditional Christian view of Israel's election may remind us of the Queen's attitude toward tea in *Alice in Wonderland:* "Tea yesterday, and tea tomorrow, but never tea today!" Precisely here, the "shock of the present tense" in Romans 9–11 exerts its enduring, foundational importance for Christian-Jewish relations. To the degree that Christians submit themselves to this shock, they will turn to their Jewish neighbor and see one who is God's beloved—not *only* in the primordial past and eschatological future—but *also* and *above all* in the abiding *now* of covenant history.²⁴

Soulen's "shock of the present tense" helps illuminate Aquinas's engagement of Paul's descriptions of the Jewish people in a way that highlights the significance of the question of the theological status of circumcision after the passion of Christ in Aquinas's thought. Aquinas not only affirms the election of this chosen people but goes in the opposite direction of the standard Christian view by connecting the doctrine of election with a positive affirmation of the theological status of Jewish observance of circumcision after the passion of Christ. Indeed, Aquinas's positive affirmations are directly related to his encounter with Paul's present tense language about Israel's prerogatives in the era after grace.

---

22. Soulen, "'They are Israelites.'"
23. Ibid., 2–3.
24. Ibid.

The Privileged State of the Jews as a Light for Those in Darkness

In lecture four of chapter 2, Aquinas comments in detail on the idea that the Jews are not justified by *hearing* the Law, but by *doing* the Law. When commenting upon Paul's words in 2:17, "But if you are called a Jew and rest in the law," he treats the Jews' present privileged state as it relates to the Law. In doing so, Aquinas does not say that the Jews *were* privileged before the age of grace. Rather, he speaks of the Jews enjoying a privileged state even now, after the passion of Christ.

The prerogative of the Jews is threefold: they are the people to whom the Law was given,[25] and for this reason, the name "Jew" is an honorable name. Second, the Jews enjoy a "prerogative in regard to the law" itself in two senses.[26] The reception of the Law brought stability to their knowledge and will,[27] especially in their worship and knowledge of one God. Third, the Jews enjoy a privileged state in regard to the "fruit of the law" (*fructu legis*) or the effect of the Law.[28] The Law not only secures worship and knowledge of one God but also the moral capacity "to select not only good from bad things but also better from less good."[29] This is why a Jew asked Christ "Which is the greatest commandment?"[30]

Additionally, their reception of the Law is a light for others who need the help of the Law.[31] These others "find themselves in three different situations, so far as knowledge of the law is concerned."[32] Aquinas then presents three groups that need the fruit or light of the Law. The first group consists of those "entirely ignorant of the Law, because they lack natural talent, just as a man is physically blind, because he lacks visual power."[33] Some persons "cannot be given the light of knowledge enabling them to see by themselves what to do." "Rather," explains Aquinas, "they must be

---

25. *Ad Rom.* 2.4.224.
26. *Ad Rom.* 2.4.226.
27. *Ad Rom.* 2.4.226.
28. *Ad Rom.* 2.4.227.
29. *Ad Rom.* 2.4.228.

30. Aquinas understands the effect of the Old Law to equip its doers with a sophisticated level of practical reasoning about the good that seems lacking in those who only have the natural law as guide because conclusions about the natural inclinations are so obscured by habitual sin.

31. *Ad Rom.* 2.4.227.
32. *Ad Rom.* 2.4.229.
33. *Ad Rom.* 2.4.229.

led, as the blind are, by commanding them to do this or that, even though they do not understand the reason for the command." In Aquinas's view, some lack the capacity to understand the good. Aquinas then introduces a subgroup of the ignorant: "others are ignorant through lack of training or not enlightened by teaching." However, for these people, "a wise man" can offer "the light of training, so that they will understand what is commanded." Citing Luke 1:79 ("to give light to those who sit in darkness and the shadow of death"), Aquinas says that those who know the Law and train others are a light in the darkness.[34] The second group consists of "those who are on the way to knowledge they have not yet attained . . . through lack of full instruction."[35] These are "the foolish" that need correction or those who have "not yet received wisdom" but are beyond a stage of ignorance. Another group that requires such instruction are children.[36] The third and final group that benefits from the Law is a group that is advanced in knowledge but that still requires instruction from the wise in order to possess authoritative sayings of wisdom "as their rule pattern."[37] Throughout Aquinas's discussion of the privileged state of the Jews in relation to the Law, there is no indication that any aspect of the Mosaic Law has come to an end or is an offense to the sacrifice of Christ as it is described in the Hebrews commentary. Although it is not explicit, Aquinas seems to imply that the Jewish observation of the Law is a source of moral knowledge for the nations in the era after grace.[38]

Of course Aquinas also understands Paul to, in a sense, level the playing field among Jews and Gentiles in regard to sanctifying grace. Paul shows that the Jews were not justified by the "things in which they gloried,"[39] which included circumcision and Law.[40] "Jewish law heard or accepted

---

34. *Ad Rom.* 2.4.229.

35. *Ad Rom.* 2.4.230.

36. *Ad Rom.* 2.4.230.

37. *Ad Rom.* 2.4.231.

38. After discussing the privileged state of the Jews in regard to the Law and its fruit, Aquinas also discusses their failures. He presents somewhat of a catalogue of errors of the Jews in order to make the more general point that though "observance of the Law by good works is an occasion for others to honor God, so its transgression by evil works is an occasion to blaspheme: 'That they may see your good deeds and glorify God'" *Ad Rom.* 2.4.235 .

39. *Ad Rom.* 2.1.169.

40. However, Aquinas does understand the Law to justify in a qualified sense. Justification can be taken in regard to "doing what is just" because, for example, "the publican

was not enough for salvation."[41] Consequently, Gentiles and Jews need the power of the gospel's grace for salvation.[42]

Near the end of chapter 2, Aquinas encounters a statement by Paul that seems to indicate that the ceremonial aspect of the Law retains theological value for Jews after the passion of Christ. The present tense of the statement from 2:25, "Circumcision profits indeed," seems to push Aquinas to say more about the positive theological value of the rite, and he explains that circumcision "remits original sin."[43] *Prima facie*, the comment could be taken to mean that the ceremonial law remits original sin even now, after the passion.

But Aquinas explains that the meaning of Paul's statement actually refers to the value of circumcision *in the past*.[44] For this interpretation, he appeals to Galatians 5:2, which operates as a marker for the era after grace, a time in which the practice of circumcision no longer has status. "However, the Apostle's statement that 'if you receive circumcision, Christ will be no advantage to you' refers to the era after grace; but now he is referring to the time before the passion of Christ, when circumcision had status."[45]

---

performed a work of justice by confessing his sin." In this way, also, doers of the Law will also be justified "by performing the justice of the law." Third, justification can be considered in regard to the cause of justice, so that a person is said to be justified, when he newly receives justice, as in Romans 5:1: *Since we are justified by faith, we are at peace with God.*'" This is the sense in which doers of the Law are *not* justified. Aquinas explains that both the ceremonial works of the Jews and what he calls "moral works" *cannot* confer justifying grace. 2.3.212

41. *Ad Rom.* 2.3.210.
42. *Ad Rom.* 2.1.169.
43. *Ad Rom.* 2.4.238.

44. Later, Aquinas will clarify how circumcision removed original sin for Jews *who had faith in Christ*. Aquinas also adds a third condition for the way in which the ceremonial law can be observed which might be called the Christological and apostolic form of observance of the ceremonial law. Aquinas actually discusses two ways of being under the ceremonial law. 1) The first way did not sanctify because it was observed out of fear and not faith. Those who observe out of fear lack faith and thus they also lack grace. 2) The second way the ceremonial law is observed is "voluntarily" through faith and love and this is how Christ and the apostles observed the ceremonial and moral aspects of the Law. Grace is obtained through this voluntary form of observance of the Law. Aquinas mentions Christ's observation of the ceremonial law in *Ad Rom.* 6.3.497–8. Aquinas also makes this distinction in the commentary on Galatians. This distinction between those who observe the Old Law out of fear and those who observe it voluntarily is not mentioned in the Hebrews commentary which posits that the Old Law was only observed out of fear, whereas, the new is observed in charity.

45. *Ad Rom.* 2.4.238.

The Ceremonial Law as Present Spiritual Benefit for Jews (Romans)

Before the passion of Christ, the value of circumcision was, in addition to enclosing the Jewish people in the worship of the one God, that it removed original sin in so far as it prefigured the coming of Christ. After grace, the value of circumcision is negative: it renders Christ no advantage. It should be noted that here, Aquinas uses the Galatians 5:2 reference to appeal to the shift of time from before the passion to the era after grace. Indeed, Aquinas sees Galatians 5:2 as the most important authority for grounding the teaching that the ceremonial law is now dead and deadly. In the famous question addressing the duration of the ceremonial law in the *Summa theologiae*, Ia-IIae q. 103.4 (Whether, since Christ's passion the legal ceremonies can be observed without committing mortal sin?), Aquinas's response begins with a citation of Galatians 5:2: "The Apostle says (Gal. 5:2): 'If you be circumcised, Christ shall profit you nothing.' But nothing save mortal sin hinders us from receiving Christ's fruit. Therefore since Christ's passion it is a mortal sin to be circumcised, or to observe the other legal ceremonies."[46]

However, in the Romans commentary, Aquinas seems to detect a problem. He does not follow the citation of Galatians 5:2 with an explanation of the full consequences of the standard position for the observant Jew as he does in the *Summa theologiae*: the teaching that observing the ceremonial law becomes dead in the era after grace and brings mortal sin. Although he reads Paul's statement that "circumcision profits indeed" through the lens of Gal. 5:2, and claims the rite profited only in the past, it is not declared dead and deadly.

As I hope to show, after this first reflection, Aquinas departs from the view that circumcision only had value before Christ. Indeed, later in the commentary, Aquinas will recognize that the claim that circumcision is no longer of value is similar to an objection Aquinas thinks Paul himself raises and then defeats—and this seems to function throughout the rest of the commentary as a sort of "literal Pauline *ratio*" for the continuing validity of Jewish observation of circumcision. Whereas, the literal meaning of circumcision was, as the Old Testament clearly teaches, it enclosed the Jews in the worship of the one God, now Aquinas begins to see this literal meaning affirmed in Paul's present tense affirmations of the rite, even after the passion of Christ.

---

46. Ia-IIae q. 103.4. I return to this connection chapter 9.

"What is the Value of Circumcision?"

Near the end of the second chapter of his commentary on Romans, Aquinas contrasts "inward and outward Judaism," based on Paul's words that circumcision in one who breaks the Law becomes "uncircumcision."[47] Aquinas understands Paul to argue that inward Judaism amounts to keeping the moral precepts, while an "outward Jew" is one who *only* keeps the ceremonial law and neglects the moral law. Based on Paul's language of "uncircumcision" it seems that circumcision profits *only* if the Law, i.e., the moral precepts, are also observed. "He is truly a Jew," explains Aquinas, "who is one *inwardly*, i.e., whose heart is possessed by the precepts of the Law, which the Jews professed."[48]

In chapter 3, Aquinas presents what he refers to as Paul's objection to his own teaching on outward Judaism. After Paul has argued that the Gentile, just like a Jew, can obtain the status of being a "true Jew," by observing the moral precepts, Aquinas says Paul "objects to his own doctrine."[49]

According to Aquinas, the objection is represented by Paul's rhetorical question, "Then what advantage has the Jew?" Aquinas then summarizes Paul's rhetorical question in his own terms in order to further clarify his view of Paul's objection to outward Judaism: "If what I say is so, i.e., that the true Jew and true circumcision are not something outward but inward in the heart, 'Then what advantage has the Jew,' i.e., what has been given to him more than others? *It seems to be nothing*."[50] He then puts the question in even more precise terms and asks: "Or what is the value of circumcision, i.e., outward?" and states, "it seems from his previous teaching [on outward Judaism] that there is no value."[51] *Videtur quod non* is a formula used to introduce a scholastic objection. That Aquinas uses the phrase to introduce the latter part of the objection (i.e. that circumcision has no value) shows he thinks there is a difficulty regarding the value of circumcision in the era after grace.

In his response to the objection that it seems circumcision has no value, Aquinas seems to shifts away from the traditional position that the

---

47. *Ad Rom.* 2.4.243.
48. *Ad Rom.* 2.4.244.
49. *Ad Rom.* 3.1.246.
50. *Ad Rom.* 3.1.247. [Emphasis added]
51. *Ad Rom.* 3.1.247.

The Ceremonial Law as Present Spiritual Benefit for Jews (Romans)

Jewish observances become dead after the passion of Christ.[52] Aquinas appeals directly to Paul's answer to his own rhetorical question in order to reject the idea that circumcision in the era after grace is superfluous. Aquinas understands Paul to answer his own objection, "What is the value of circumcision, i.e., outward?" with Paul's own emphatic and immediate reply in Romans 3:2: "Much in every way!" Aquinas writes, "when [Paul] says 'Much in every way' he answers the objection [that circumcision has no value]."[53]

This Pauline affirmation of the theological status of the ceremonial law after Christ's passion then compels Aquinas to embark on a lengthy defense of the advantage of outward Judaism. Aquinas explains that "when [Paul] says 'Much in every way!' he answers the objection: first, in regard to Judaism's prerogative; secondly, in regard to the value of circumcision." While Aquinas does not think the rites provide justifying grace, he appears to hold that circumcision remains valuable as a prerogative of the Jewish people. Indeed, in his extended reply to the objection that circumcision is superfluous, Aquinas is concerned to state, in four ways, the positive theological status of this Jewish rite *in the present tense*.

First, Aquinas attempts to elaborate on why circumcision is of value in the era after grace by linking the rite to the election of Israel—that the Jewish people are God's special possession. Aquinas writes, "[the idea that there is no advantage to the Jew] is not fitting, since the Lord had said: 'The Lord, your God, has chosen you to be a people for his own possession' Dt 7:6."[54] For Aquinas, the election of Israel is the ground of the ongoing value of circumcision and the first thing that comes to mind upon consideration of the meaning of Paul's "Much in every way!" The advantage is grounded in the theological claim that God has chosen this people.

Second, Aquinas states that another reason that the idea of circumcision is superfluous is not fitting in the era after grace is because God imposed it upon this chosen people. It is "not fitting" to say there is no value in circumcision because, Aquinas writes, "[circumcision] was imposed by God, Who says: 'I am the Lord, your God, who teaches you unto profit.' Is 48:17."[55]

---

52. Ia-IIae q. 103.4
53. *Ad Rom.* 3.1.248.
54. *Ad Rom.* 3.1.247.
55. Ibid.

Aquinas then adds a third theological defense against the idea that there is "no value" to this significant Jewish rite after Christ. That he understands Paul's "Much in every way!" to solidly defeat the objection that there is no advantage to the Jew and no longer a theological value in circumcision becomes clear as he elaborates upon the advantage of the prerogatives of the Jews in the present by listing a series of advantages. Aquinas argues that Judaism's "advantage is both quantitative, which is indicated when [the Apostle] says, 'much,' and numerical, which is indicated when he says, 'in every way.'"[56] He then outlines several advantages including, "contemplating divine matters," by which he means their being given revealed knowledge of God, and "the provision of temporal things," by which he means deliverance from Egypt. The third advantage is "advantages relating to their ancestors" which he explains are "the promises to their offspring." In reference to these "promises" he cites Romans 9:4, which states, "They are Israelites, and to them belong the sonship, the glory, the covenant."[57] Each advantage of the Jews is described in the present, not in the past, which indicates that Aquinas understands these advantages of the election of Israel as an ongoing reality.

Fourth, Aquinas adds that, "In each of these there is no small advantage, but great and important ones, which are summed up when [the Apostle] says, 'much.'"[58] The great and important Jewish advantage that Aquinas specifies as a chief advantage (*praecipue amplius*), is that "[the Jews] *are* entrusted the oracles of God, being His friends: 'I have called you friends' Jn 15:15."[59] Their chief advantage is expressed in their closeness to God. This is because man's "greatest good lies in knowing and clinging to God and being instructed by God."[60] Here, Aquinas's remarkably positive and present tense affirmation of the Jews as the friends of God now is reminiscent of Pope John Paul II's positive language about the Jews as "elder brothers."[61] To cite John 15:15 to support the idea that the Jews *are* entrusted with knowledge of God and enjoy a closeness to God seems to raise the theological status of Israel after the era of grace to a level not com-

---

56. *Ad Rom.* 3.1.249.

57. *Ad Rom.* 3.1.249. I show below that Aquinas thinks the covenant mentioned here, in 9:4, is the old covenant.

58. Ibid.

59. *Ad Rom.* 3.1.250.

60. *Ad Rom.* 3.1.249.

61. Bruce Marshall, "Elder Brothers," 113–29.

monly affirmed in the history of Christian theology. Such a status is usually viewed as a feature of Israelite history that has passed away.

Advantages of the Jews Despite Unbelief in Christ

Next, Aquinas considers the challenge of unbelief in Christ to this doctrine. He makes the argument that God's faithfulness would actually be compromised if the prerogatives of Israel were annulled due to unbelief in Christ. He does this when he considers an objection he understands Paul to raise regarding the advantage of the Jew.

The objection is represented by Paul's question, "What if some were unfaithful?"[62] Aquinas then restates the objection in his own terms: the unfaithfulness of Israel seems manifest in their ingratitude and lack of belief in God. Would not such unbelief mean the annulment of their prerogatives?[63] Aquinas then builds the strength of the objection by explaining that someone could belittle the Jews' prerogative on the basis that they were ungrateful to God's message and lack belief. He writes, "Someone could belittle the Jews' prerogative by citing their ingratitude, through which they would seem to have set aside the value of God's message." He then explains that this is exactly why the [the Apostle] takes the time to suggest the objection, "What if some were unfaithful?" and Aquinas once more explains the objection, in his own terms: "Does this show that the Jew has no advantage?"[64] Aquinas then sharpens the objection by pointing out the difficult nature of the unbelief he thinks is assumed by the question. Jewish unbelief is not only lack of belief in God's message, but also lack of belief in the mediators of the message: the Lawgiver himself, the prophets, and even the Son of God.[65] Aquinas then lends biblical support to the objection by stringing

---

62. *Ad Rom.* 3.1.251.

63. *Ad Rom.* 2.4.253.

64. *Ad Rom.* 3.1.252.

65. *Ad Rom.* 2.4.253. Aquinas's description of this objection seems rather reminiscent of the punitive supersessionism of the *adversus Iudaeos* tradition. Again, Soulen defines punitive supersessionism as follows: "According to punitive supersessionism, God abrogates God's covenant with Israel on account of Israel's rejection of Christ and the gospel." See Soulen, *The God of Israel*, 30. Paula Fredriksen's summary of Tertullian's view of the Jews reveals a sharp contrast between the punitive supersessionism of the *adversus Iudaeos* tradition and Aquinas's argument here: "By continuing in their fleshly observances—even after the resurrection of Christ, whom their own prophets had said they would murder; even after the punitive destruction of their city and their Temple, the only

together witnesses from the Old and New Testaments concerning unbelief: "For they did not believe the Lawgiver: 'They had no faith in his promises' Ps 106:24 or the prophets: they are a rebellious house Ez 2:6." The objection even becomes more pointed with the last citation of the words of Christ to the Jews: "... Or the Son of God: 'If I tell the truth, why do you not believe me?'"[66]

In his reply to this sharp objection to Jewish prerogatives Aquinas unpacks a robust theology of God's promise to Israel. He bases his reply to the objection that the prerogatives of Israel are threatened by Jewish unbelief on Paul's answer to the rhetorical question "Does their unfaithfulness nullify the faithfulness of God?" which is, "Let it not be!" Aquinas explains Paul's "Let it not be!" by appealing to the idea of the faithfulness of God. He cites Hebrews 10:23: "God is faithful in keeping His promises: 'He who promised is faithful.'"[67] Here, Aquinas recognizes that God's faithfulness is the foundation of the election of Israel and it is a foundation that remains steadfast in the face of the vice of unbelief in the Son of God: "[God's] faithfulness would be nullified, if it happened that the Jews had no advantage, just because some have not believed." Aquinas goes on, "For God promised to multiply that people and make it great," and then cites Genesis 22:16: "I will multiply your descendants."[68] God's faithfulness cannot be nullified, explains Aquinas, because "it is unfitting for God's faithfulness to be nullified on account of men's belief."[69]

Aquinas then goes on to state how the prerogatives of Israel relate to God's promise to the Jewish people. He argues that the prerogatives cannot be taken away without compromising God's faithfulness. Aquinas

---

place where they could enact most of their wrong-headed ancestral practices; even after being driven out of their native land in punishment for their rejection of God's son—the Jews confirmed all the reasons why God had given them the Law to begin with. They were stiff-necked, stubborn, belligerent, utterly unrepentant. Accordingly, concluded Tertullian, Israel was punished forever with exile. Indeed, their permanent displacement had been instigated by Christ himself, who in the Psalms had demanded of his Father, 'Scatter them in your might.' (Psalm 59:12; *Against Marcion* 3.23, 1–4)." Fredriksen, *Augustine and the Jews*, 226. For a summary of the view see A. Lukyn Williams, *Adversus Iudaeos*. Aquinas's rejection of ideas similar to punitive supersessionism in *Ad Rom.* 2.4.253 seem to sit in tension with statements he will make later in the commentary when discussing the fall or trespass of the Jews in *Ad Rom.* 11.2.881.

66. *Ad Rom.* 3.1.252.
67. *Ad Rom.* 3.1.254.
68. *Ad Rom.* 3.1.253.
69. *Ad Rom.* 3.1.254.

The Ceremonial Law as Present Spiritual Benefit for Jews (Romans)

understands Paul to exclude the objection that there is now, after Christ, no longer an advantage to the Jew by arguing against "the unsuitable conclusion it engenders." Aquinas states: "For if the Jews' prerogative were abrogated (*praerogativa Iudaeorum tolleretur*) on account of the unbelief of some, it would follow that man's unbelief would nullify God's faithfulness—which is an unacceptable conclusion."[70]

The perpetuity attributed to the prerogatives of Israel, which includes the ceremonial law, is wrapped up with the very faithfulness of God. To claim that the prerogatives of Israel are annulled is "an unacceptable conclusion" because it calls into question the faithfulness of God. "God's justice, which involves keeping His promises," writes Aquinas, "is not changed on account of sin."[71] He then cites Proverbs 8:8: "All the words of my mouth are righteous." And Psalm 145:13: "The Lord is faithful in all his words . . . ."[72] For Aquinas, the perpetuity of the value of the prerogatives is connected to God's promise to this people, which he will keep because God is "faithful in all [God's] words" and does not lie.

Aquinas's defense of the prerogatives expands the notion of God's promise to Israel well beyond the temporal definition afforded it in the Hebrews commentary. In the Hebrews commentary, the promise to carnal Israel is described as limited to the physical and temporal. In the Romans commentary, the promise is understood as a promise that Israel be a people that will be multiplied and made great. Aquinas attributes to the Jews' advantage a perpetual quality that was absent from the Hebrews commentary. The promise, of course, includes the Davidic promise for an eternal kingdom, which Aquinas understands as fulfilled in Christ.[73] But the fulfillment of the promise through the eternal priesthood of Christ does not also entail the rendering void of the prerogatives of Israel.

Indeed, Aquinas articulates a rather succinct argument that problematizes the logic behind punitive and economic supersessionist views of

---

70. *Ad Rom.* 3.1.253. [Emended]: "Deinde cum dicit Numquid incredulitas, excludit dictam obiectionem ducendo ad inconveniens, quia si propter incredulitatem aliquorum praerogativa Iudaeorum tolleretur, sequeretur quod incredulitas hominis fidem Dei evacuaret, quod est inconveniens." Larcher translates *tolleretur* as "taken away" but it can also mean abrogate. For Aquinas, *tolleretur* can mean "to take off, carry off, make away with, kill, destroy, to abolish, annul, abrogate, cancel." Deferrari, *Latin-English Dictionary*, 1043.

71. *Ad Rom.* 3.1.257.

72. *Ad Rom.* 3.1.257.

73. *Ad Rom.* 3.1.256; 258.

the prerogatives of Israel. First, recall that punitive supersessionism is the idea that Israel's prerogatives are taken away or revoked due to the sin of unbelief and God then replaces Israel with the Church as the new elect people. Aquinas clearly refutes punitive supersessionist thinking since this view holds that God abolishes the prerogatives of Israel as punishment for the rejection of Christ. Aquinas says this is an unacceptable conclusion because it nullifies God's faithfulness.

Second, recall that economic supersessionism assumes that with the advent of Christ, the old sacraments are both fulfilled and obsolete and God replaces Israel with the Church, the people of the new sacraments. The unspoken premise of Aquinas's above argument is that the prerogatives of Israel, which include circumcision and Law, remain a present benefit to the Jewish people in the era after grace.[74] This premise contradicts the "double sense of fulfillment" identified by both Isaac and Soulen, that claims the Law is rendered void or obsolete.

Therefore, while Aquinas's argument here in 3.1.253 *explicitly* denies the logic of punitive supersessionism, which would annul the prerogatives as punishment for Jewish unbelief in Christ, it also *implicitly* denies the logic of economic supersessionism, which demands the annulment of the prerogatives due to the advent of Christ. Both punitive and economic forms of supersessionist logic require the evacuation of Israel's prerogatives. But according to Aquinas, such an abrogation would actually annul (*evacuo*) God's faithfulness.

Aquinas's argument against the abrogation of the *praerogativa Iudaeorum* calls the traditional Christian teaching on Christ's fulfillment of the Law into question. The sort of fulfillment theology that entails the voiding of the prerogatives, such as the type found in the Hebrews commentary, seems to be in tension with this part of the Romans commentary.[75] God's promise to carnal Israel cannot be transferred to a new regime without calling into question God's justice.

---

74. As I shall demonstrate below, Aquinas explicitly states in his comments upon Romans 9:4–5 that the ceremonial law is a *present spiritual benefit*.

75. Ironically, in 3.1.253, Aquinas uses the same verb, *evacuo* (in the imperfect active subjunctive form, *evacuaret*) to describe the unacceptable effect that the nullification of the prerogatives would have on God's faithfulness that he uses to describe the nullification of the imperfect Priesthood and ceremonial law in the Hebrews commentary: the perfect renders the imperfect *evacuo*: *Secunda ratio probat quod etiam ipsum evacuat, quia perfectum evacuate imperfectum*. *Ad Hebraeos* 7.3.349. In the Romans commentary, however, to annul (*evacuo*) the ceremonial law is to annul the faithfulness of God.

The Ceremonial Law as Present Spiritual Benefit for Jews (Romans)

At the close of chapter 3 and throughout chapter 4, Aquinas returns to the theme that the ceremonial law could not confer grace and justify, but his discussion seems to reflect the above strong affirmation of circumcision in the era after grace. Aquinas discusses circumcision in greater detail, emphasizing both its literal and prefiguring functions, and states the rite was instituted for four purposes that had to do with divine worship. The first reason for the institution of circumcision was to signify the faith and obedience by which Abraham submitted to God "so that those who accepted the circumcision of Abraham should observe his faith and obedience."[76] The second reason was to express in bodily sign "something that was to occur spiritually, namely, just as superfluous skin was removed from the organ of reproduction, which is the chief servant of concupiscence, so every superfluous desire should be removed from man's heart . . . ."[77] The third reason, according to Aquinas, was to distinguish the children of Israel from all the other nations.[78]

Aquinas then lists a fourth purpose: these rites prefigured Christ.[79] It is from this relation to Christ that the rite was able to remove original sin. "But through faith in Christ, of which circumcision was a sign, it removed original sin and conferred the help of grace to act righteously."[80] Aquinas then explains why baptism is more fitting than circumcision and refers again to the figurative reason for the rite:

> It is clear from what has been said, why circumcision had to be changed. For it was a sign of something to come. But the same

---

76. *Ad Rom.* 4.2.347.

77. *Ad Rom.* 4.2.347.

78. *Ad Rom.* 4.2.347.

79. *Ad Rom.* 4.2.348. In 5.6.463, Aquinas also states that the ceremonial precepts were multiplied to prevent the Jews from cultivating alien gods. The Law operated at two levels: for the proficient, who are called *mediocres*, or ordinary people; and for the perfect. The ceremonial law had the affect of restraining the people in divine worship, and with respect to moral precepts, they were advanced toward justice. For the perfect, on the other hand, the ceremonies functioned as a sign.

80. *Ad Rom.* 4.2.349. Regarding the power of circumcision to confer grace and remove original sin, Aquinas explains the multiple views on the question. He lists the positions and explains problems with each one. It should be noted that Aquinas does not always hold that circumcision did not have effective power to remove guilt as he does here. Andrew Hofer, O.P., has shown that in the *Scriptum super Sententiis* Aquinas holds that circumcision removed original sin. Andrew Hofer, "The Circumcision of the Lord," 63. I am grateful to Fr. Hofer for sharing with me his unpublished dissertation. See also Schenk, "Covenant Initiation."

> sign does not suit the present, past and future. Therefore, baptism, as the sign of present grace, produces a more copious and more beneficial effect of grace, because the closer the agent is in time and place, the more effectively it works.[81]

However, it seems significant that Aquinas does not say that the fulfillment of the sign also entails that its literal meaning in relation to the faith of Abraham, and its distinguishing the Jews from the nations, is rendered void for Jews. The concept of fulfillment surfaces again when Aquinas comments upon Paul's rhetorical question "Do we therefore overthrow the Law?" Aquinas explains that "someone might claim that he is overthrowing the aforementioned law . . . in as much as we say that men are justified without the works of the law?"[82] Yet Aquinas argues that the Apostle Paul cannot be opposed to Christ's words in Matthew 5:18, which he then cites: "Not an iota, not a dot, will pass from the law." "On the contrary," writes Aquinas, "we uphold the law, i.e., by faith we complete and fulfill the Law, as Matt 5:17 says, 'I have come not to abolish the law but to fulfill it.'"[83] Aquinas then explains how the faith of Christ "upheld and fulfilled" both the ceremonial and moral precepts of the Law:

> This is true as regards the ceremonial precepts because, being figures, they were *upheld and fulfilled* [*statuuntur et adimplentur*] by the fact that the truth signified by them is shown forth in the faith of Christ [*in fide Christi exhibetur*]. This is also true as regards the moral precepts, because the faith of Christ confers the help of grace to fulfill the moral precepts of the Law and even adds special counsels, through which moral precepts are more safely and securely kept.[84]

---

81. *Ad Rom.* 4.2.350. Brian Davies offers one of the most succinct summaries of Aquinas's view of the importance of the new sacraments: "For Aquinas, however, the important sacraments are 'the sacraments of the New Law,' by which he means the Christian sacraments. Why? Because, so he thinks, these cause grace while the sacraments of the Old Law did not. The sacraments of the Old Law, he argues, predated the death of Christ by which justifying grace comes, and they were signs representing faith in Christ only in the sense that they anticipated what was to come. They looked forward to something which was not yet. The sacraments of the New Law, on the other hand, signify something actually present. The sacraments of the Old Law 'fulfilled the function of prefiguring grace' while those of the New Law 'are appropriate as manifestations of a grace that is already present.'" Davies, *The Thought of Thomas Aquinas*, 354.

82. *Ad Rom.* 3.4.321.

83. *Ad Rom.* 3.4.321.

84. *Ad Rom.* 3.4.321. [Emphasis added]

The Ceremonial Law as Present Spiritual Benefit for Jews (Romans)

What Aquinas *does not say* here speaks volumes when considered against the backdrop of the position as stated in the Hebrews commentary. Although the ceremonial precepts are fulfilled, Aquinas does *not* say they are destroyed, as he does in the Hebrews commentary. Rather, Aquinas states that the ceremonial precepts are "fulfilled and upheld" by the faith of Christ. Where the prefiguring function is affirmed in the Romans commentary, the hard consequences for the observant Jew in the era after grace do not surface. Aquinas does not take the time to argue for the distinction between how the moral precepts remain and the ceremonial become void, and then dead and deadly in the era after grace. Nowhere in the Romans commentary does Aquinas argue that the Law is dead, nor does he state the more negative conclusion that the observances are deadly.[85] Indeed, Aquinas seems to link the fulfillment of the ceremonial law not only to the passion but also to the faith of Christ.

Aquinas's vigorous theological defense of the prerogatives of Israel becomes more pronounced in chapter 9 of the commentary, where he comments upon the prerogatives of Israel for the third time and explicitly argues that the ceremonial law is a *present* spiritual benefit.

The Spiritual Benefits of the Jewish People in the Era of Grace

Aquinas discusses the prerogatives of Israel once more in chapter 9. In the context of explaining Paul's sadness concerning Jewish unbelief in Christ, Aquinas describes the Jews as a "deteriorating people."[86] However, he does not say Jewish dignity is a thing of the past but goes on to speak of the dignity of the Jews in the present tense. Aquinas explains that the greatness of the Jews is demonstrated in several ways:

First, their dignity is from their being Israelites according to the flesh. Aquinas states: "'They are Israelites,' i.e., descending from the stock of Jacob who was called Israel Gen 32:28. This pertains to their greatness, for it says in Dt 4:7: 'Neither is there any nation so great as to have their gods coming

---

85. Another telling example of this is Aquinas's treatment of the Pauline statement "For the end of the Law is Christ," in Romans 10:4. When commenting upon this verse in the Romans commentary Aquinas only comments upon how the Law could not bring to perfection (i.e. it could not bring sanctifying grace) and its prefigurative function. *Ad Rom.* 10.1.819.

86. *Ad Rom.* 9.1.744.

to them.'"[87] Aquinas once again acknowledges God's election of this particular people and names it as a benefit in the present.[88]

Second, the Jews enjoy a dignity from "God's blessings," which include a number of "spiritual blessings" or "benefits" which we may identify as benefits 1–5.

1. The first spiritual benefit is Israel's sonship, as opposed to other nations: "to them belongs the sonship: hence it says in Ex (4:22): Israel is my son, my firstborn."[89] The blessing seems to concern the idea that this particular people is considered the firstborn son of God.[90] Aquinas seems to attribute Jewish distinction from the nations as possessing an ongoing theological significance.

2. The second blessing from God is explicitly described as a future spiritual benefit. Aquinas explains that this "spiritual blessing refers to the future when he says: *the glory,* namely, of the sons of God promised to them."[91] Next, Aquinas introduces another classification of spiritual benefits from God, referred to as figures of present spiritual benefit. Aquinas frequently uses the term *figura* throughout his works to refer to the symbolic meaning of the ceremonial law as foreshadowing Christ. However, this is the only place in his work where he employs the phrase "figure of present spiritual benefit" (*figura praesentis spiritualis beneficii*) to refer to these rites and this novelty seems to indicate something important.[92]

---

87. *Ad Rom.* 9.1.743.

88. *Ad Rom.* 9.1.745.

89. *Ad Rom.* 9.1.744.

90. In particular, it is their sonship as opposed to the other nations: "the spiritual men who arose among that people: but as to worldly men he stated above (8:15) that they received the spirit of slavery in fear." The sonship therefore refers to the distinction of these "spiritual men" (Israel) from what Aquinas sees as "worldly men" or nations that were in slavery and in fear.

91. *Ad Rom.* 9.1.744.

92. *Ad Rom.* 9.1.744: "... *beneficia figuralia, quorum tria sunt figura praesentis spiritualis beneficii* ...." Larcher's original translation of these benefits reads, "*were* figures of present spiritual benefit" rather than "*are* figures of present spiritual benefit." The Italian Dominican Study Edition of the Romans commentary translates these benefits in the present tense. See Tommaso d'Aquino (san), *Commento al Corpus Paulinum (expositio et lectura super epistolas Pauli apostoli)* vol. 1–3—*Seconda Lettera ai corinzi-Lettera ai galati* (ESD-Edizioni Studio Domenicano, 2006), 601. I am indebted to my colleague, James Stroud, for pointing this out to me. Additionally, the Aquinas Institute editors (2012) of the commentary emended Larcher's translation of the spiritual benefits to the present tense.

The Ceremonial Law as Present Spiritual Benefit for Jews (Romans)

3. Circumcision. The first "figure of present spiritual benefit" is identified as the covenant mentioned in Romans 9:4, which Aquinas says refers to "the pact of circumcision given to Abraham, as is recorded in Gen 17." Here, Aquinas explicitly states that circumcision is a *present* spiritual benefit (*praesentis spiritualis beneficii*). That circumcision is described as a present figure that remains connected in any way to a spiritual benefit after the passion of Christ is incredibly significant given Aquinas's standard teaching, as represented in Ia-IIae q. 103 a. 4, and the commentary on Hebrews, that the rites *were* figures. In identifying the covenant of Romans 9:4 as the pact of circumcision Aquinas also diverges from the standard biblical commentary of his day, the *Glossa ordinaria*, which is careful to state that the covenant mentioned in Romans 9:4 refers to "the New Testament" covenant, *not* the old.[93]

4. Law. The fourth blessing from God is the second figure of present spiritual benefit: the Law given through Moses.

5. Divine Worship. The fifth blessing from God is the third figure of present spiritual benefit: divine worship. All these spiritual benefits of Jewish worship confer dignity on the Jews after the passion of Christ.

Aquinas's affirmation of the spiritual benefits of Judaism sits in tension with the negative idea of an ongoing deterioration of the Jews as the cause of Paul's sadness. Nevertheless, circumcision, law, and worship are described as blessings from God despite Jewish unbelief in Christ. Jewish observances are referred to as rites that are connected to a present spiritual benefit and that somehow retain a figural meaning.

---

93. *Ad Rom.* 9.1.744. Aquinas considers the possibility that Paul might be referring not to the covenant with Israel but to the new covenant: "although this could be referred to the new covenant preached first to the Jews. Hence, the Lord Himself said: *I was sent only to the lost sheep of the house of Israel* (Mt 15:24); *and Jer (31:31): I will make a new covenant with the house of Israel*." Despite the alternative interpretation Aquinas offers regarding the reference to the covenant—that it "could be" the new covenant—he thinks the "pact of circumcision" is the literal meaning. That he mentions the possibility of it being the new testament seems to be a nod to the standard medieval interpretation, the *Glossa ordinaria* on Romans, which explicitly states that this reference to the covenant means the new covenant and not the old: "*the glory*—because they are a peculiar people, or because of what they do through miracles. *The testament*—the New Testament. *The legislation*—which the Old Testament presented through figures . . . ." Nevertheless, by listing circumcision first he seems to deliberately move away from this interpretation. See Michael Scott Woodward, trans., *The Glossa Ordinaria on Romans*, 138–39.

Aquinas on Israel and the Church

The Certainty of God's Promise to Israel

The final reflection in the Romans commentary that I want to highlight is when Aquinas comments on Paul's famous words in Romans 11:29, "For the gifts and the call of God are without repentance." Here, Aquinas once again secures the perpetuity of the election of Israel by grounding it in God's unchanging promise.[94] In particular, he does this when he responds to an objection he raises to the idea that God's call can change.[95] Indeed, Aquinas explains the objection as follows: "God's call seems to be changed sometimes, since it is written 'Many are called but few are chosen' Mt 22:14."

In his reply, Aquinas explains that the ongoing election of Israel is secured by the nature of God's promise, which is a promise that is, because of God's predestination, "as good as given." Commenting upon Romans 11:29, "For the gifts and the call of God are without repentance," Aquinas says that: "it should be noted that 'gift' is taken here for a promise made according to God's foreknowledge or predestination, and 'call' is taken for election." "Because both are so certain," explains Aquinas, "whatever God promises is as good as given and whomever [God] elects is somehow already called."[96]

---

94. *Ad Rom.* 11.4.926.

95. In the Hebrews commentary, Aquinas actually argues for the opposite position when drawing upon Augustine. He argues that God's providence is different than God and that while God does not change, his providence can. The difference between these two texts is that in the Romans commentary, Aquinas is more aware of the robust depth and perpetuity of the promise to carnal Israel while in the Hebrews commentary the promise is defined narrowly, as a temporal and physical phenomenon.

96. *Ad Rom.* 11.4.926. Aquinas adds an eternal/temporal distinction regarding God's promise in order to explain that a promise from God can "change" in the sense that human persons can cast off God's grace. Aquinas says this change is not because God's eternal acts change, but because man changes when he throws off God's grace. Nevertheless, what Aquinas says concerning God's promise to Israel seems secured by his argument that the unbelief of the Jews cannot nullify God's justice in *Ad Rom.* 3.1.257. As Aquinas states in 3.1.257, if the election of the Jews was abrogated on account of their unbelief in God in Christ (i.e. "change in man"), this would be unacceptable because it calls into question God's faithfulness. In other words, when Aquinas does address Jewish unbelief in light of God's promise in *Ad Rom.* 3.1.257, the conclusion he draws seems to employ a notion of promise that is not dislocated from the idea of God's justice regarding the promise to the particular people, the Jews.

The Ceremonial Law as Present Spiritual Benefit for Jews (Romans)

3. THE EMERGING TENSION IN THE PAULINE COMMENTARIES

At several places in his commentary on Romans, Aquinas seems to allow present tense, positive descriptions of Israel to shape his views of the goodness of Jewish worship even in the face of unbelief. Aquinas affirms the ongoing Jewish election and advantage of circumcision and argues that abrogating the prerogatives of Israel would compromise God's faithfulness, which is "an unacceptable conclusion." When Aquinas discusses God's covenant with Israel, which he links to the rite of circumcision, he even affirms this observance as a blessing from God and a present spiritual benefit.[97]

And yet, it is not clear how exactly the spiritual blessings of the Law and circumcision can be said to remain figures not to mention spiritually beneficial if the exact relationship of the rites to the Christian faith is not specified. In the Romans commentary, Aquinas does not explain how the rites can be said to remain figures in relationship to Christ's passion.

If one reads Aquinas's commentary on Romans 9–11, especially chapter 9:1–5, in isolation from the rest of the lecture, not to mention the organic unity Aquinas understood Paul's letters to possess, this positive role might seem as if it is representative of his view. However, when read in context, the picture seems more complex.

When read against the background of Aquinas's words about the ceremonial law in the Hebrews commentary, major portions of the Romans commentary contradict the more negative view. When read in the context of the Hebrews commentary, it becomes clear that Aquinas shifts away from the standard view that the ceremonial law no longer has status and argues at length that circumcision possesses theological significance for the Jewish people in the era after grace. Reading Aquinas in context of these two lectures highlights a tension in the commentaries: How can Aquinas hold that the ceremonial law is a present spiritual benefit to Jews in the era after grace and at the same time that which causes spiritual death of observant Jews? How can the rites by which the Jews are made the friends of God also serve to cut them off from God?

In the Romans commentary, Aquinas's defense of the prerogatives of Israel undermines the teaching that the observance of the ceremonial law is superfluous and a mortal sin after the passion of Christ. In fact, he says the opposite. Aquinas states that circumcision possesses a theological value;

---

97. *Ad Rom.* 11.4.926.

that law, and cult are a present spiritual benefit to the Jewish people; and that these cannot be abolished without compromising God's faithfulness. Aquinas's extended reflections on Israel's present tense prerogatives may even have pushed him to leave out the negative conclusion of the traditional teaching: that observance of the ceremonial law is now a mortal sin. Despite frequent references to the Old Law in the age of grace, nowhere does Aquinas say that its observance brings spiritual death. Aquinas's view represents a departure from the claim, based in Galatians 5:2, that circumcision no longer has a status after the passion of Christ.

Aquinas's sensitivity to the multifaceted literal sense of Scripture allows him to respond to the present tense of Paul's words about Israel. These positive descriptions afford Aquinas with multiple opportunities to step away from the position that the ceremonial law is simply dead after the passion of Christ. The first step away is when Aquinas affirms the prerogative of the Jewish people as a light to the nations. The second is Aquinas's defense of the great value of Jewish election and circumcision against the claim based in Galatians 5:2 that circumcision no longer has value. The third is when Aquinas presents the argument that to abrogate the prerogatives of Israel would nullify God's promise and undermine God's justice, which is "an unacceptable conclusion." The fourth is where the covenant with Israel, which is said to include rite of circumcision, is described as a blessing from God and a present spiritual benefit. The last is Aquinas's claim that the election and call of Israel is a promise from God that is "as good as given." In each case Aquinas allows what Soulen has referred to as the "priority of the present tense" descriptions of Israel to shape his interpretation of prerogatives of the Jewish people in a way that allows for a more benevolent view of the ceremonial law in era after grace that might be referred to as "fulfilled and upheld."

Although the emerging tension in the commentaries presents difficulties for making sense of Aquinas's thought, the positive view in the Romans commentary is a robust theological defense of Judaism after the passion of Christ. Aquinas's view provides premodern support for Karl Thieme's defense of Jews against the Nazis: that the Jew can remain pleasing to God despite unbelief in Christ.

6

The Ceremonial Law as Fulfilled, Dead, and Deadly (Galatians)

THE GALATIANS COMMENTARY CONTAINS a number of topics directly related to the question at the heart of supersessionism, whether with the advent of Christ, the ceremonial law becomes expired or obsolete. In the Galatians commentary, Aquinas comments upon the Apostle Paul's teaching on Christ's fulfillment of the Law as well as Paul's observance of the Law; the question on Gentile observance of the Law debated by the Jerusalem Conference in Acts 15; the Antioch incident between Paul and Peter; and the controversy between Jerome and Augustine on the Jewish apostles' observance of the ceremonial law. As Aquinas comments upon each of these topics it becomes clear that he understands the ceremonial law to have been destroyed (*destruxi*) by the Apostle Paul's teaching.[1] Aquinas thinks the Jerusalem conference in Acts 15 approved Paul's teaching and declared that the old sacraments were superfluous in the apostolic age, and deadly thereafter, *not only* for Gentiles and Jewish believers in Christ, but *for all* who observe the old sacraments, including Jews.

---

1. *Ad Galat.* 2.5.100.

1. PRIMARY THEME AND DIVISION OF THE GALATIANS COMMENTARY

The prologue and the greeting indicate that the cessation of the ceremonial law after the passion of Christ is a major theme of the Galatians commentary.[2] Aquinas's selection of Leviticus 26:10 as the interpretive key of Paul's message makes this especially clear: "The new coming on, you shall cast away the old."[3]

Aquinas understands this verse to express the teaching in Paul's letter to the Gentile Christians at Galatia. For Aquinas, these Gentile Christians had fallen into the same error as the Jewish Christians in Paul's letter to the Hebrews.[4] The problem in both cases was that believers in Christ were seeking to observe the ceremonial law along with the gospel.[5] Aquinas therefore understands the letter to address not simply the cessation of the rites of the

---

2. Aquinas uses "insufficiency," "cessation," and "abandonment" a number of times to describe the ceremonial law. *Ad Galat.* 1.1.15: "insufficientiam legalium"; 1.1.2: ". . . epistola ad Galatas, in qua agitur de cessation sacramentorum veteris testamenti"; ". . . si observantia legalium dimissa, observantiae Evangelii Christi ferventer insistamus." Like Aquinas's use of term *legalia* in the Hebrews commentary, he does not define the rites in detail. *Ad Hebraeos, Prologus* 5. In general, he uses *legalis* to refer to the Law, human law, or the Law of the Old Testament. In this context it is of course the Law of the Old Testament to which he refers. According to Deferrari, Aquinas's use of the phrase *observatio legalis* refers to the "observance of the prescriptions of the Old Testament." Aquinas is more than likely referring to three specific rites or "legal observances" that can be considered under the broader category of *caeremoniae veteris legis* (or ceremonies of the Old Law): these rites include the sacraments of circumcision and Passover, and observance of dietary regulations. In Ia-IIae q. 101.4, "observances" *are only one category* of *caeremoniae veteris legis* or ceremonies of the Old Law. Aquinas divides the ceremonies of the Old Law into four categories: 1) *sacrificia* or sacrifices; 2) *sacra* or sacred things; 3) *sacramenta* or sacraments; and 4) *observantiae* or observances. Associating "legal observances" with category 3 and 4 in particular seems justified by a reading of the Aquinas's description of the Antioch dispute between Paul and Peter, in which Aquinas discusses ceremonial law as rites at length (*Ad Galat.* 2.1). As I show below Aquinas understands the decision among the apostles at Acts 15 as a decree on not observing the rites of the Law. See also the note on this same topic in chapter 4.

3. *Ad Galat.* 1.1.1.

4. "He wrote this letter against the errors of those converts from Judaism who wanted to preserve the legal observances along with the gospel, as though Christ's grace was not sufficient for salvation." *Ad Heb.* 1.1.6.

5. However, this does not mean that Aquinas's teaching does not also apply to Jews, a point I attempt to make clear below.

The Ceremonial Law as Fulfilled, Dead, and Deadly (Galatians)

Law. Rather, the teaching of Galatians is that the old sacraments must be cast away because of the grace available in the new sacraments of the Church.[6]

That the theme of the commentary is the cessation of the old sacraments due to the arrival of the new sacraments is clearly indicated by Aquinas's view of the place of Galatians after the Corinthian letters in the canon of the New Testament:

> The order of this epistle is fitting in that, after the two epistles to the Corinthians, in the first of which it is a question of the sacraments of the Church, and in the second, of the ministers of these sacraments, there should necessarily follow the epistle to the Galatians, treating of the termination of the sacraments of the Old Testament.[7]

For Aquinas, Hebrews treats the origin of grace in Christ the head of the Church. Romans treats the manifestation of the grace of Christ in the Church. The Corinthian letters treat the new sacraments of the Church and its ministers. Galatians treats the teaching that these new sacraments must *not* be observed along with the old:

> [T]he Apostle plainly is arguing against them that if the death of Christ is the sufficient cause of our salvation, and if grace is conferred in the sacraments of the New Testament, which have their efficacy from the passion of Christ, then it is superfluous to observe, along with the New Testament, the rituals of the Old Law in which grace is not conferred nor salvation acquired, because the law brought nothing to perfection (Heb. 7:19).[8]

Therefore, for Aquinas, the primary theme of the letter is Paul's teaching that the efficacy of the new sacraments renders the old sacraments superfluous.[9]

---

6. *Ad Galat.* 1.1.2: ". . . sacramentorum veteris testament."
7. *Ad Galat.* 1.1.2.
8. *Ad Galat.* 1.1.14.
9. Aquinas's discussion of the ceremonial law is scattered throughout the chapters. Since the great majority of the content is found in chapters 1 through 4, my thematic examination of the commentary focuses there.

2. THE CEREMONIAL LAW AS FULFILLED AND DESTROYED

Aquinas's view of Paul's claim that it is now superfluous to observe the ceremonies along with the New Testament seems to indicate that Aquinas understands Paul to rebuke believers in Christ who thought the observance of the ceremonial law was necessary for salvation. For the most part, the commentary does consists of Aquinas's comments on what he views as Paul's response to the particular error of Gentile Christians at Galatia who, under pressure from Peter and Jewish converts, had stubbornly left the faith and sought "to be preserved by carnal observances."[10] In Aquinas's view, the Galatian Gentile believers abandonment of the new sacraments for the old amounted to turning away from Christ and to another gospel.

However, Aquinas also thinks that Paul and the Jerusalem conference in Acts 15 declared that the old sacraments were superfluous in the apostolic age, and deadly thereafter, *not only* for Gentile and Jewish Christians, but *for all* who observe the old sacraments, including Jews. In Aquinas's view, Paul's teaching is based on the fact that the Law was temporal and carnal because it served to prefigure Christ. Once Christ fulfilled the carnal Law it was destroyed and its observance is now sinful for Christians as well as Jews.

"Before the Faith, the Jew was Greater": The Temporality of the Law

Aquinas understands Paul's reference to the Gentile Christians turning to another gospel to mean their observation of the old sacraments. However, when Aquinas explains the evil of this act he is careful to once again guard against the Manichean idea that the Old Law is in and of itself evil.[11]

The Old Law, explains Aquinas, is not evil because it is "a good message." The Law is good "only insofar as it does announce some good things, namely, temporal and carnal."[12] The Old Law is not perfect because it only announces goods that are "small and slight." The New Law, on the other

---

10. *Ad Galat.* 3.2.125. That Aquinas thinks Jewish converts, rather than Jews, are the false brethren is clear from 4.5.239: "certain false brethren, converted from Judaism, went about the churches of the Gentiles, preaching the observance of the law."

11. *Ad Galat.* 1.2.19. He relies upon the imperfect/perfect distinction to avoid what he identified in the Hebrews commentary as the Manichean view that the Old Testament is evil.

12. *Ad Galat.* 1.2.19.

The Ceremonial Law as Fulfilled, Dead, and Deadly (Galatians)

hand, announces goods that are greatest and perfect. The reason the goods of the New Law are perfect is because these goods are not carnal but spiritual. "The New Law," says Aquinas, "is perfectly and in the full sense a Gospel, i.e., good message, because it announces the greatest goods, namely, heavenly, spiritual and eternal."[13]

Aquinas then anticipates an objection to the claim that the Old Law was in any sense a good Law. Since the Law seems to have accomplished so little, what purpose did it actually serve? Aquinas then cites Paul's rhetorical question from Romans 3:1. For Aquinas, to ask what purpose the Old Law served is reminiscent of Paul's question, "What advantage then does the Jew have; or what is the profit of circumcision?"[14]

This question, explains Aquinas, is solved by showing how the fourfold purpose of the Old Law corresponds to the four consequences of sin enumerated by Bede: wickedness, weakness, passion, and ignorance. First, the Old Law restrained men from the wickedness of sin by forbidding it and punishing it. Second, the Old Law disclosed human weakness because "men gloried in two things: knowledge and power."[15] Third, the Old Law was given to tame the "concupiscence of a wanton people" in order that they would be "worn out by various ceremonies" so they would not fall into idolatry.[16] Fourth, the Old Law was given as a "figure of future grace." Indeed, the Law was significantly "interposed . . . between the law of nature and the law of grace."[17]

Although Aquinas goes onto argue that the Law "was a pedagogue" and the Jews "were benefited" his explanation of the purposes of the Law certainly lacks the theological defense of the advantage for the Jew after the grace of Christ prominently displayed in the Romans commentary.[18] The ways in which Law benefited the Jews are consistently described in the past tense, *before* faith came. "What benefits did the Jews derive from the law before faith came by grace?"[19] Aquinas's second answer draws upon his earlier defense of the fourfold purpose of the Law: The Jews were protected from idolatry by being kept under the Law. Unlike his replies to the "What

---

13. *Ad Galat.* 1.2.19.
14. *Ad Galat.* 3.7.163.
15. *Ad Galat.* 3.7.165.
16. *Ad Galat.* 3.7.165.
17. *Ad Galat.* 3.7.165.
18. *Ad Galat.* 3.8.175; Cf. 3.8.178–9.
19. *Ad Galat.* 3.8.176.

advantage then does the Jew have?" in the Romans commentary, there is no mention of the present theological value of the Law as a light to the nations or circumcision and Law as present spiritual benefit to Jews after the grace of Christ.

When Aquinas comments upon Paul's statement in Galatians 3:28 "there is neither Jew nor Greek, there is neither slave nor free, there is neither male nor female" he returns to the rhetorical question of Romans 3:1 once more.[20] First, Aquinas paraphrases his interpretation of what Paul might have thought about the meaning of verse 28: "as if to say: truly have I said, that as many of you as have been baptized in Christ Jesus have put on Christ, because there is nothing in man that would exclude anyone from the sacrament of the faith of Christ and from baptism."[21] For Aquinas, "There is neither Jew nor Greek" means: "Since you have been baptized in Christ, the rite from which you came to Christ, whether it was the Jewish or the Greek, is no ground for saying that anyone occupies a less honorable place in the faith."[22]

Then he presents a possible objection to his interpretation of the claim that "there is neither Jew nor Greek" by drawing once again upon Romans 3:1–2: "What advantage then does the Jew have? Much in everyway."[23] Aquinas states that what Paul said in Romans 3:1–2 seems to contradict Galatians 3:28 (there is neither Jew nor Greek)—it seems there is no advantage to the Jew if there is no distinction between Gentile and Jew in Christ. In the *respondeo* Aquinas says that Jews and Greeks

> can be considered . . . according to the state in which they *were* before faith. In this way, the Jew *was greater* because of the benefits he derived from the law. In another way, according to the state of grace; and in this way, the Jew *is not* greater. And this is the sense in which it is taken here."[24]

Here, Aquinas is commenting directly upon the advantage of the Jews after the passion of Christ. Jewish advantage is affirmed, but only as something in the past: "Before the faith, the Jew was greater." The picture of the Law

---

20. *Ad Galat.* 3.9.186. He also cites Romans 10:12 as well, which states "There is no distinction of the Jew and Greek; for the same is Lord over all." "Et Rom. X,12: *non est distinctio Iudaei et Graeci, et cetera.*"

21. *Ad Galat.* 3.9.185.

22. *Ad Galat.* 3.9.186.

23. *Ad Galat.* 3.9.186.

24. *Ad Galat.* 3.9.186.

The Ceremonial Law as Fulfilled, Dead, and Deadly (Galatians)

that begins to emerge from the commentary is similar to that of Hebrews: the Law was imperfect but beneficial for the Jews *only in the time before the coming of the New Law*.

Aquinas's view of the temporality of the Law is also expressed in the idea that it can be changed due to the fact that the source of its authority is angels, not Christ. He explains that there are three kinds of teachings each with different forms of authority. The first is that of the philosophers who arrive at knowledge of their doctrine with their own reason guiding them.[25] The second *doctrina* is "that which has been delivered by angles, as the Old Law."[26] The Old Law, explains Aquinas, was not issued by a human will but by angels. The third *doctrina* "was given immediately by God Himself, as the teaching of the Gospel."[27] Aquinas then quotes Hebrews 1:2 and explains why the first and second type of teaching can be "changed and revoked" because these are not given directly from God:

> Now, a teaching passed on by a man can be changed and revoked by another man who knows better, as one philosopher refutes the sayings of another, or by an angel who has a more penetrating knowledge of the truth. Even a teaching handed down by one angel could be supplanted by that of a higher angel or by God. But a teaching that comes directly from God can be nullified neither by man nor angel.[28]

The Gospel teaching has come directly from God and is therefore so great that "if a man or even an angel preached another Gospel . . . he is anathema."[29] The Old Law, on the other hand, is given by angels, not directly by God, and can therefore be changed. Although the Old Law is indeed higher than man it is not grounded in the same authority as the New Law. As in the Hebrews commentary the Law is not closely connected with God's election of the Jews or God's faithfulness as it was in the Romans commentary. Rather the Law is associated with its angelic mediators and it passes away due to a change of time. The Old Law "had a time fixed by God determining how long it was to endure and how long the heir, i.e., the Jewish people, were to be under it."[30]

25. *Ad Galat.* 1.2.25.
26. *Ad Galat.* 1.2.25.
27. *Ad Galat.* 1.2.25.
28. *Ad Galat.* 1.2.25.
29. *Ad Galat.* 1.2.25.
30. *Ad Galat.* 4.1.196.

The Prefiguring Function of the Ceremonial Law

In addition to the temporality of the Law, the prefiguring function of the Old Law is discussed in the Galatians commentary. Aquinas understands Christ's words in Matthew 5:17 to mean that the figures of the Old Law are now fulfilled.[31] To observe the ceremonial law after the passion is "absurd and the greatest of troubles."[32] To observe the ceremonial law after the passion is to cling to an old sign after having already arrived at the destination to which it pointed, which is to misuse it:

> But the New Testament and the Gospel of Christ are not ordained to the Old, but contrawise, the Old Law is ordained to the new law, as a figure to the truth. Consequently the figure ought to be converted into the truth, and the Old Law to the Gospel of Christ, not the truth into the figure, or the Gospel of Christ into the Old Law.[33]

To illustrate this point, Aquinas draws upon an analogy about the relationship between a man and an image of a man: "This is plain from the way we ordinarily speak; for we do not say that a man resembles the image of a man, but contrawise, that the image resembles the man . . . ."[34] He then cites the Leviticus text once more: "the new coming on, you shall cast away the old."[35] For Aquinas, to observe the ceremonial law after the passion is an attempt to turn the Gospel into the Old Law.

Aquinas also argues that the words that encapsulate the apostolic message of the letter, "The new coming on, you shall cast away the old," indicate a rationale for a casting away of the ceremonial law based on its "oldness": "In these words the Lord suggests a fourfold oldness (*quadruplicem vetustatem*).[36] The first and second forms of oldness are directly related to the rationale behind the casting away of the ceremonial law.[37] The first old-

---

31. *Ad Galat.* 4.1.200.
32. *Ad Galat.* 1.2.21.
33. *Ad Galat.* 1.2.21.
34. *Ad Galat.* 1.2.21.
35. *Ad Galat.* 1.2.21.
36. *Ad Galat. Prologus* 1.
37. The third oldness is of guilt. Aquinas understands this guilt as a result of "not confessing . . . sins" but this is made new by "the newness of justice." Although he does not spell out this justice, it is safe to assume he means the sanctifying justice that comes only through Christ. The fourth oldness is punishment of sin in the body, which the newness of glory will remove. *Ad Galat. Prologus* 1.

The Ceremonial Law as Fulfilled, Dead, and Deadly (Galatians)

ness is that which Isaiah referred to in Isaiah 26:3: "The old error is passed away."[38] The teaching of Christ removes the error of the old. The second oldness of the Law refers to the prefiguring function of the rites which, for Aquinas, announced the new covenant in Jeremiah 31:22. Aquinas explains that, "Here he shows first of all that the first testament is old and that it is made new by the newness of grace or of the reality of Christ's presence."[39] Aquinas's use of the Jeremiah text functions in the same way it does in the Hebrews commentary: to refer to the change of time, when the grace of the new covenant appears in Christ. It is because of this grace of the New Testament, Aquinas explains, that "the Old Testament should be cast out, so that with the fulfillment of the truth, the figure may be abandoned, and with the attainment of these two, grace and truth, one may arrive at the truth of justice and glory."[40]

The Cessation of the Ceremonial Law

Aquinas not only sees the old sacraments as fulfilled but he also understands them to terminate with the coming of Christ.[41] The prefiguring function of the Law therefore also points toward the Law's cessation and replacement by better sacraments. If the Old Law justified, it was only because it prefigured Christ: "Again, if there were any in the Old Law who were just, they were not made just by the works of the Law but only by the faith of Christ . . . although some who observed the work of the law in times past were made just, nevertheless, this was effected only by the faith of Jesus Christ."[42] The difference between the sacraments is essentially a matter of when and how they are configured to the appearance of the grace of Christ: "Hence the sacraments of the Old Law were certain protestations of the faith of Christ, just as our sacraments are, but not in the same way, because those sacraments were configured to the grace of Christ as to something that lay in the future; our sacraments, however, testify as things containing a grace that is present."[43] Now that justifying grace is present in the new

38. *Ad Galat. Prologus* 1.
39. *Ad Galat. Prologus* 1.
40. *Ad Galat.* 1.1.2.
41. Aquinas makes the distinction between the permanent moral precepts and the temporary ceremonial law in *Ad Galat.* 2.4.94.
42. *Ad Galat.* 2.4.94.
43. *Ad Galat.* 2.4.94.

sacraments, the prefiguring function of the old sacraments as figure of the future reality is exhausted and no longer necessary.

Because the Old Law pointed forward to Christ, observing the Law after Christ is "something that cannot be done without sin."[44] However, there is a difference in the gravity of the sin for those that observe the Law. Aquinas uses harsh language to describe the error of Gentile observance of the ceremonial law.[45] The termination of these rites is especially serious for the Galatians who were Gentile believers.[46] If the foolish Galatians would read the Law they would realize that it should be abandoned: "You have either read the law or not. If you have read it, you ought to know the things written in it. But those things prove that it should be abandoned."[47] In Aquinas's view, the Law contains "certain things which clearly indicate that the law must not be retained."[48] To assume the burden of the Law is "a mark of exceeding stupidity" as is clear from the fact that the apostles themselves abandoned the Law at the Jerusalem conference in Acts 15:10.[49]

The Apostle's Pious Destruction of the Carnal Law

Lastly, Aquinas views Paul as one who destroyed (*destruxi*) the ceremonial law. Paraphrasing what he takes as Paul's own view, Aquinas writes, "I destroyed the law understood carnally by judging and teaching it spiritually."[50] Yet Aquinas sees how such an idea seems to contradict the claim that the Law is good and not evil: "one might regard [Paul] as a destroyer of the law and consequently impious according to Psalm 118:126: They have dissipated your law . . . ."[51] Aquinas replies by explaining how Paul actually destroys the Law without being impious. When anyone destroys a law by means of the law itself, he is indeed a prevaricator of the law, but not impious: "For a law is destroyed by means of the law when the law

---

44. *Ad Galat.* 2.5.100.

45. *Ad Galat.* 4.7.248. Aquinas views Acts 15:10 as the apostolic rejection of the ceremonial law: "This is a yoke which neither our fathers nor we have been able to bear." I will treat Aquinas's view of the Jerusalem conference below.

46. That Aquinas thinks the Galatians are Gentiles is clear in 3.1.123.

47. *Ad Galat.* 4.7.248.

48. *Ad Galat.* 4.7.249.

49. *Ad Galat.* 3.2.121.

50. *Ad Galat.* 2.5.100.

51. *Ad Galat.* 2.6.103.

itself contains some local or temporary precept, such that the law should be observed for such a time or in such a place and no other, and this fact is expressed in the law."[52] If someone were to *not* use that law after the said time and place, explains Aquinas, then he "destroys the law by means of the law itself...."[53] "In this way," says Aquinas, "the Apostle destroyed the law." Aquinas paraphrases his view of Paul's thinking on the matter: "I somehow destroyed the Law, but by means of the Law; because through the Law I am dead to the Law, i.e., by the authority of the Law I have rejected the Law, as being dead to the Law."[54] This authority, according to Aquinas, is "cited in many places in Sacred Scripture," chief of which is Jeremiah 31:31: "I will make a new covenant with the house of Israel...."[55] In a sense, the "terms" for the abolishment of the old covenant are therefore included in that same old covenant. For Aquinas, the old covenant is therefore abolished by the new covenant because this old covenant clearly foretold such abolishment.

3. AQUINAS ON THE JERUSALEM CONFERENCE, ANTIOCH INCIDENT, AND CONTROVERSY BETWEEN JEROME AND AUGUSTINE

In Aquinas's view, the dispute between Peter and Paul at Antioch (frequently referred to as the Antioch incident) raises the issue of apostolic authority and the unity of the gospel as it relates to the observance of the ceremonial law. He begins his comments on the Antioch incident by first highlighting Paul's commendation of the authority of the gospel as it relates to the other apostles in matters "where they opposed his teaching."[56] For Aquinas, Galatians reveals how Paul demonstrated that he not only instructed Peter regarding the implications of the gospel for the observance of the ceremonial law, but that he did so based on apostolic authority of the Jerusalem conference.[57] Indeed, before Aquinas even begins to comment on the dispute between Peter and Paul he takes the time to explain why the conference is the authoritative basis of Paul's rebuke.

52. *Ad Galat.* 2.6.103.
53. *Ad Galat.* 2.6.103.
54. *Ad Galat.* 2.6.103.
55. *Ad Galat.* 2.6.103.
56. *Ad Galat.* 2.1.51.
57. *Ad Galat.* 2.3.76.

Aquinas on the Apostolic Decree that the Ceremonial Law is No Longer of Value

Aquinas explains the circumstances of the Jerusalem Conference of Acts 15 in detail.[58] He takes the time to do so because Paul famously references the Conference in Galatians 2:1, when he tells of his confrontation with Peter, and because Aquinas understands Paul to have established and defended his authority at the conference.[59]

In Aquinas's view, the Jerusalem Conference results in what he views as an apostolic decree on the value of circumcision. It is this decree that serves as the ground of Paul's rebuke of Peter's error at Antioch. Aquinas understands Paul's words in Galatians 2 to report the time, place, witnesses, and motive of the apostolic conference of Acts 15. Though he views Paul and the apostles as equals in the Church, he privileges Paul as *the* apostle who taught the others and not vice versa. The other apostles greatly benefit from Paul's perfect conversion, which included direct instruction by Christ.[60] Paul "neither received the Gospel from man nor learned it by man."[61]

However, Aquinas also views the apostles as called from out of the synagogue by the Holy Spirit to a shared faith in the gospel. The "conversion" of the apostles from the synagogue is mentioned in 2.1.66. And when

---

58. Larcher translates *collatione* as "conference" or "discussion."

59. Aquinas explains that the Galatians had been so deceived by false teachers that they believed that Paul did not "enjoy the same authority as the other apostles, as having neither been taught by Christ nor lived with Him, but sent by them as their minister." See *Ad Galat.* 1.1.6.

60. "Furthermore, his conversion was perfect with respect to his understanding, because he was so instructed by Christ that there was no need to be instructed by the apostles; hence he says, *Neither went I to Jerusalem*, i.e., to be instructed by them." *Ad Galat.* 1.4.44. Aquinas is aware of Paul's stay with the apostles in Damascus and Jerusalem mentioned in Acts 9 and includes this fact as an objection to his position that Paul was *not* instructed by the apostles but received his teaching directly from Christ. His reply is simply that Paul, although he did go to Jerusalem to see Peter, did not go for instruction. Aquinas repeats this in 1.4.47 in order to reinforce the idea that Paul did not seek instruction from Peter but obtained his teaching from Christ. He states in his own words what he believes Paul meant to say: "Although I did not go to the apostles to be instructed by them in the beginning of my conversion, because I had already been instructed by Christ, yet, being moved by a feeling of charity, *after three years*, i.e., after my conversion, I went to Jerusalem, because I had long desired to see Peter, not to be taught by him but to visit him . . . ."

61. *Ad Galat.* 2.2.69.

The Ceremonial Law as Fulfilled, Dead, and Deadly (Galatians)

Aquinas comments upon the possible meanings of Paul's words that God "separated me from my mother's womb and called me by his grace," he explains that the "womb" is the "college of Pharisees." The Pharisees trained Paul in Judaism. "Therefore," says Aquinas, "the synagogue was his mother . . . its womb are the Pharisees. And from this womb he was separated by the Holy Spirit unto faith in the Gospel . . . ."[62]

Paul's teaching on faith in this gospel was confirmed at the Jerusalem conference where he conferred with Peter, James, and John, among others. Paul conferred with these senior apostles on the gospel and the observance of the Law.[63] The discussion at the conference concerned the teaching of false brethren that held "you cannot be saved without circumcision."[64] Aquinas argues that Paul, on the other hand, had always taught that faith is of value but "neither circumcision nor uncircumcision profits anything . . . ."[65] This is why Aquinas explains that after Paul's conversion he began to preach that the ceremonial law was not to be observed by Gentiles: "immediately after his conversion [he] began to preach things odious to the Jews, especially the vocation of the Gentiles and that they should not observe the justifications of the law."[66] It should be noted that here, Aquinas understands Paul's teaching on the gospel to include a prohibition of the observance of the ceremonial laws (or legal justifications) *as a specifically Gentile vocation*. Paul's teaching on the gospel is that *the Gentiles* must not be compelled to observe the rites of the Law.

Jewish Christians, on the other hand, can *and should* observe the legal ceremonies.[67] This is made clear in a comment Aquinas makes on why Paul allowed Timothy to be circumcised but prevented Titus from being circumcised. When Aquinas explains why Timothy, a Jewish "convert" to Christianity, was circumcised but not Titus, a Gentile, he reiterates his point about the Gentile vocation for nonobservance. However, he then adds a significant justification for what seems like a Jewish Christian vocation to observe the Law in the middle period that is based on obedience to the Law. Aquinas writes,

62. *Ad Galat.* 1.4.41.
63. *Ad Galat.* 2.1.56.
64. *Ad Galat.* 2.1.62.
65. *Ad Galat.* 2.1.63.
66. *Ad Galat.* 2.1.57.

67. This observance is only allowed in what Augustine calls the "middle period" or the apostolic age.

> But the special reason why Timothy was circumcised and Titus not, was that Timothy was born of a Gentile father and Jewish mother, whereas Titus' parents were both Gentiles. And *the opinion of the Apostle was that those born of a Jewish parent on either side should be circumcised*, but those born entirely of Gentile parents should on no account be circumcised.[68]

For Aquinas, Paul's teaching required Jewish Christians to continue observing the Law in the middle period because of their Jewish identity.[69] At least in the case of Timothy, Paul taught Jewish believers in Christ to follow the ceremonial law. Aquinas even refers to these Jewish believers as an *ecclesia* led by Peter. He views Peter as a pillar of what he calls the *Ecclesia Iudaeorum fidelium* or "Church of the Jewish believers."[70] However, as Aquinas moves into the discussion of the Jerusalem Conference, there is no mention that a Jewish Christian should observe the rite of circumcision because of their Jewish parent.

According to Aquinas's reading, Paul's aim at the conference was to gain apostolic support for his teaching on the Law. Paul "wanted to confer with them, in order that when his hearers heard that his teaching was in agreement with that of the other apostles and approved by them, they would hold to it more firmly."[71] The result of the conference, in Aquinas's view, is that Paul's teaching is approved rather than the opinion of the false brethren. At the Jerusalem conference, Paul won apostolic approval of his controversial teaching that was "odious to the Jews." Aquinas paraphrases Paul's view of the outcome of the conference as follows: "contrary to the opinion of the adversaries who came up to Jerusalem to oppose me in this matter, it was I that the Apostles approved."[72]

Aquinas then moves to a description of the decree issued by the conference. When he describes the apostles' decree to approve Paul's teaching

---

68. *Ad Galat.* 2.1.63.

69. For Augustine, the ceremonial law should be observed by Jewish Christians in order to avoid scandalizing the Jews in the middle period but is ultimately a matter of indifference for the Jewish Christian—the Law can be observed as an expression of Christian freedom and respect for the ancient customs but is not necessary. Augustine Ep. 82, cited in White, *Correspondence*, 153. In Titus's case the rationale to not circumcise is the rejection of the doctrine that circumcision is necessary for salvation for Gentiles. Paul allows Timothy to be circumcised in Acts 16:3; Titus is refused circumcision by Paul in Galatians 2:3–5.

70. *Ad Galat.* 2.2.74–5.

71. *Ad Galat.* 2.1.59.

72. *Ad Galat.* 2.2.71.

The Ceremonial Law as Fulfilled, Dead, and Deadly (Galatians)

he *does not* mention that nonobservance of the Law was the particular vocation of Gentiles. As Aquinas draws upon a citation of John Chrysostom's view of the Law, his description of the apostolic decree seems to implicitly broaden the rule of nonobservance of the Law to include *all* who observe the rites, including Jewish Christians like Timothy.

Aquinas explains the outcome of the conference as follows: "The discussion occasioned the decree handed down by the apostles on not observing the rites of the Law, as is had in Acts (15:28)."[73] Immediately after describing the terms of the decree, Aquinas explains the rationale for the decision that the rites are "not to be observed" by appealing to John Chrysostom's view of circumcision as a sign of the promise with Abraham that was fulfilled and completed by the passion of Christ:

> The reason why these rites were not to be observed after the passion of Christ is assigned in the following way by Chrysostom: "For it is evident that the instrument drawn up for any promise or pact binds only until the pact and promise are fulfilled; but when fulfilled, the instrument no longer binds on that point." Now circumcision is an instrument of the promise and pact between God and believing men. Hence it was that Abraham underwent circumcision as a sign of the promise, as is said in Genesis (11:26). And because the promise was fulfilled and the pact completed by the passion of Christ, neither the pact holds after the passion nor is circumcision of any value.[74]

Here, Aquinas states the terms of the apostolic decree as a decision on "not observing the rites of the Law" in general, with no mention of the qualification of Gentile vocation. Chrysostom's view of circumcision and Aquinas's interpretation of Paul's teaching on nonobservance of the rites as a Gentile vocation are clearly different. Chrysostom's view that the rites are not to be observed at all and that circumcision is no longer of value is not the same as the more nuanced Pauline teaching that only Gentiles should not observe the Law and Jewish Christians that have Jewish parents should be circumcised. The distinction between a Jewish Christian obligation to Torah in the middle period and a Gentile vocation of nonobservance seems to dissolve into one general principle of nonobservance of the rites.

Nevertheless, Aquinas then argues that Paul's teaching was vindicated at the conference and that his preaching "was not changed nor did the

---

73. *Ad Galat.* 2.1.61.
74. *Ad Galat.* 2.1.61.

apostles add to it." He then paraphrases his understanding of Paul's view of the decree in a way that seems to blend together the Gentile vocation of nonobservance with Chrysostom's view that the rites should no longer be observed:

> I say that the result of my discussion with them about the teaching of the Gospel was that my teaching and opinion remained unaltered concerning the non-observance of legalism, i.e., the Gentiles would not be compelled to observe the rites of the law[.] ... [T]his discussion occasioned the decree handed down by the apostles on not observing the rites of the law.[75]

Aquinas seems to attempt a synthesis of Paul's teaching on the Gentile vocation of nonobservance of the rites with his view that the conference of Jerusalem decreed that the rites should not be observed in general because circumcision no longer has value.

Overall, the recounting of the conference and its decision is part of what Aquinas views as Paul successfully defending his authority and the authentic gospel message.[76] Though he asserts there was no change made to Paul's teaching, his exposition of the meaning of the decree handed down by the apostles at the Jerusalem conference seems to undermine his comments that Paul's teaching was that nonobservance of the rites was a specifically Gentile vocation. The rationale of the apostles, which Aquinas explains by relying upon the citation of Chrysostom, explicitly states that the observance of the ceremonial law is no longer of value. Aquinas's reliance upon Chrysostom's description of the rationale indicates that he thinks the decision of the apostles' is that the ceremonial law is dead for all. As the quote from Chrysostom made clear, circumcision *was* a sign of the promise. Now, after the passion, the pact is fulfilled and completed. The passion completes the promise and the rites are no longer of value.

For Aquinas, therefore, the question before the Jerusalem conference concerned whether Gentiles should observe the ceremonies but the decision that was handed down is a general prohibition on observance of circumcision based on the idea that the sacraments of the Old Law are superfluous after the passion.

---

75. *Ad Galat.* 2.1.61.
76. *Ad Galat.* 2.1.60.

The Ceremonial Law as Fulfilled, Dead, and Deadly (Galatians)

Aquinas's View of the Antioch Incident

After establishing the validation of Paul's teaching by the Jerusalem Conference, Aquinas comments upon Paul's rebuke of Peter at Antioch. For Aquinas, Paul shows how he "helped Peter by correcting him."[77] Aquinas summarizes Paul's narration as follows. After regularly eating the food of the Gentiles, Peter withdrew from the Gentiles when certain Jews arrived, and "adhered to the Jews alone and mingled among them."[78] Peter did so, reasons Aquinas, because he feared the Jews. Although this fear was not "a human or worldly fear but a fear inspired by charity, namely, lest they be scandalized, as is said in a Gloss."[79] Peter "became to the Jews as a Jew, pretending that he felt the same as they did in their weakness."[80] "What resulted from this pretense," says Aquinas, is "the rest of the Jews consented who were at Antioch, discriminating between food and separating from the Gentiles."[81] "Prior to this act," explains Aquinas, "they would not have done this." In order to avoid scandalizing the Jews, Peter pretended to feel the same way the Jews did and observe the laws. The Gentiles were then compelled to observe the legal justifications and the truth of the gospel was being undone.[82]

Paul's rebuke was just and fitting, explains Aquinas, because "in cases where danger is imminent, the truth must be preached openly and the opposite never condoned through fear of scandalizing others . . . ."[83] Aquinas

---

77. *Ad Galat.* 2.3.76. Aquinas sides with Augustine, who also viewed Peter as being in the wrong for withdrawing from Gentile table fellowship.

78. *Ad Galat.* 2.3.79–80.

79. *Ad Galat.* 2.3.80. He goes onto explain that Peter "became to the Jews as a Jew, pretending that he felt the same as they did in their weakness. Yet he feared unreasonably, because the truth must never be set aside through fear of scandal." Aquinas's reference to Peter's "fear of scandal" motivated by charity actually resembles Jerome's view of the reason for Peter's fear. Peter Gorday explains: "[Jerome] took the tack of interpreting the 'fear' felt by Peter 'of those from the circumcision' mentioned by Paul (Gal. 2:14) as a reference not to cravenness on Peter's part but to a fear that he would lose his Jewish converts if he acted unwisely in the crisis (Ep. 112, 8). He enters not into a lie, contended Jerome, but into 'honest diplomacy' intended to display the wisdom of the apostles . . . ." Gorday points out that the idea that Peter caved to the circumcision group out of a craven fear is actually from the anti-Jewish tradition of the Marcionite prologues. Gorday, "Jews and Gentiles," 215.

80. *Ad Galat.* 2.3.88.

81. *Ad Galat.* 2.3.81.

82. *Ad Galat.* 2.3.83.

83. *Ad Galat.* 2.3.83.

understands Peter to have an obligation to not compel the Gentiles to eat such foods. This is because Aquinas thinks Peter was instructed by God to no longer live as the Jews do: "he had been instructed by God that although he had previously lived as the Jews do, he should no longer discriminate among foods: 'That which God has cleansed, do not thou call common' (Acts 10:15)."[84] Paul's rebuke of Peter is restated and then paraphrased by Aquinas with echoes of Acts 10 in the background:

> If you, being a Jew, by nature and race, live after the manner of the Gentiles and not as the Jews do, i.e., if you observe the customs of Gentiles and not of Jews, since you know and feel that discriminating among foods is of no importance, how do you compel the Gentiles, not indeed by command, but by example of your behavior, to live as the Jews do?[85]

In Aquinas's view, the idea that the ceremonial law is no longer to be observed is a teaching revealed to Peter by God in Acts 10:15.[86] Peter *did not* observe the rites prior to the arrival of the Jews and ate with Gentiles because "the inspiration of the Holy Spirit Who had said to him: 'That which God hath cleansed, do not thou call common,' as is had in Acts 10:15."[87] Aquinas's Peter is therefore aware that the ceremonial law is of no importance and need not be observed. While Aquinas's understanding of Peter's observance of the Law is rather straightforward (he did not observe it after his dream; he did observe it when under pressure from Jewish Christians), his view of Paul's position on the Law is more complex. As I show below, Aquinas departs from Augustine on this important point: whether Paul actually observed the ceremonial law and whether he taught that Jews could observe it in the apostolic age.

From Superfluous to Deadly: Aquinas on the Controversy between Jerome and Augustine

In his discussion of the debate between Aquinas and Jerome, it becomes clear that Aquinas follows Augustine on two important points but also

---

84. *Ad Galat.* 2.3.85.

85. *Ad Galat.* 2.3.85.

86. As far as I can tell, in his exchange with Jerome, Augustine does not use Acts 10:15 to argue that Peter knew the Law was no longer important.

87. *Ad Galat.* 2.3.79.

The Ceremonial Law as Fulfilled, Dead, and Deadly (Galatians)

departs from Augustine in a significant way. Aquinas says that Paul's rebuke of Peter "occasioned no small controversy between Jerome and Augustine . . . ."[88] The controversy concerned the proper interpretation of Galatians 2:11–14.[89] The discussion dominated a series of letters exchanged between these church fathers "from opposite ends of the Latin-speaking Roman Empire," sometime between 394 and 419.[90] "As their writings clearly show,"

---

88. *Ad Galat.* 2.3.86.

89. Peter Gorday points out that the controversy between Jerome and Augustine centered upon finding answers to lingering questions about the Antioch incident: "To be sure, on one level Paul's narrative posed no problem for Augustine and Jerome. They were quite clear in their agreement about the final implications for faith and practice of the encounter between the two apostles at Antioch. Christians may on no account feel bound to observe Jewish ritual law as a required, inherent part of their discipleship. In Christ, the Law has been dethroned as the means of salvation. On another level, however, questions remained about what had really been going on in the encounter between the two apostles. Was it a straightforward matter of the clash of two opposed points of view, in which one man was right and the other wrong? Was the outcome a simple submission of one to the other? Further, was Peter not only theologically wrong but also morally flawed in his behavior? Was Paul arrogant, or worse, inconsistent, in administering the rebuke? Was there a triumph here of the Gentiles' understanding and practice of the gospel over that of their Jewish fellow believers? Or were there deeper, hidden dimensions of the meeting of Peter and Paul, in which a more fundamental unity, even concord, was more significant than their opposition? Furthermore, and more basically, was the abrogation of the law as the means of salvation a simple, straightforward matter? Why then did not only Peter but [also] Paul . . . continue on occasion to observe its requirements? The answers arrived at by Jerome and Augustine to these questions, based in part on their historical reconstructions of the special circumstances affecting Paul's theology, then enabled them to arrive at somewhat different understandings of the continuing significance of the law of Moses in the history of salvation." Gorday, "Jews and Gentiles," 205–6.

90. Augustine wrote the first letter in the exchange after he read a copy of Jerome's commentary on Galatians (written in 388). Augustine believed Jerome had given an unsatisfactory and dangerous interpretation of Galatians 2:11–14. The danger was that Jerome suggested that the Jewish apostles had acted under a pretense in observing the ceremonial law, which would mean the biblical authors sometimes lie. Carolinne White provides a helpful overview of the letters exchanged: "It was his disagreement on this point in particular which was to lead to the famous controversy, prolonged because their letters were often lost or delayed and because of Jerome's refusal to reply to the question at issue; the discussion of the critical passage of Galatians is restricted to Ep. 28 (which never reached Jerome), Ep. 40 (largely a repetition of Ep. 28), Jerome's lengthy Ep. 112 and Augustine's final answer in his Ep. 82—the other letters written while the dispute raged are largely devoted to expressions of love and respect or indignation and to the question of the extent to which criticism is permissible between Christian friends." Augustine writes letter 40 only because there is no response to the first letter, 28. For an introduction to the letters see White, *The Correspondence between Jerome and Augustine*, 2–3; 120–32. For a concise summary of the debate see ibid., 43–7. See also Nanos, *The*

explains Aquinas, "they are seen to disagree on four points."[91] Aquinas then lists and comments upon each of the four disagreements, two of which will be discussed below.[92]

First, Augustine and Jerome disagreed as to the time of the justifications, namely when they should be observed. Aquinas explains that Jerome distinguishes two periods for the observation of the legal justifications: 1) *before the passion of Christ* and 2) *after the passion*. For Jerome, explains Aquinas, "the legal justifications were living before the passion of Christ, i.e., had validity, inasmuch as original sin was removed through circumcision, and God was pleased with sacrifices and victims."[93] After the passion, explains Aquinas, Jerome held that the legal justifications were "not only not living i.e. dead (*mortua*), but what is more, they were deadly (*mortifera*), so that whoever observed them after the passion of Christ sinned mortally."[94]

Augustine, on the other hand, distinguishes three periods. The first period is 1) *before the passion of Christ*. Here, and in agreement with Jerome, the legal justifications were living before the passion. The second period is 2) that time "*immediately following the passion of Christ, before grace was promulgated* . . . ."[95] Aquinas describes Augustine's view of this "time of the apostles in the beginning" as follows:

Irony of Galatians; Nanos, "Peter's Hypocrisy (Gal. 2:11–21) in the Light of Paul's Anxiety (Rom. 7)"; Boyarin, *Border Lines*, 209; Gorday, "Jews and Gentiles, Galatians," 199–236; Childs, *Biblical Theology of the Old and New Testaments*, 293.

91. *Ad Galat.* 2.3.86.

92. The third and forth points of the disagreement between Augustine and Jerome are less relevant to my argument that Aquinas thinks the Law is now dead and deadly for all Jews and thus will be included here. The third point on which Jerome and Augustine differ is the sin of Peter. Jerome, explains Aquinas, claims Peter did not sin because he withdrew from the Gentiles out of charity not mundane fear. Aquinas, however, claims that Peter sinned venially. He sinned on account of a lack of discretion by leaning toward the Jews in order to avoid scandalizing them. Finally, the fourth point which Jerome and Augustine differ is on Paul's rebuke. Jerome claims that Peter pretended to observe the legal justifications and Paul pretended to rebuke him. Jerome said this was done by mutual consent, explains Aquinas, so that each might exercise his care over their respective mission, Gentiles and Jews. Augustine, however, claims Peter really sinned by observing the justifications because this action was a source of scandal to the Gentiles. Paul did not sin in rebuking him because no scandal followed from his rebuke.

93. *Ad Galat.* 2.3.86.

94. *Ad Galat.* 2.3.86.

95. *Ad Galat.* 2.3.86.

The Ceremonial Law as Fulfilled, Dead, and Deadly (Galatians)

> During this period, says Augustine, the legal justifications were dead (*mortua*) but not yet deadly (*mortifera*) to the converted Jews, so long as the ones observing them placed no hope in them. Hence the Jews observed them during that period without sinning. But had they placed their trust in them when observing them after their conversion, they would have sinned mortally; because if they had placed their trust in them so as to believe that they were necessary for salvation, then, as far as they were concerned, they would have been voiding the grace of Christ.[96]

In the time of the apostles the Law is therefore dead for all Jews or of no value. However, it is not yet deadly and converted Jewish Christians as well as Jews observed the ceremonial law during this time. These "Jews observed them during that period without sinning," says Aquinas.[97] In order to explain how these Jews observed the Law without sinning, Aquinas relies upon what might be referred to as the "two ways" of observing the ceremonial law in the middle period or apostolic age.

Jewish Christians could have observed the rites of the Law in the time of the apostles without having sinned so long as they did not "place their trust in them so as to believe that they were necessary for salvation."[98] Here, Aquinas makes a distinction between 1) *observing the Law* and 2) *being of the Law*. "Observing the law" is simply one who fulfills or obeys the law, "so that one who fulfills is not under a curse." However, to be "of the works of the Law" is to place trust and hope in these works.[99]

It is this latter form of observance—being "of the works of the Law"—that Aquinas, following Augustine's view, believes is unacceptable. This distinction allows Aquinas to say that it is not the Law in and of itself that suddenly becomes sinful but rather the belief that the Law saves: "Therefore, inasmuch as the law begets a knowledge of sin and offers no help against sin, they are said to be under a curse, since they are powerless to escape it by those works."[100]

For Aquinas, these "two ways" of observing the Law in the apostolic age (or middle period) also functions to explain how Christ himself observed the Law. Aquinas says that "a difficulty comes to mind" concerning

---

96. *Ad Galat.* 2.3.86. Aquinas actually refers to this middle period as the "third period" but I am reordering them according to chronology in order to simplify the presentation.
97. *Ad Galat.* 2.3.86.
98. *Ad Galat.* 2.3.86.
99. *Ad Galat.* 3.4.136; Cf. 5.5.318.
100. *Ad Galat.* 3.4.136.

Christ and the Law when Paul's says "If you are led by the spirit, you are not under the Law" in Galatians 5:18.[101] The difficulty is that "if Christ is not only spiritual but the giver of the Spirit, it seems unbecoming to say that He was made under the Law."[102] Aquinas's *respondeo* relies upon the "two ways" of observing the Law in the middle period. He explains that "to be under the Law" can be taken in two ways: "under" can denote mere observance of the Law, which is the sense in which Christ was made under the Law, because he was circumcised and presented in the temple. Aquinas then cites Matthew 5:17 "I am not come to destroy but to fulfill." And "under" can also denote oppression, in the sense that one is oppressed by fear of the Law. "But neither Christ nor spiritual men are said to be under the Law in this way."[103] For Aquinas, the "mere observance" of the Law, without trust in it, by Christ can therefore be considered a form of "fulfillment" of the Law. This middle period is the only time in which the ceremonial law can be observed by Jews and Jewish Christians after the passion of Christ.

Lastly, Aquinas explains that Augustine posits a third period: 3) *after the grace of Christ had been proclaimed*. It was during that period, according to Augustine, that these legal justifications became both "dead and deadly" *to all* who observed them.[104] The "reasoning that underlies these statements," explains Aquinas, is that

> if the Jews had been forbidden the legal observations right after their conversion, it might have seemed that they had previously been on equal footing with idolaters, who were immediately forbidden to worship idols, and that just as idolatry had never been good, so too the legal observances. Therefore, under the inspiration of the Holy Spirit, the legal observances were condoned for a short time for the reason given, namely, to show that the legal observances had been good in the past. Hence says Augustine, the fact that the legal justifications were not forbidden right after the passion of Christ showed that the mother, the synagogue, was destined to be brought in honor to the grave. But whosoever did not observe them in that manner would not be honoring the mother, the synagogue, but disturbing her grave.[105]

---

101. *Ad Galat.* 4.2.208.
102. *Ad Galat.* 4.2.208.
103. *Ad Galat.* 4.2.208.
104. *Ad Galat.* 2.3.86.
105. *Ad Galat.* 2.3.86.

The Ceremonial Law as Fulfilled, Dead, and Deadly (Galatians)

In order to avoid any semblance of the Manichean idea that the legal observances were evil, a special condoning of the legal observances is declared for the apostolic age. By allowing for the observance of the ceremonial law in the apostolic age the Church shows its respect for the ancient customs. The sacraments of the synagogue are honored and respected in this way but are nonetheless, in Augustine's view, destined to expire.

It is important to emphasize that Aquinas understands the observance of the ceremonies after the promulgation of grace as a mortal sin for Jews and not Jewish Christians. As I argued in chapter 2, the reason Matthew Levering misses the primary concern in Wyschogrod's critique of Aquinas is because he thinks Aquinas's teaching that the observance of the ceremonial law is a mortal sin after the passion applies only to baptized Jews. For Levering, Aquinas does not condemn Jewish observance of the Law.[106]

Levering fails to recognize the consequence of Aquinas's adoption of Augustine's teaching that after the final period (after the grace of Christ had been proclaimed), the observance of legal observances is deadly for all. Aquinas states the consequences of observing the Law after the middle period in 5.1.278: "*To observe the legal ceremonies after grace had been preached is a mortal sin for the Jews. But during the interim, i.e., before the preaching of grace, they could be observed without sin even by those who had been converted from Judaism, provided they set no hope on them.*"[107] There is no question in Aquinas's mind that the legal observances were always sinful for Gentile Christians, but after the expiration of the middle period that comes with the promulgation of the gospel, these observances are forbidden for Jewish Christians *and* Jews.

The second point on which Jerome and Augustine differed was on the reason the apostles observed the ceremonial laws. Jerome argues that the apostles only observed the rites out of pretense. For example, they did not really observe the Sabbath, but simply rested. Augustine, on the other hand, argues that the apostles definitely intended to observe the legal justifications. However, they did so without putting their trust in them as though they were necessary for salvation.

Aquinas adopts Augustine's position here again, and explains the rationale. In the apostolic age, both Jews and Jewish Christians can safely observe the ceremonial laws: "This was lawful for them to do, because they

---

106. "Aquinas does not condemn the observance of Torah by Jews who do not believe in Jesus Christ." Levering, *Christ's Fulfillment*, 161fn60.

107. *Ad Galat.* 5.1.278.

had been Jews. Nevertheless, they observed them before grace was proclaimed. Hence just as certain other Jews could safely observe them at that time without putting any trust in them, so too could the apostles."[108]

As is well known, Aquinas sides with Augustine on both of these points. However, there is a significant difference between Augustine's interpretation of Paul's observance of the Law and Aquinas's own interpretation. Although they arrived at different answers to the question, both Jerome and Augustine assumed that the apostles observed the Law after the passion of Christ. As Peter Gorday explains, the question that preoccupied them concerned whether "the abrogation of the law as the means of salvation [was] a simple, straightforward matter? Why then did not only Peter but [also] Paul . . . continue on occasion to observe its requirements?"[109] Augustine's words to Jerome in Epistle 82 demonstrate that he thought Paul's observance of the Law was a fact: "I believe that the Apostle Paul did all these things honestly, and without dissimulation; and yet if any one now leave Judaism and become a Christian, I neither compel nor permit him to imitate Paul's example, and go on with *the sincere observance of Jewish rites*, any more than you, who think that Paul dissembled when he practiced these rites, would compel or permit such a one to follow the apostle in that dissimulation.[110] For Augustine, Paul observed the ceremonies and meant

---

108. *Ad Galat.* 2.3.87. Aquinas's view that the Jewish apostles actually practiced the ceremonial law and his view of the three periods is basically the same as Augustine. Augustine writes, concerning Paul's observance of the ceremonial law: "Paul was without doubt a Jew and when he became a Christian he did not give up the practices of the Jews which that people had accepted as being lawful and suitable for the times. That is why he undertook to perform these things although he was already and apostle of Christ: he did so in order to show that they were not harmful to those who wished to observe them in the way they had received them from their parents by means of the Law even after they had come to believe in Christ. He wanted to show that Christians ought not to set their hope of salvation in these things because the salvation which was signified by those sacraments had already come through the Lord Jesus. And so he judged that they were in no way to be imposed upon the Gentiles because such a heavy and unnecessary burden might repel them, unaccustomed as they were, from the faith. Consequently, Paul was not rebuking Peter for observing the traditions of his fathers which could be performed without deceit or inconsistency if Peter wished (for although these customs were now superfluous they were not harmful); but he criticized him for forcing the Gentiles to live as Jews, which he could only do by himself observing these traditions as if they were still necessary for salvation even after the coming of the Lord." Augustine, Ep. 40, in White, 77–8.

109. Gorday, "Jews and Gentiles," 205–6.

110. Augustine, Epistle 82, cited in White, *Correspondence (394–419)*, 120–32. [Emphasis added]

The Ceremonial Law as Fulfilled, Dead, and Deadly (Galatians)

to do so. For Jerome, the apostles also observed the ceremonies but did so under pretense. Both Fathers viewed Paul as observing the rites.

As is clear from his presentation of Augustine's view, Aquinas understands Augustine to hold that the Jewish apostles actually observed the Law without sinning in the middle period. Unlike Augustine and Jerome, however, Aquinas does not think that Paul observed the Law. Although Augustine and Aquinas agree that Jews and Jewish Christians who observed the Mosaic Law without putting hope in it avoided sinning during the middle period, they differ on 1) whether the Apostle Paul observed the Law during the middle period; and 2) whether Paul taught that Jews should abandon the Law in the middle period.

First, Aquinas holds that Paul, and Peter, actually abandoned the Law during the middle period. Peter did so at the direct instruction of the Holy Spirit. Aquinas views the cessation of the ceremonial law to have begun almost immediately with Paul and Peter's conversions. He views both apostles as having been called out by the Holy Spirit from the synagogue and into a "life without the law." Aquinas thinks Paul himself abandoned the Law and encouraged others to do likewise. He claims that Paul lived without the Law himself, had abandoned a life of the Law, and that he taught Jews to do so as well. When Paul admonishes the Galatians to "Be as I am," Aquinas describes Paul's thinking as follows: "'Be as I am,' i.e. live without the law, because I, who had the law and was born in the law, am *now* as you formerly were, namely, without the law."[111]

Second, Aquinas teaches that the Apostle Paul destroyed the Law through his teaching that the old covenant had been fulfilled by the new covenant. He also interprets Paul to have taught Jews that the ceremonies should not be observed, and that the Jerusalem Conference approved this teaching. Additionally, in *Ad Gal.* 5.2.295, Aquinas argues that Acts 21:21 proves that Paul was suffering Jewish persecution *because* he taught that the legal ceremonies *should not be observed* even in the apostolic age: "For the Jews persecuted Paul precisely *because he taught that the legal ceremonies should not be observed.*" He then cites James' report to Paul in Acts 21:21 of what the Jews were saying about Paul's teaching: "They have heard of you that you teach those Jews who are among the Gentiles to depart from Moses; saying that they ought not to circumcise their children nor walk according to custom."[112] Augustine rightly interprets the charge reported by

---

111. *Ad Galat.* 4.4.227. [Emphasis added]
112. *Ad Galat.* 5.2.295. [Emphasis added]

James against Paul as a *false* description of Paul's teaching.[113] Aquinas, on the other hand, interprets James's report as an *accurate* description of what Paul was teaching.

Yet the differences between Aquinas and Augustine on these points are not as important as their shared view that the fulfillment of the ceremonial law also means that it was destined to expire, and that Jewish Christians were not destined to endure. Because of his adoption of Augustine's interpretation of the middle period, Aquinas assumed that the Church of the circumcision was simply not meant to continue. His view of the destiny of the Jewish Christians is mentioned in passing when he comments on the meaning of the Jewish Christian Church's (or Church of the circumcision) practice of selling their goods. Such a practice was allowed because the Church of the circumcision, which was in Jerusalem, was "not destined to endure."

> Now the reason why the custom prevailed in the early Church for those in the Church of the circumcision to sell their goods and not those in the Church of the Gentiles was that the believing Jews were congregated in Jerusalem and in Judea, which was soon to be destroyed by the Romans, as later events proved. Hence the Lord willed that no possessions were to be kept in a place not destined to endure. But the Church of the Gentiles was destined to grow strong and increase, and therefore, by the inspiration of the Holy Spirit, it came about that the possessions in it were not to be sold.[114]

Aquinas's view of the destiny of the Church of the circumcision operates as an extension of the Augustinian idea that the Holy Spirit allowed believing Jews and Jews to observe the ceremonial law but only for a limited time. After the middle period those who observe the ceremonies were not destined to grow strong and increase.

---

113. Augustine writes, in Epistle 82: "It is clear, in my opinion, that James gave this advice so that those Jews who had continued to be zealous for the Law after coming to believe in Christ should know that what they had been told about Paul was false, namely that the commandments prescribed by God and granted to their fathers by Moses should be regarded as condemned as sacrilegious by the teaching of Christ. . . . Plotting to rouse hatred and persecution against him, they accused him of being an enemy of the law and the divine commandments and the only way Paul was able to avoid the hatred awakened by their false accusation was by himself performing these rites, which he was thought to condemn as sacrilegious." See Augustine, Epistle 82, in White, *Correspondence (394–419)*, 150–51.

114. *Ad Galat.* 2.2.75.

4. FULFILLED, DESTROYED, AND DEADLY: THE ECONOMIC SUPERSESSIONISM OF THE GALATIANS COMMENTARY

In the Galatians commentary, Aquinas clearly views the ceremonial law as dead in the apostolic age and deadly thereafter. Although he acknowledges the historical value of the Law in securing the Jewish people against the danger of idolatry, and serving as a pedagogue that provided knowledge of sin, this value is lost once the prefiguring function of the Law is fulfilled by the reality that it prefigured. The fulfillment of the ceremonial law also brings about its completion, and it is a completion that requires what Aquinas refers to as the "destruction" of the ceremonial law.

Aquinas thinks Paul's message about the sinfulness of observing the ceremonial law is directed toward the Gentile Christians of Galatia. However, he also thinks Paul's teaching also applies to all who observe the Law after the passion of Christ, including Jews. This is clear from Aquinas's approval of Augustine's "middle period" where the ceremonial law becomes dead and deadly for all after the promulgation of grace.

Aquinas's view of the ceremonial law in the Galatians commentary is at odds with his positive theological view of the Law in the era after grace in the Romans commentary. In the Romans commentary, Aquinas takes the time to articulate a theologically positive answer to the question "What is the value of circumcision?" His replies state that the ceremonial law (including circumcision) is an advantage for the Jew in the present tense, and a fundamental aspect of God's promise to Abraham. Moreover, in the Galatians commentary, Aquinas argues that observance of the ceremonial law after the promulgation of grace is a mortal sin, yet in the Romans commentary, he describes it is a present spiritual benefit.

The conflicting visions of the ceremonial law that emerge from Romans and Galatians amount to what might be called rival versions of the fulfillment of the ceremonial law. On the one hand, Aquinas's Romans commentary represents a view of fulfillment that emphasizes the ongoing theological significance of Judaism; the law is "fulfilled and upheld." On the other hand, the Galatians commentary represents a view of fulfillment that could be referred to as "fulfilled, destroyed, and deadly." In this latter form of fulfillment, the Jewish Law is declared as superfluous, destined to expire, and then deadly to anyone who observes the rites in the era after grace.

7

The Replacement of Israel as *Societas Sanctorum* (Ephesians)

IN THE EPHESIANS COMMENTARY, Aquinas views Israel as a "society of the saints" that enjoyed special election as God's people. However, in ways similar to the Galatians commentary, Aquinas describes the ceremonial law as "destroyed" after the passion of Christ. In the Ephesians commentary, Christ is described as the one who destroys the Law rather than the Apostle Paul. Aquinas argues that Christ brings about a convergence between Jews and Gentiles by destroying the ceremonial law and uniting the two groups together into one body, the Church, the true heir of Israel's promises. For this reason, the Ephesians commentary reveals that, for Aquinas, the replacement of Israel with the Church is the result of Christ's fulfillment and cancellation of the ceremonial law.

1. PRIMARY THEME AND DIVISION OF THE EPHESIANS COMMENTARY

In Aquinas's view, Paul's intention in writing the letter is strengthening the faith of the Ephesian believers.[1] He selects Psalm 75:4, "I have strengthened its pillars," as the interpretive key verse of the letter in order to empha-

---

1. *Ad Eph. Prologus* 1.

The Replacement of Israel as Societas Sanctorum (Ephesians)

size Paul's aim of building up ecclesial unity among Jews and Gentiles as one body.[2] For Aquinas, these "pillars" represent the Jewish and Gentile believers in the Church. Christ's establishment of unity between these two groups is the primary theme of the commentary.

Aquinas divides the six chapters of Ephesians into two parts: chapters 1 through 3 and 4 through 6. Overall, chapters 1 through 3 concern the divine blessings of God through which the Church's unity is established and preserved. Chapters 4 through 6 consist of Paul's admonishment to the Ephesians to maintain this unity. In chapter 2, Aquinas comments upon the effects of Christ's supreme power, including how it destroys slavery to sin and the alienation between Jew and Pagan. The result of Christ's power is that all races have access, by Christ, in the Spirit, to the Father. As Christopher Baglow has observed, for Aquinas, the relationship between Jewish and Gentile Christians becomes the major theme of chapter 2 but also serves as a concrete pole that bounds his exposition of the entire letter.[3] Chapter 2, as well as chapter 3, lecture one, contains the majority of Aquinas's comments on the ceremonial law and the Jews and Gentiles before and after their convergence in the Church.

2. PAUL'S JEWISH "NATIONALITY"

In the first lecture, Aquinas begins by commenting upon Paul's identity as a Christian in religion (*religio*) and a Jew in nationality (*nation*). Aquinas's opening comments on Paul's identity indicate that the theme of Jew and Gentile is a prominent one throughout the commentary. As I argue below, these two aspects of Paul's identity seem to correspond to the Gentile Christian and Jewish pillars of the Church: "Of the church at Ephesus he rightfully can claim: 'I have strengthened its pillars'—I who am an Israelite in nationality, a Christian in religion, an Apostle in dignity."[4] Paul's identity as "Israelite in nationality" and Christian in religion functions as a sort of microcosm of the Jewish and Gentile Ephesian believers and foreshadows the sort of convergence these two groups will exhibit when they are unified by Christ into one body.

Although Aquinas refers to Paul's Christian religion and his Jewish nationality as present parts of his identity, he is also careful to guard against

---

2. *Ad Eph.* Prologus 1.
3. Baglow, "*Modus Et Forma*," 165.
4. *Ad Eph.* 1.1.1.

the idea that Paul's Judaism is from any observance of the ceremonial law. Citing 2 Corinthians 11:22, Aquinas says that Paul is a Jew by birth because he "sprung from Abraham's seed in the tribe of Benjamin."[5] The caveat he adds to this citation hints at what sort of Judaism Aquinas imagines to exist in the Church in the age of grace. Although Paul is a Jew by birth, his Christian faith also means he is dead to the Law: "A Jew by birth, 'for I am an Israelite sprung from Abraham's seed.' . . . A Christian in religion, 'for I, through the Law, am dead to the Law, that I may live to God . . . .'"[6] For Aquinas, Paul's Judaism is a nationality and not a religion. It is based on his birth but no longer has anything to do with the observance of the Law. Aquinas's view of Paul's Judaism seems as if it is an extension of the picture of the Apostle's identity that emerged from the Galatians commentary: Paul is viewed as having been called out of the synagogue to faith in Christ, no longer observing the rites of the Law after conversion.

In addition to Judaism as a nationality, Aquinas also mentions a second attribute of Paul's Judaism. Paul's Judaism is also characterized by the contemplation of God: "Everyone who proclaims saving wisdom, like Paul, must be an Israelite in his contemplation of God, a Christian in his religious faith, an Apostle in his function's authority."[7] Although Aquinas views Paul as having left the works of the Law behind, he maintains a twofold connection to Paul's Judaism through the idea of "nationality" as well as the "contemplation of God."

Aquinas therefore posits a sort of nonreligious Judaism that is independent of the Law. Aquinas's view of Paul's identity may suggest a sort of archetype for the particular type of Jewish Christians he envisions as so crucial to the unity of Jew and Gentile discussed in the Ephesians commentary. Aquinas will eventually argue that Jews are built along with Gentiles as two walls of the temple that is the body of Christ.

Therefore, in the Ephesians commentary, Aquinas seems to articulate a different type of Jewish Christian than the Jewish Christian (or "Church of the Jews") presented in the Galatians commentary. The Jewish believers in Christ of Galatians observed the Law but these Christians were destined not to endure after the expiration of the Augustinian middle period.[8]

---

5. *Ad Eph.*, 1.1.1.
6. *Ad Eph.*, Prologus 1.
7. *Ad Eph.*, Prologus 1.
8. Recall Aquinas's view of the Church of the Jewish believers in Galatians: "Now the reason why the custom prevailed in the early Church for those in the Church of the

The Replacement of Israel as Societas Sanctorum (Ephesians)

However, as I show below, the Jewish believers in Christ in the Ephesian Church are united to the Gentile believers and both are viewed as central to the formal cause of the Church being unified and increasing. Nevertheless, it is important to first discuss Aquinas's view of the state of the Jews before their convergence into the body of Christ and then return to these different views of the importance of Jewish Christians.

3. THE CONVERGENCE OF JEWS AND GENTILES INTO THE TEMPLE OF CHRIST'S BODY

In chapter 2, Aquinas comments on how Paul expounded upon the convergence of the Jews and Gentiles and their assimilation into Christ's body. Before touching upon the blessings of the unity established between Jews and Gentiles by Christ, he outlines the condition of both groups before their conversion.

The Sinful Condition of Jews and Gentiles before their Convergence

For Aquinas, Paul taught that Jews and Gentiles were in a state of "sin and paganism" before they received the blessings of Christ.[9] All are under sin. Yet Aquinas explains that the Jews and Gentiles were in a state of sin in different ways.[10] According to Aquinas, Paul designated two causes for Gentile sin. Gentiles were in sin because of "worldly causes," and because of the demons they worshiped. These demons tempt "the children of despair" away from faith in eternal realities. While the Gentiles sin from both worldly causes and the worship of idols, Jews sin only from worldly causes.[11]

The worldly causes of sin affecting both groups are threefold: sins of the heart, sins of action, and original sin.[12] The "sins of the heart" con-

---

circumcision to sell their goods and not those in the Church of the Gentiles was that the believing Jews were congregated in Jerusalem and in Judea, which was soon to be destroyed by the Romans, as later events proved. Hence the Lord willed that no possessions were to be kept in a place not destined to endure. But the Church of the Gentiles was destined to grow strong and increase, and therefore, by the inspiration of the Holy Spirit, it came about that the possessions in it were not to be sold." *Ad Galatas* 2.2.75.

9. *Ad Eph.* 2.1.72.
10. *Ad Eph.* 2.1.80.
11. *Ad Eph.* 2.1.80.
12. *Ad Eph.* 2.1.80.

sist of the "carnal desires of our flesh" by which Aquinas means "inner concupiscence."[13] The "sins of action" are "nothing else than a manifestation" of the sins of the heart, or inner concupiscence.[14] The last worldly cause of sin is original sin, and Aquinas thinks Paul hinted at this with the phrase "and we were by nature children of wrath."[15] Both Gentile and Jew suffer from original sin.[16] However, the Jews enjoyed cleansing from original sin through circumcision. In the Ephesians commentary, Aquinas states his early view on circumcision: it instrumentally cleansed the individual from original sin. He does not specify, as he does in his mature thought, that the cleansing power of circumcision comes *only* because implicit or explicit faith in Christ.[17]

Israel as a *Societas Sanctorum* and Gentiles as Strangers to the Promises

When Aquinas comments upon Paul's words that the Gentiles were formerly at a disadvantage because they were alien to "Israel's way of life" he takes the time to outline the good things of Israel in which the Gentiles had

---

13. *Ad Eph.* 2.1.81.

14. *Ad Eph.* 2.1.82: These sins of action amount to "doing what the flesh delights in" especially in food, and sexual relations. Another manifestation of the sin of action is in the thoughts or appetitve faculty of the soul. The sins of action in the appetitve faculty include: ambition for honors and for one's own excellence.

15. *Ad Eph.* 2.1.82.

16. *Ad Eph.* 2.1.82.

17. In Valkenberg's concise words this "latter" view was that "the sacraments of the Old Law *cannot* be said to cause grace by themselves, but only as much as they prefigure Christ." The late view appears in *Summa theologiae* III 62.6 ad 3; 70.4 and *ad Romanos* 4.2. As far as I can see, the late view includes two changes to the early view. As Richard Schenk has noted, Aquinas's late view is "that the rite was . . . like non-covenantal religious practices, at best an occasion of the implicit (or even explicit) faith in Christ. It was by this Christological faith alone that the rite of circumcision had mediated grace . . . ." The second point was made clear for me by Andrew Hofer: "Aquinas ascribes to the sacrament of circumcision the grace that removes all sin and enables one to resist all sin." Aquinas's early view (*Libri Sententiarium* IV d. 8, q. 1, a. 2, qua. 5) was that circumcision removed original sin in and of itself. Valkenberg writes, "Old Testament circumcision removes original sin and is a sign of Christian spiritual circumcision. It is not just a sign of future removal of sin, it is not only valued as a prefiguration of the Christian dispensation, but it really removes original sin even before the passion of Christ." Andrew Hofer, "The Circumcision of the Lord," 259–78. See Schenk, "Covenant Initiation, 555–93. Valkenberg and Schoot, "Thomas Aquinas and Judaism," 58–59.

The Replacement of Israel as Societas Sanctorum (Ephesians)

no share. In doing so, Aquinas positively affirms the covenants of Israel as the promises of God in very much the same way that he does in the Romans commentary. However, it should become clear as the chapter unfolds, that the positive affirmation of the covenants of Israel as the promises of God fade after the passion, and are ultimately relativized when their election is described only as something formerly held.

Paul "recounts the good things" of which the Gentiles were deprived. Overall, in their sinful state the Gentiles were deprived of two things: 1) a "share in the sacraments," and 2) a "knowledge of God."[18] According to Aquinas, the greatest injury the Gentiles suffered was their ignorance of the knowledge of God.[19] However, Aquinas only mentions the former deprivation in passing. He spends more time lecturing upon "three sacraments" of Israel that the Gentiles did not have.[20] When Aquinas uses the term *sacramenta* in the context of the Old Law, he is usually referring to circumcision.[21] But here, Aquinas employs the term in a broad way that includes both the promises of the old and new covenants.

18. *Ad Eph.* 2.3.105.

19. *Ad Eph.* 2.3.107. Aquinas is careful to maintain a distinction between the natural knowledge of God and the knowledge of God that we have by faith: "'And without God in this world' means without the knowledge of God. 'God has shown himself in Judah' (Ps 76:2), but not among the Gentiles: 'Not in the passion of lust, like the Gentiles that do not know God' (1 Thes 4:5). This must be understood of the knowledge obtainable through faith, for Romans 1 (21) speaks of their natural knowledge: 'Although they knew God, they neither glorified him as God nor give him thanks.'" He also asserts, however, in *Ad Hebraeos*, that such Gentile knowledge of God is only a knowledge of God from God's effects. God "is not able to be comprehended by a creature except through His effects." *Ad Heb.* 9.1.422.

20. Aquinas's positive description of Israel's sacraments is reminiscent of the treatment of the prerogatives in *Ad Romanos* 3.1.

21. Cf. *Ad Romanos* Prol. 12 and *Ad Galatas* 1.1.2. In Ia-IIae q. 101.4, Aquinas's use of *sacramenta* usually occurs, in the context of the Old Law, as one aspect of the ceremonial law. He divides the ceremonies of the Old Law into four categories: 1) *sacrificia* or sacrifices; 2) *sacra* or sacred things; 3) *sacramenta* or sacraments; and 4) *observantiae* or observances. All of these categories are referred to together as *caeremoniae veteris legis*. The 1) *sacrificia* include sacrificial animals offered by the Levite priesthood. 2) *Sacra* include instruments such as the temple, tabernacle and the vessels. 3) *Sacramenta* include circumcision, "without which no one was admitted to the legal observances" (102.5) and the eating of the paschal banquet. Aquinas actually refers to the paschal banquet as an observance but it is treated in the same article on sacraments, indicating that the Passover, for him, may fit into both *sacramenta* and *observantiae* categories. 4) *Observantiae* mostly refers to dietary regulations, which include the prohibition of blood and fat of animals. According to Aquinas, the latter two precepts, which are the 3) sacrament of circumcision and 4) observances both function together to consecrate the Jewish people

The first sacrament of Israel the Gentiles lacked was the "promise of a Christ." Though he does not use the term covenant, Aquinas seems to have in mind the Davidic covenant.[22] Here, Aquinas does *not* define the promise of Christ as Abraham's seed as he did in the Galatians commentary. Rather he treats Abraham's promise as a third and separate sacrament that I will outline below.

The second sacrament seems to consist of two covenants enjoyed by Israel, or the people whom he refers to as a *societas sanctorum* or "society of the saints." Aquinas takes note of the fact that Paul refers to testaments in the plural and chooses to interpret this as meaning the old and the new covenants: "He says testaments in the plural since the old testament was offered to the Jews and the new was promised."[23] When Aquinas cites Sirach 44:25, he makes clear that the first covenant of the second sacrament of Israel is the old covenant established by God: "The Lord made his covenant rest upon the head of Jacob" which he says, "can be understood of the old testament."[24] Throughout this section of his commentary, Aquinas insists upon pointing toward the old covenant in a way that emphasizes the Jews as God's elect people. He cites Deuteronomy 7:2–3 "You shall not make any league with them, nor show them mercy. Neither shall you make marriages with them."[25] Aquinas then cites John 4:9: "Jews do not communicate with Samaritans" to reinforce that no other people were chosen from among the nations in this way. Aquinas says that Gentiles were deprived because they were not part of this society and did not enjoy its covenants.[26] Even Gentile proselytes were still not considered to have equal citizenship, since, if they became proselytes of this society, they were accepted to partake of God's covenants as "strangers of the testaments" rather than as citizens.[27]

Aquinas mentions the second covenant of the second sacrament of Israel when he cites Baruch 2:35, "And I will make an everlasting covenant

---

to the worship of God. Indeed, in Ia-IIae q. 102.6 Aquinas affirms the literal, rational cause for the *observantiae* of the Law as "a special prerogative of that people." All of these precepts are ceremonial in character in the sense that they give public expression to divine worship.

22. *Ad Eph.* 2.3.106. Aquinas references Jeremiah 23:5: "I will raise up for David a just branch; and a king shall reign and shall be wise."

23. *Ad Eph.* 2.3.106.
24. *Ad Eph.* 2.3.106.
25. *Ad Eph.* 2.3.106.
26. *Ad Eph.* 2.3.106.
27. *Ad Eph.* 2.3.106.

The Replacement of Israel as Societas Sanctorum (Ephesians)

with them," and then Romans 9:4 to connect this promise to the Israelites: "the latter [or new covenant] was granted to those 'to whom belong to the adoption as children, the glory and the giving of the Law.'"[28] Thus far, Aquinas has identified two of three sacraments of Israel to which Gentiles did not have access.

The third sacrament that the Gentiles were deprived of is what Aquinas refers to as "another blessing" for Israel.[29] Aquinas then references Paul's words that the Gentiles had no "hope of the promise," which he defines as "the hope of future goods."[30] Aquinas then cites Galatians 3:16, "To Abraham were the promises made and to his seed."[31] This hope of the promise of future goods is Abraham's seed.

What Aquinas does not say about Abraham's seed is significant. Aquinas's use of the Galatians 3:16 reference to God's promise to Abraham's seed is different than his use of the same verse in the Galatians commentary. In the Galatians commentary the promise to Abraham's seed is defined exclusively as the promise for the new covenant justification of all peoples in Christ.[32] In the Ephesians commentary, however, the promise for Christ is not associated with Abraham but with the Davidic covenant and promise for a King. The new covenant is listed as a distinct sacrament (the second sacrament of Israel) from the promise to Abraham's seed (third sacrament of Israel). Aquinas's choice to distinguish between Abraham's promise of future goods and the new covenant despite his appeal to the Galatians 3:16 text is one sign that in the Ephesians commentary there is more interest in

---

28. *Ad Eph.* 2.3.106. Here, Aquinas reads Romans 9:4 as an exclusive reference to the new covenant promised to Israel and not the old. Aquinas's use of the Romans 9:4 text in the Romans commentary differs from his use here. In the Romans commentary, he not only mentions Israel's "sonship" or adoption, and the glory, and giving of the Law, but he also mentions the "covenant." Secondly, in the Romans commentary he offers two definitions of this covenant that indicates it can be either the new or the old covenant: "the covenant [is] the pact of circumcision given to Abraham, as is recorded in Gen. 17, although this could be referred to the new covenant first preached to the Jews."

29. *Ad Eph.* 2.3.106.

30. *Ad Eph.* 2.3.106.

31. *Ad Eph.* 2.3.106.

32. Aquinas also does this in III 70 a. 1–2. Valkenberg summarizes Aquinas's view from this question of the promise made to Abraham as a promise for Christ: "Through circumcision Abraham differentiated himself as a believer from the non-believers, moving out from his homeland and his family, on the promise of God that in and through his offspring, which is Christ, all nations of the earth would be blessed." Valkenberg, "Aquinas and Judaism," 58.

God's multiple promises to Israel—an interest that was absent in both the Galatians and Hebrews commentaries.

In the Ephesians commentary, Paul's language about the Gentiles living as strangers of the plural promises and covenants seems to influence Aquinas to explore multiple possibilities of the literal sense of the promise to Abraham. Aquinas adopts a more expansive view of Israel's covenants that includes affirmation of aspects of the literal meaning of the covenants: enclosing Israel in the knowledge and worship of the one God. God's promises and covenants to Israel are not limited exclusively to a Christological interpretation. This is not to say that Aquinas thinks that the covenant with Abraham does not also prefigure Christ or is something separate from the future and eternal good that is Christ. It is to say that, here, Aquinas affirms the promise of Christ as a Davidic promise to Israel without replacing the literal meaning. The sacraments of Israel, the society of saints, are presented as a matrix of God's covenants that include the explicit promise of Christ's kingdom, the benefits of the Old Law, the promise of a new covenant, and undefined "future goods" for Abraham's seed.

However, as I show below, Aquinas highlights the special election of the Jew not because his aim is to offer a treatment of the multiple literal meanings of God's promise to Abraham. Rather, his main intention is to follow what he views as Paul's teaching on how Christ unifies these two estranged groups that are Jews and Gentiles and the idea that the Law, which separated these two peoples, is destroyed by Christ.

Christ's Abolishment of the Ceremonial Law

In addition to presenting the conditions of Jew and Gentile before faith in Christ, Aquinas also treats of the justification of Jews and Gentiles and the blessing of being assimilated into Christ.[33] After discussing the blessing of justification, Aquinas moves on to treat how such justification overcomes hostility and establishes unity between Jews and Gentiles.[34]

---

33. *Ad Eph.* 2.2.88.

34. God's mercy is the efficient cause of the blessing of justification. The exemplary cause of the blessing of God's mercy is the life of Christ. Aquinas then explains that the final cause or purpose of the blessing granted in Christ for Jews and Gentiles can be taken in two ways, depending upon how one interprets "ages to come." Aquinas says the phrase "age to come" can mean "in this age" or "the one to come." If one takes it to mean "this age," the text means God shows the blessings of Christ in the age to come by giving gifts of grace to the early saints in order that "later generations would more easily

The Replacement of Israel as Societas Sanctorum (Ephesians)

Aquinas understands Paul to show how Gentiles "have converged with the Jewish people" and "are drawn close to God."[35] The Gentiles are now partakers of the goods previously denied them. These goods include the covenants that consisted of Israel's way of life. Because of the blessing of the grace of justification, Gentiles now participate and share in the covenants of Israel not as strangers but citizens.[36] Aquinas then outlines the 1) cause, 2) method, and 3) purpose of the convergence of Jew and Gentile.

As he proceeds to discuss these elements of how the Gentiles "share" in the covenants with the Jews, it becomes increasingly clear that Aquinas means "share" in covenants with Jewish believers in Christ. He does not address the theological status of Israel's way of life in the era after grace, amidst the building up of the spiritual edifice of the Church. As he describes the deconstruction of the ceremonial law and the building of the walls of the Church, the *societas sanctorum* fades out of view and is replaced by the new community of believers.

First, the cause of the convergence of the Jew and Gentile is Christ, who Aquinas says, is the cause of peace. When commenting upon Paul's phrase, "For he is our peace, who has made both one," Aquinas says "this is an emphatic way of speaking to better express the reality, as though he said: 'Rightly do I say that you are drawn near each other, but this occurs through Christ since he is the cause of our peace.'"[37] The result of this convergence is that Christ made both Gentiles and Jews one: "he has made both one, joining into unity both the Jews who worshiped the true God and the Gentiles who were alienated from God's cult."[38]

Next, Aquinas spends a great deal of time explaining the method of convergence of Jew and Gentile, which is indicated by Paul's words "breaking down the middle barrier of partition."[39] Christ's method in unifying Jews and Gentiles in one body involves "removing what is divisive" or that

---

be converted to Christ." However, the final cause or purpose of the blessing of God can also be taken to mean God's purpose in showing the "abundant riches of his grace." This mercy even exceeds the mercy and grace God has bestowed in the world in the interim. God's purpose in the blessing of the grace of justification can therefore be to bring to perfection "the next life" or the eternal age. *Ad Eph.* 2.2.89–90.

35. *Ad Eph.* 2.4.110.
36. *Ad Eph.* 2.4.109.
37. *Ad Eph.* 2.5.111.
38. *Ad Eph.* 2.5.111.
39. *Ad Eph.* 2.5.112.

which prevented Jews and Gentiles from mixing together in the past.[40] Aquinas then presents an analogy in order to explain the phrase "breaking down the middle barrier of partition." Before Christ came this wall was a high barrier separating the two peoples:

> To understand the text we should imagine a large field with many men gathered on it. But a high barrier was thrown across the middle of it, segregating the people so that they did not appear as one people but two. Whoever would remove the barrier would unite the crowds of men into one multitude, one people would be formed.[41]

Aquinas's illustration provides a metaphor for why the ceremonial law is destroyed by Christ in the creation of the Church.

The field represents the world crowded with men, and the barrier that runs down this middle of the field of men is explained as the carnal observances of the Old Law: "the Old Law can be termed such a barrier, its carnal observances kept the Jews confined . . . ."[42] The people segregated by the observances are the Jews and Gentiles.

Aquinas gives two reasons why the carnal observances were a barrier of partition. First, Aquinas explains that Paul uses *paries maceriae* or "barrier of partition" and not a *paries muri* or a "wall," for a reason.[43] The Old Law was a barrier because it was not "mortared together with charity, which is, as it were, the cement unifying individuals among themselves and everyone together with Christ."[44] Rather, as Augustine holds, the Old Law is a law of fear that persuades by threats. Those who kept it, did so out of love "belonged by anticipation . . . to the New Testament which is the law of love."[45] It is for this reason that the barrier of partition was not meant to last permanently but only for a time: "A barrier of partition," says Aquinas, "is one in which the stones are not mortared together with cement; it is not built to last permanently but only for a specified time."[46]

In addition to the barrier as a metaphor for the ceremonial law that temporarily separated these two peoples, the barrier also prefigured Christ.

40. *Ad Eph.* 2.5.112.
41. *Ad Eph.* 2.5.112.
42. *Ad Eph.* 2.5.112.
43. *Ad Eph.* 2.5.113.
44. *Ad Eph.* 2.5.113.
45. *Ad Eph.* 2.5.113.
46. *Ad Eph.* 2.5.113.

The Replacement of Israel as Societas Sanctorum (Ephesians)

Aquinas writes, "Christ was figured (*figurabatur*) through the Old Law: 'Behold he stands behind our wall' (Cant. 2:9)."[47] "Christ, however, has put an end to this barrier," writes Aquinas.[48] Christ has made these two people one by the method of "breaking down the middle barrier."[49]

As he does in several places in the Pauline commentaries, Aquinas recognizes that the claim that the Law has been destroyed seems to be in tension with positive descriptions of the Law. It seems Paul's words "breaking down the barrier of partition" that is the ceremonial law appears contrary to Christ's own words about fulfilling but not destroying the Law in Matthew 5:17. He says, "A problem arises here since [Paul] says 'breaking down the barrier of partition' and, on the contrary, Matthew 5:17 states: 'Do not think that I have come to destroy the Law (*solvere legem*) or the prophets. I have not come to destroy, but to fulfill.'"[50]

Aquinas's reply explains the meaning of "fulfill" by relying upon the idea that the Law Christ said he did not come to destroy was the moral commandments: "I reply. The Old Law contained both moral and ceremonial precepts. The moral commandments were not destroyed (*non solvit*) by Christ but fulfilled in the counsels he added and in his explanations of what the Scribes and Pharisees had wrongly interpreted."[51] Christ fulfilled (*adimplevit*) the moral commandments when he said "your justice must abound more than the Pharisees" and then cites Christ's commandment to love enemies (Matt 5:43–44).

However, regarding the ceremonial precepts, Christ "fulfilled them with regard to what they prefigured." Christ's fulfillment of carnal Law added "what was symbolized to the symbol."[52] This fulfillment brings about the cessation of the literal meaning of the ceremonial law: "He abolished the ceremonial precepts with regard to what they were in themselves."[53] Christ breaks down the barrier of the Law in and of itself for a positive purpose: he destroys the enmity Aquinas says the commands caused between Jew and Gentile. Aquinas says, "It should be understood, therefore, that in saying breaking he refers to the observance of the carnal Law. To

---

47. *Ad Eph.* 2.5.113.
48. *Ad Eph.* 2.5.113.
49. *Ad Eph.* 2.5.113.
50. *Ad Eph.* 2.5.114.
51. *Ad Eph.* 2.5.114.
52. *Ad Eph.* 2.5.114.
53. *Ad Eph.* 2.5.114.

break down this barrier of partition is to destroy the hostility between the Jews and Gentiles."[54] The hostility was the result of anger and jealousy that had sprung up between these two peoples. By abolishing the carnal Law (*lex carnalis*) Christ has also abolished this animosity.[55] Christ, abolished this barrier in his incarnation and death. "In fulfilling the Old Testament figures, he killed the hostility that had arisen through the Law between Jews and Gentiles."[56]

The result of the destruction of the barrier of partition is that all the sacrifices "were fulfilled and came to an end."[57] "Christ was symbolized through the Old Law.... Christ, however, has put an end to this barrier . . . ."[58] Through the precepts of the New Testament "the law was cut off."[59] "It is as if Paul said: I affirm that Christ in his flesh was 'making void the law of commandments' as the imperfect is made void by the perfect and the shadow by the truth."[60] Faith in Christ is "the truth of those symbols."[61]

After discussing this method of the destruction of the carnal Law at length, Aquinas then treats the purpose of the convergence. Because Christ took the place (*succedens*) of the Law the two people can be reconciled into "one new man, making peace." The purpose of the convergence is the same as the purpose of the grace of justification: because Christ put an end to the barrier of the ceremonial law, "the Jews and Gentiles became one people."[62] This union is possible only because that which divided the two peoples has been destroyed: "since the law divided they could not be united in that

---

54. *Ad Eph.* 2.5.114.

55. Aquinas says Christ destroys the ceremonial law and not only the hostility between the Jew and the Gentile. Baglow's interpretation of Aquinas's view makes this point clear: "The barrier of religious custom, so often in human history a cause for division, is torn down by Christ who fulfills the end of religious custom by achieving what it attempted." Baglow, 176.

56. *Ad Eph.* 2.5.119.

57. *Ad Eph.* 2.5.114.

58. *Ad Eph.* 2.5.112.

59. *Ad Eph.* 2.5.115: "Et hoc *decretis*, id est, praeceptis novi testamenti, per quae excluditur lex." [Emended.] Lamb translates *excluditur*, which Aquinas uses only once in the commentary, as "was annulled" but a better translation may be "was excluded," "was cut off," or "was removed."

60. *Ad Eph.* 2.5.115.

61. *Ad Eph.* 2.5.116.

62. *Ad Eph.* 2.5.112.

law."⁶³ In Baglow's terms, the carnal Law posed a "dilemma" to the unity of the human race.⁶⁴

Throughout his description of Christ's abolishment of the carnal Law, Aquinas emphasizes the prefiguring function of the rites. This is clear from Aquinas's exposition of the symbolic meaning of the barrier of partition, as well as from his description of the "novelty" of Christ. Aquinas explains that this novelty, or newness, is expressed in both the manner of Christ's conception and his command "love one another as I have loved you."⁶⁵ The newness is also expressed in the grace he bestows, and Aquinas then cites Galatians 6:15: "neither circumcision nor uncircumcision has any meaning, but a new creature."⁶⁶ After the destruction of the Law, the grace of Christ renders circumcision superfluous.

4. THE FOUNDATION AND CONSTRUCTION OF THE TEMPLE OF CHRIST'S BODY

After indicating how the Gentiles have "been admitted to spiritual blessings together with the Jews" by the removal of the barrier, Aquinas says Paul goes on to teach that the new blessing enjoyed by the Gentiles is not of less eminence than the Jews.⁶⁷ Aquinas is referring to the share of blessings in Christ in the Church. Each group has "equal access to Christ's blessings." This is why Paul says that the Gentiles are "no more strangers and foreigners." Both are conformed to the whole Trinity and in no way lack a share in spiritual goods.⁶⁸ Aquinas explains this equal access by drawing upon two analogies used for the growth and increase of the faithful in Scripture: the Church as a building with Jews and Gentiles as its two walls.

To understand Paul's words that Gentiles are no longer strangers and foreigners to Israel's promises and covenants, Aquinas says one must realize "that the community of the faithful are sometimes referred to as a house in the Scriptures."⁶⁹ Aquinas briefly comments about the ways in which a

---

63. *Ad Eph.* 2.5.116.
64. Baglow, *Modus et Forma*, 174.
65. *Ad Eph.* 2.5.116.
66. *Ad Eph.* 2.5.116.
67. *Ad Eph.* 2.6.122.
68. *Ad Eph.* 2.6.123.
69. *Ad Eph.* 2.6.124.

Church can be compared to a city and a house.[70] But he spends more time commenting upon how the Church is a "building" (*aedificium*) and his use of this metaphor makes clear his view of the promises of Israel after the passion of Christ in the Ephesians commentary.

Aquinas's treatment of the building metaphor expresses well the theme of unity in the Ephesians commentary. Aquinas understands Paul to teach that the Ephesians can be likened to a building or *aedificium*, based on Paul's words, "built upon the foundation of the Apostles."[71] In Aquinas's view, Paul's use of the metaphor is meant to clarify his teaching about how the Church is constructed. This "building" consists of two key parts, a foundation and two walls.

First, Aquinas explains what he terms the primary and secondary foundations of the building.[72] The secondary foundation of the building is made up of the apostles of the new covenant and the prophets of the old covenant. It becomes clear as Aquinas explains the relationship between these two pieces of the secondary foundation that Aquinas thinks that the entity formed by God's commanding (Old Law given through prophets) and God's helping grace (New Law given through apostles) is the Church. He even correlates prophets and apostles as they relate to the prefigurement of Christ in Israel's worship and Christ's fulfillment of that worship as proclaimed by the apostles. Aquinas writes, "What the prophets foretold was to come, the apostles proclaimed as accomplished."[73] There is a unity or "harmony between the two"[74] that is clearly Christological. Each relates to Christ through their respective function of either prefiguring Christ or announcing Christ's fulfillment of the figure. The one who was to come, or the truth of the figure, is therefore the primary or "principal foundation" that supports and unites the prophets and apostles.[75] For Aquinas, the foundation of the Church is the unity of Israel's Law and the apostles preaching

---

70. Aquinas briefly comments upon how the Church is like a city in its public acts of faith, hope, and love, and how it is like a home in that it is ruled by the Father. He quotes 1 Timothy 3:15: "that you may know how to behave thyself in the household of God, which is the church of the living God." At other times the community of the faithful (*collegium fidelium*) is called a city, and Aquinas cites Psalm 121:3: "Jerusalem, which is built as a city."

71. *Ad Eph.* 2.6.126.
72. *Ad Eph.* 2.6.126.
73. *Ad Eph.* 2.6.128.
74. *Ad Eph.* 2.6.128.
75. *Ad Eph.* 2.6.129.

The Replacement of Israel as Societas Sanctorum (Ephesians)

as these relate to Christ's coming or having come. The reason why Christ is "called a cornerstone" is precisely on account of the convergence of both [Jews and Gentiles]. He writes, "As two walls are joined at the corner, so in Christ the Jewish and Gentile peoples are united."[76] This building grows into a "holy temple" when the number of the disciples multiplies greatly as it did in Acts 6:7 and when its members make progress in good works. However, the "perfection and completion" is achieved when the two walls of the temple, Jews and Gentiles, "are built together," into a holy temple.[77] This takes place through what Aquinas describes as a sharing in the covenants and promises of Israel.

5. THEY WERE SET APART: THE SPECIAL ELECTION OF ISRAEL AS A THING OF THE PAST

When Aquinas comments upon Paul's statement that the Gentiles are now "fellow heirs" he returns once again to the subject of Israel's threefold sacraments but this time uses the term "prerogatives" to describe the three sacraments of the Jews, and how these have now also been received by Gentiles.[78] When Aquinas says Jews share the covenants and are co-partners with Gentiles, he means Jewish believers in Christ. However, unlike his view of the prerogatives in the Romans commentary, Aquinas describes the prerogatives of the Jews in the past tense, as things the Jews formerly held. Aquinas begins by saying, "it should be recognized that the Jews enjoyed three prerogatives with respect to the Gentiles."[79]

The first prerogative he mentions is justification through faith: "*they had* the promised inheritance: 'For not through the Law was the promise to Abraham or to his seed, that he should be heir of the world; but through the justice of faith' (Rom. 4:13)."[80] The third sacrament mentioned above which pertained to the promise to Abraham is defined here only according to Romans 4:13 as the justice brought by Christ. The second prerogative of the Jews is their special election. "Another [prerogative] *was* their special

---

76. *Ad Eph.* 2.6.129.

77. *Ad Eph.* 2.6.132.

78. Aquinas uses "prerogatives" to reference his earlier discussion of the three sacraments of Israel. He therefore seems to use "sacraments," "promises," and "prerogatives" as interchangeable terms. See *Ad Eph.* 3.1.142

79. *Ad Eph.* 3.1.142.

80. *Ad Eph.* 3.1.142.

election, they *were* set apart from the Gentiles: 'The Lord thy God hath chosen thee to be his peculiar people of all peoples that are upon the earth' (Deut. 7:6)."[81] Finally, they had "the promise of Christ" and Aquinas then cites God's promise to Abraham in Genesis 12:3 that "in thee shall all the kindred of the earth be blessed."[82]

At one time, these three prerogatives were promises and covenants that the Jews had and that Gentiles did not enjoy. Aquinas reiterates this when he cites Ephesians 2:12, concerning the notion that the Gentiles were aliens and strangers.[83] However, Gentiles have now been made the co-heirs of the prerogatives, including the special election. The Gentiles "have received them," that is, received each prerogative by faith.[84] Again, Aquinas lists each prerogative received by the Gentiles. First, when Paul says that the Gentiles are "fellow heirs" (*cohaeredes*) with the Jews, this refers to the heavenly inheritance of justification by faith.[85] Next, and most importantly, when Paul says "of the same body" Aquinas says this refers to the fact that Gentiles are also fellow heirs to the election of "the chosen community of believers" (*speciale collegium fidelium*).[86] But Aquinas immediately states that this same body is "one body," by which he means the body of Christ. Third, Gentiles are admitted to a participation in the promised grace and this is clear from when Paul says they are "co-partners of his promise, the promises made to Abraham."[87] Gentiles have received justification, admission to the chosen community of believers, and because of this, they are co-partners of the promise. Though the language of fellow heirs and co-partners of the promise is employed, the society of the saints that is Israel is described as having had these promises in the past. The promises of Israel now belong to the community of believers. The inheritance has been passed along to the new community of those justified in Christ.

---

81. *Ad Eph.* 3.1.142. Aquinas's discussion of each of the prerogatives appears in a list of things they *held*. Lamb's translation emphasizes this.

82. *Ad Eph.* 3.1.142.

83. *Ad Eph.* 3.1.142.

84. *Ad Eph.* 3.1.142.

85. *Ad Eph.* 3.1.142.

86. *Ad Eph.* 3.1.142.

87. *Ad Eph.* 3.1.142.

The Replacement of Israel as Societas Sanctorum (Ephesians)

6. FULFILLED AND DESTROYED: THE ECONOMIC SUPERSESSIONISM OF THE EPHESIANS COMMENTARY

Aquinas's view of the Law in the Ephesians commentary shares characteristics with the commentaries on Hebrews, Romans, and Galatians. Ephesians is similar to the lectures on Hebrews and Galatians in its description of Christ's destruction of the ceremonial law. Aquinas insists that the ceremonial law is a barrier to the unification of Jew and Gentile. The destruction of the ceremonial law in Christ's immolated and resurrected Jewish flesh is the method by which Christ removes the barrier of the Jewish rites, overcomes hostility, and unites Jew and Gentile. The replacement of Israel with the church is the result of Christ's fulfillment and destruction of the ceremonial law. For this reason, the commentary clearly contains economically supersessionist view of the Jewish people.

However, Ephesians is similar to the Romans commentary in two ways. In the Ephesians commentary, Aquinas affirms the special election of Israel and melds the election with the covenants as promises from God. The special election of the Jewish people is a covenant or promise from God. He even refers to Israel as a *societas sanctorum*. Second, although Aquinas understands Christ as abolishing the ceremonial law, *he does not say* that the Law is now deadly or that its observance by Jews is a mortal sin, despite one of the most extended and detailed treatments of how Christ "tears down" the observances, as Baglow puts it. There is also no mention of the Augustinian middle period in Ephesians and in the Romans commentary.

The view of the ceremonial law after the passion of Christ in the Ephesians commentary can therefore be said to represent somewhat of a middle position between Aquinas's view in Romans and his view in Galatians and Hebrews. In the Ephesians commentary, the ceremonial law is *not* affirmed as "fulfilled and upheld" as it is in the Romans commentary, but it is also *not* declared "fulfilled, destroyed, and deadly" (i.e., Galatians and Hebrews). Rather, the view in Ephesians is that the ceremonial law is "fulfilled and destroyed" after the passion of Christ.

Nevertheless, Aquinas's argument that the passion of Christ fulfills and destroys the ceremonial law undermines 1) his positive affirmation of the special election of Israel as a promise of God as well as 2) his attempt to say how Jewish Christians exist as a second wall of the temple of the body of Christ.

Aquinas's argument that Christ has destroyed the ceremonial law, when considered in the context of two other claims, implies that God has broken God's promise to Israel to be a special people and has replaced the *societas sanctorum* with the community of believers who have received Israel's promised Christ. Aquinas's teaching that Christ completely destroys the ceremonial law, combined with his description of the Jews' special election as a thing of the past, and the notion that Jewish and Christian believers have received Israel's special election and promises implies that Israel is no longer the elect. Rather, the fellow heirs of the election are the Jewish and Christian believers united in the one body of Christ. After the passion of Christ, the body of Christ becomes "the chosen community of believers" (*speciale collegium fidelium*).[88] Taken together, these claims imply that the promise of the special election of Israel as a *societas sanctorum* now applies to the body of Christ.

Aquinas's teaching on the replacement of Israel with the Church also problematizes his comments upon the Jews and Christians of the Ephesian church as the two walls of the temple of Christ's body. When Aquinas refers to Jews and Gentiles as co-heirs of the promises, he means that there is now a convergence between Jewish believers in Christ and Gentile believers in Christ. These believing Jews and Gentiles are the elect co-heirs of the promises of Israel.

Yet it is not clear how the Jewish wall of the temple of Christ's body, which is built together with the Gentile wall, can be said to be a Jewish wall. It may seem that the Jewish Christians of Ephesians practice the Law but only during the middle period and without placing their hope in this Law—Aquinas chooses to adopt this view of the Jewish Christians in the Galatians commentary.

But such a middle period is absent in the Ephesians commentary. The Jewish Christian described in the Ephesians commentary is foundational to the unity and growth of the Church. The Jewish Christians of Ephesians are described as a fundamental aspect of the Church's very construction and growth as they are united together with Gentiles into one body.

In the Galatians commentary, on the other hand, Aquinas adopts Augustine's view that after the middle period expires, the observance of circumcision becomes deadly. The Jewish Christian of the Galatians commentary is not permanent. The Jewish Christian believers of Galatians, which he refers to there as the Church of the circumcision, or *ecclesia*

---

88. *Ad Eph.* 3.1.142.

The Replacement of Israel as Societas Sanctorum (Ephesians)

Iudaeorum fidelium (Church of the Jewish believers)[89] observe the Law and are viewed by Aquinas as "not destined to endure."[90]

When Aquinas speaks of the Jewish wall of the temple of Christ's body he does *not* have in mind the Church of the circumcision of the Galatians commentary. If Aquinas did adopt the Galatians view of the Jewish Christian it would seem one wall of the temple of Christ's body was not destined to endure. In the Ephesians commentary, with its emphasis on the unity of Jewish and Christian believers in the Church, there is no discussion of how Jewish Christians could observe the Law without putting their trust in it, i.e., without sinning.

In what way then is the second wall of the temple of the body of Christ a Jewish wall in the Ephesians commentary? Aquinas's understanding of Paul's Jewish nationality may provide an answer to this question.[91] It seems that when Aquinas speaks of the Jewish Christian that exists as a permanent part of the Church of the Ephesians, he may have in mind the idiosyncratic Judaism he attributed to Paul at the outset of the commentary. Paul is only Jewish in "nationality" and "contemplation."[92] This odd view of Judaism is dead to the Law. It could be the case that for Aquinas, the Jewish believers of the Ephesian Church are also Jewish only "from birth" and no longer observe the ceremonial law since Christ destroyed this barrier.

Nevertheless, even if Aquinas's peculiar Pauline Judaism is shared by all the Jewish believers of the Ephesian Church, it is still not clear how the Jewish wall of the Church remains fundamental since it is not clear how one remains Jewish without the observance of the Law. Both versions of Aquinas's "Jewish Christian" seem impermanent. One is explicitly impermanent since the Law-observant Jewish believer of the Galatians commentary is permitted to observe the Law in the middle period but is not destined to endure. The other is implicitly impermanent since the nonobservant "Jewish" believer of Ephesians would, without the Law, soon be absorbed into the Gentile wall of the Church.

---

89. *Ad Galatas* 2.2.74–75.
90. *Ad Galatas* 2.2.75.
91. *Ad Eph. Prologus* 1.1.1.
92. *Ad Eph. Prologus* 1.1.1.

8

Rival Versions of Christ's Fulfillment of the Law

The Tension in Aquinas's Thought between Galatians 5:2 and Romans 3:1–2

A COMPARISON OF AQUINAS's thought on the ceremonial law after Christ in the commentaries with his teaching in the *Summa theologiae*[1] reveals a tension in his thought on the ceremonial law. The tension is caused by what Aquinas understands as a difficulty in Pauline statements concerning the value of circumcision after the passion of Christ. Aquinas understands the value of the ceremonial law after the passion of Christ to hang on whether Paul teaches that circumcision is "superfluous" for all in the era of grace (Gal 5:2) or "advantageous" (Rom 3:1-2) for the Jewish people. In the Romans commentary, Aquinas recognizes that Paul defends the Law as a spiritual benefit for Jews even after Christ, and uses this teaching to reject the traditional view in Ia-IIae q. 103 a. 4, and based in Galatians 5:2, that circumcision no longer has value for Jews.

---

1. English translations are from the Benziger edition unless otherwise noted. *Summa Theologica*, trans. Fathers of the English Dominican Province. Citations of the *Summa theologiae* will appear in the text and footnotes as: Ia-IIae q. 103.2 ad. 1, where "Ia-IIae" stands for *Prima Secundae* etc., "q. 103" stands for question 103, "2" for the article, and "ad." for "reply objection."

1. REVISITING THE DISCUSSION OVER THE QUESTION OF SUPERSESSIONISM IN AQUINAS'S THEOLOGY

In my analysis of the commentaries I asked whether Aquinas consistently teaches that the ceremonial law becomes *mortua et mortifera* or whether he attributes some sort of theological value to the rites after the passion of Christ? I discovered three views of fulfillment of the ceremonial law in the relevant Pauline commentaries: 1) fulfilled, destroyed, deadly (Hebrews and Galatians); 2) fulfilled and destroyed (Ephesians); and 3) fulfilled and upheld (Romans).

My study of Aquinas's commentaries on Paul supplies a perspective for comparing the *Summa theologiae* not only as it relates to the Romans commentary, which a few scholars have done, but also to the commentaries on Hebrews, Galatians, and Ephesians. Since my primary task in this chapter is a comparison of Aquinas's thought on the ceremonial law after Christ in the commentaries and the *Summa theologiae* it is necessary to briefly engage the three Thomists who have, with varying degrees of detail, commented upon the relationship between the *Summa theologiae* and Romans commentary.

Boguslawski, Marshall, and Levering on the Relationship between the Romans Commentary and the *Summa theologiae*

Although these scholars provide illuminating comparisons of the *Summa theologiae* and the Romans commentary they either 1) do not attend to the teaching in the *Summa theologiae* on the cessation of the ceremonial law or 2) overlook the particular point in Aquinas's teaching on the duration of the ceremonial law in the *Summa theologiae* that is in tension with his more positive teaching on the ceremonial law in the Romans commentary.

Boguslawski rightly argues that Aquinas's commentary on Romans 9 through 11 provides a positive view of the Jews and avoids Augustinian supersessionism, which he defines as the deconstruction of Israel's prerogatives to Christological prefigurements.[2] As I argued in chapter 5, Aquinas's view of the fulfillment of the ceremonial law in the Romans commentary can be referred to as "fulfilled and upheld." Nevertheless, while it is clear that this special delineation for the Jewish people exists in Aquinas's Romans commentary, it is not clear from Boguslawski's presentation how

2. Ibid., xv.

such delineation exists in the *Summa theologiae*, as he does not address Aquinas's teaching on the fulfillment and cessation of the ceremonial law after Christ in Ia-IIae q. 103.4. Although Boguslawski highlights positive aspects of Aquinas's views concerning the teaching on the Jewish people in the *Summa theologiae*, it is not clear that these aspects "overcome supersessionism." In fact, my below examination of the treatise on law demonstrates that Aquinas's teaching in the *Summa theologiae* actually strengthens Augustine's view that the Law is dead after the passion of Christ by buttressing it with Pauline authority.

Unlike Boguslawski, who views the relationship between the *Summa theologiae* and the Romans commentary as works of Aquinas that share complimentary views of Israel and the Law that avoid supersessionism, Marshall thinks the Romans commentary is in tension with the teaching on the ceremonial law in the *Summa theologiae*, which largely corresponds to what I have described above as the "fulfilled, destroyed, and deadly" view of the ceremonial after the passion of Christ. Nevertheless, he does not provide an in-depth analysis of Romans or demonstrate the source of the tension in these two works of Aquinas.

When it comes to explaining how the view of the positive language about the Jewish people in the Romans commentary is related to Aquinas's teaching in the *Summa theologiae*, Marshall and Boguslawski depart in significant ways. Whereas Boguslawski views the teaching in the *Summa theologiae* as complimenting the positive view of Jewish election in the Romans commentary, Marshall thinks that the teaching in the *Summa theologiae* actually undermines the positive view of Jewish election in the Romans commentary.

Both scholars overlook the particular point in Aquinas's teaching on the duration of the ceremonial law in the *Summa theologiae* that is in tension with his more positive teaching on the ceremonial law in the Romans commentary. Levering's view of the relationship between the *Summa theologiae* and the Romans commentary deserves more attention since he has treated the concept of fulfillment of the Old Law in Aquinas at length.

Levering on How Aquinas's Teaching on Christ's Fulfillment and Transformation of Israel's Law is Influenced by Pauline Texts

Levering has shown that the concept of the fulfillment of the Old Law plays an incredibly significant role in Aquinas's theology of salvation. He provides a helpful summary of the historical reasons why Aquinas attended to the Old Law and how he did so with originality. Drawing upon the work of M. D. Chenu and Beryl Smalley, Levering rightly explains that Aquinas's interest in the Mosaic Law was influenced by a "growing enthusiasm for the Old Law among medieval theologians."[3] Levering points out that one sign of the growing importance of the Old Testament is a shift that occurs in Aquinas's theology of salvation between his *Commentary on the Sentences* (1256) and his *Summa theologiae* (early 1270s).[4] Levering points out that there is almost no discussion of the Old Law in the *Sentences*. However, by the time Aquinas writes the *Summa theologiae* he includes a massive and detailed treatment of the Old Law.

Levering explains that Aquinas's treatment of the fulfillment of the Law in the *Summa theologiae* mirrors an important source: the *Summa Fratris Alexandri*. The *Summa Fratris Alexandri* proposes three classes of precepts: moral, judicial, and ceremonial. Each set of precepts functioned to "confer goodness in accord with the 'branches of charity': love of neighbor in the moral precepts; punishment of evildoers in judicial precepts; and preparation for worship of God in the ceremonial precepts."[5] Most significantly, argues Levering, the *Summa Fratris Alexandri* views each set of precepts as being fulfilled in different ways by Christ: Christ fulfills the moral laws by perfect knowledge of the good; perfect execution of the good; and perfect revelation of the good after the fall.[6] Christ fulfills the judicial laws by teaching not to resist evil rather than exacting retribution. Christ fulfills the ceremonial laws as the "end or term" of the ceremonial laws. In this way, Levering writes, Christ shows what they prefigure, and he manifests their inner meaning. Aquinas adopts from *Fratris Alexandri* the threefold division of the Mosaic Law and the claim that Christ fulfills the Law. However, Levering points out that the novelty of Aquinas's position is

---

3. This surge of interest lay in a number of factors, which include "combat with the Catharist heresy, which rejected the Old Testament, to the development of increasingly complex legal and political institutions." Levering relies upon Marie-Dominique Chenu, "The Old Testament in Twelfth-Century Theology." The *Summa Fratris Alexandri*, whose completion preceded the *Summa theologiae* by little more than a decade, influenced Aquinas's interest in the Old Law. The treatment of the Mosaic Law in the *Summa Fratris Alexandri* was a collaborative effort on the part of Franciscan theologians, among them Alexander of Hales and his students John of la Rochelle, and William of Middleton. Levering, *Christ's Fulfillment*, 6.

4. Ibid.

5. Ibid., 7.

6. Ibid.

that "Christ fulfills the Old Law *precisely* in his passion or suffering on the cross."[7] Christ's passion is the perfect and supreme act of obedience and that fulfills the Old Law.[8]

According to Levering, Aquinas's systematic exposition of Christ's fulfillment of the Law by the passion is influenced by his reading of Pauline texts. Indeed, Levering points out that the commentaries "assisted his mature theological expression."[9] Levering identifies the Commentary on John as an influence upon Aquinas's view, and Augustine's *Against Faustus* is identified as a key source.[10]

---

7. Ibid. [Emphasis added]

8. Levering shows how the fulfillment of the Law should be interpreted in light of Israel's threefold office of prophet, priest, and king. I unfortunately do not have the space to present Levering's detailed account of all the ways in which Aquinas understands the fulfillment of the Law in the *Summa theologiae*. It should suffice for my purposes to note that Christ's act of obedience in the passion is what fulfills the ceremonial precepts. Christ's act of obedience flows from the supernatural grace that infused Christ's soul at the moment of the hypostatic union. Levering explains that Christ's perfect act of obedience simultaneously fulfills all three aspects of the Old Law. Christ fulfilled the moral law because his perfect charity, displayed in his love of the Father and love of his neighbor. Christ perfectly fulfilled the ceremonial precepts in the self-sacrifice that he offered upon the cross. Finally, Christ perfectly fulfilled the judicial precepts by taking upon himself the suffering due to others. Ibid., 70–9.

9. Ibid., 8.

10. Ibid. Levering points out that although Aquinas commented upon Matthew, his treatment of Matthew 5:17 is lost. Levering also explains that "the *Catena Aurea* demonstrates that the key patristic source for Aquinas's theology of fulfillment is Augustine's *Against Faustus*, Book 19, to which his debt is enormous, although his thought develops rather than merely recapitulates Augustine's." Levering says that the view that the *Catena Aurea* is a major source is from Valkenberg, *Words of the Living God*, 188. Levering 150n38. *Catena Aurea*, vol. 1, St. Matthew, 170. However, Levering does not say how *Against Faustus* influences Aquinas, especially on the question of the cessation of the Law. He explicitly says Aquinas follows Augustine on the following: that the traces of martyrs' scars may remain in their resurrected bodies, 105; that sacraments are important for unity in religion, 121; the relationship between sacrifice and sin offering, 55–56; that Christ becomes sin and that Christ is a priest, 77; that God is author of Scripture, 90. Levering, *Christ's Fulfillment*, 150, fn. 39. The works of Augustine that Levering says Aquinas follows are cited throughout the above notes: *De Trinitate*, *De Civitate Dei*, *De Doctrina Christiana*. Despite *Against Faustus* being the key source, however, it is only mentioned there (150n.39). As I show below, one way in which *Contra Faustm* functions in Aquinas's view of fulfillment of the Law is the teaching in Ia-IIae q. 103.4 that the Law ceases after the passion of Christ. Another major influence is Augustine's debate with Jerome. Aquinas synthesizes Augustine's views from both of these works with his view of Paul's teaching in Galatians and Hebrews to say that ceremonial law is destroyed and deadly.

Rival Versions of Christ's Fulfillment of the Law

Although Levering does not explain exactly how the Pauline commentaries function in Aquinas's view of Christ's fulfillment of the Law, he does imply that the most determinative verse for Aquinas is Romans 3:31. In particular, Levering argues that Aquinas's interpretation of this verse in his Romans commentary influences his view of Christ's fulfillment of the Law. Levering points to Aquinas's interpretation of Romans 3:31 ("Do we then, destroy the Law through faith? God forbid! But we establish the Law."). Here, in the Romans commentary, Levering rightly sees that Aquinas interprets Romans 3:31 in light of Matthew 5:17 and understands it "to mean that the Mosaic Law is established (*statuimus*) by being perfected and fulfilled (*perficimus et adimplemus*) by Christ."[11]

Here, the first text that Levering points out as a Pauline source for Aquinas's view of the fulfillment of the Law is actually the same text (*Ad Romanos* 3.4.321) that I argued represented the positive view of fulfillment of the Law as "fulfilled and upheld."[12] In chapter 5 of this study, I argued that in the Romans commentary, Aquinas does not teach that the ceremonial law is destroyed, nor does he include the teaching that Jewish observance of the Law is now a mortal sin after the passion of Christ. Aquinas argues that Paul is faithful to Jesus' words in Matthew 5:18 ("Not an iota, not a dot, will pass from the Law."), and does not destroy the Law. "On the contrary," writes Aquinas, "we uphold the Law, i.e., by faith we complete and fulfill the Law, as Matt 5:17 says, 'I have come not to abolish the Law but to fulfill it.'"[13]

However, when Aquinas discusses Christ's fulfillment and cessation of the Old Law in the *Prima Secundae* he does not use either of these verses from Romans or Matthew. Indeed, Matthew 5:17 and Romans 3:31 are left out of Aquinas's treatment of the fulfillment of the Law in the treatise on law altogether.[14] I shall demonstrate below, the primary sources for Aquinas's view of the fulfillment and cessation of the Law in the treatise on law are Hebrews and Galatians. Aquinas's account of the fulfillment and cessation of the Law in the treatise on law is shaped *not* by the positive view

---

11. He cites *Ad Rom.* 3.4.321.
12. See chapter 5 of this study.
13. *Ad Rom.* 3.4.321.
14. As far as I can see, the only citation of Matthew is 5:11 and 5:22. Ia-IIae q. 100.3 "Blessed are ye when they shall revile you, etc."; Ia-IIae q. 100.9: "Whosoever is angry with his brother, shall be in danger of the judgment."

of fulfillment in Romans, but by the view that I referred to as "fulfilled, destroyed, and deadly."

Levering's account of the fulfillment of the Law does not include the more negative aspect of Aquinas's teaching. Levering claims that the Pauline texts teach that the Law is fulfilled and transformed and seems to avoid the more negative language of the Law in Hebrews.[15] This is clear from Levering's handling of the influence of both Hebrews and Galatians on Aquinas's view of fulfillment.

When discussing how Christ fulfills the Old Law as priest of Israel, Levering rightly points out that Aquinas follows the focus of Hebrews on how the passion takes place in "the context established by Israel's law." Christ, as God, who was already the principal legislator of the law of which Moses was the promulgator, "fulfills and transforms Moses' law." This perspective, according to Levering, is present in the *Summa theologiae*, as well as in Aquinas's commentary on Hebrews. However, Levering seems to avoid the fact that in the Hebrews commentary, Aquinas teaches that the Old Law is not fulfilled and transformed but fulfilled and rendered void.[16]

Indeed, the *cessatio legalium* (cessation of the Law) caused by Christ's fulfillment of these precepts is also included in Aquinas's teaching on the *Summa theologiae*. That the influence of this common medieval doctrine is overlooked in Levering's account of fulfillment becomes especially clear when one examines Aquinas's reliance upon Pauline texts from Galatians. In particular, Aquinas takes what he views as Paul's teaching on how the ceremonial law renders the grace of Christ of no benefit and synthesizes it with themes from Hebrews to support the common medieval doctrine of the *cessatio legalium* in Ia-IIae q. 103.4.

Levering understands this teaching from Galatians 5:2, which states, "If you receive circumcision, Christ will be of no advantage to you" to function as a teaching *only* for Jewish converts to Christianity and *not* Jews.[17] In a footnote he remarks that Aquinas does not take this verse to mean Jews should not observe the Law: "In this crucial discussion, Aquinas does not

---

15. Levering, *Christ's Fulfillment*, 54.

16. *Ad Hebraeos.* 7.3.361.

17. Levering, *Christ's Fulfillment*, 160n64. Levering mentions two other Galatians texts in two footnotes. He also understands Aquinas to follow Galatians 3:16 when Aquinas argues that the promise to Abraham signified the future birth of the Savior from among the descendants of Abraham. Ibid., 193, fn. 20. The third place Levering notes Galatians influence is when he rightly says that Aquinas frequently describes the Law "as a pedagogue" (he cites Ia-IIae, q. 91.5). Ibid., 193, fn. 24.

state, that Jews, who have not accepted Christ, sin by continuing to observe the Torah's ceremonial precepts."[18] As I briefly mentioned in chapter 6, which focused on the Galatians commentary, Levering misinterprets Aquinas's view of this text and in so doing, he misses how the text fundamentally influences Aquinas's view of Christ's fulfillment of the ceremonial law.

For Aquinas, Galatians 5:2 marks the middle period in which Israel's old sacraments become superfluous. Because Levering misses how this key text functions in Aquinas's account of fulfillment, he does not see why it is problematic on Aquinas's own terms to assert that the Jewish Law is "transformed," rather than abolished, after the passion.[19]

2. AQUINAS'S TEACHING ON THE CEREMONIAL LAW AFTER THE PASSION OF CHRIST IN THE *SUMMA THEOLOGIAE*

An examination of Aquinas's teaching on the ceremonial law after Christ in the *Summa theologiae* should provide a more comprehensive picture of Aquinas's thought on the ceremonial law after Christ and help clarify not only the source of the tension between his views of the ceremonial law, but the significance of the positive view of circumcision in the Romans commentary.

Because of the great size of Aquinas's treatment of the ceremonial law, my analysis must be limited to the same scope of inquiry that has guided the study throughout: whether the ceremonial law becomes expired and obsolete or retains a theological status after the passion of Christ. Aquinas addresses this question directly in Ia-IIae q. 103.1–4.[20]

---

18. Ibid., 161.

19. When commenting upon Christ's role of prophet, Levering writes, "Aquinas conceives of the content of the New Law as fulfillment, *not a destruction*, of the Old Law." "Christ *does not abolish* the commandments; rather, he shows how they can be truly obeyed in light of the supernatural destiny that he reveals." Ibid., 76. Levering reiterated this view of "fulfillment and not negation" in his recent essay on Aquinas's view of the Old Testament entitled, "Ordering Wisdom: Aquinas, the Old Testament, and Sacra Doctrina." He writes, "Christ's fulfillment of the Torah reveals the 'whole divine pedagogy of God's saving love.' Since this fulfillment is not a negation, the Old Testament remains 'a storehouse of sublime teaching on God and of sound wisdom on human life.'" See Levering, "Ordering Wisdom," 91.

20. As I explain below, Aquinas's treatment of the Old Law is the largest part of the treatise on law and contains some of the longest articles in the entire *Summa theologiae*. I do not have the space to discuss scholars who have commented upon the theological

The Setting of Aquinas's Treatment of the Ceremonial Law after the Passion of Christ in the *Summa theologiae*

M. D. Chenu observes that, towards the end of Aquinas's life, he became aware that the two forms of university teaching, *lectio* (commentary on texts) and *quaestio disputata* (disputed question), could not satisfactorily meet the requirements of theological education. According to Chenu, these two forms of teaching failed to provide beginning students with a *summa*, or summary of theology, which he defines as "organic presentation of the whole of sacred wisdom."[21] A *summa* consisted of a concise exposition of the teaching of theology adapted for students and constructed in a way that made clear "the internal relationships of the objects under consideration."[22] Like other medieval theologians, Aquinas sought to make clear the crucial interrelationship between the old and the new covenant in his *Summa theologiae*.[23] David Braine has observed that the opening of the *Summa theologiae* "makes it plain that Aquinas is speaking as a theologian, giving an exposition of sacred doctrine, intending to speak of the God of Abraham, Isaac and Jacob."[24] Aquinas consistently defended the claim that both testaments were from the good God of Israel and Father of Our Lord Jesus Christ.[25] Aquinas discusses the commandments of the good God of Israel

---

sources of the Old Law in relation to Paul in general. In my view, reading Aquinas's inaugural lectures is the best introduction to Aquinas's theology of the Old Law. For commentary on Aquinas's theology of the Old Law see the following sources. Levering, "Ordering Wisdom," 80–91. For scholarly comments on how Paul influences Aquinas's view of the Old Law in general see John Y. B. Hood, *Aquinas and the Jews*, and Jeremy Cohen, *Living Letters of the Law*. For scholarly treatments of how Paul influences Aquinas's theology in general see the following resources: The Proceedings of the IX Plenary Session of the Pontifical Academy of St. Thomas Aquinas, entitled, *Saint Thomas's Interpretation on Saint Paul's Doctrines*, 2009; Baglow, *"Modus et Forma"*; Valkenberg, *Words of the Living God*; Otto Pesch's classic lecture is also a good starting point: Pesch, "Paul as Professor of Theology."

21. Chenu, *Aquinas and His Role in Theology*, 137. That Aquinas is concerned to teach "beginners" is clear from the preface to the *Summa theologiae*.

22. Ibid., 137.

23. See Chenu, "The Old Testament in Twelfth-Century Theology"; Smalley "William of Auvergne, John of La Rochelle and St. Thomas Aquinas on the Old Law,"; Schenk, "Covenant Initiation," and "Views of the Two Covenants in Medieval Theology."

24. Braine, "Aquinas, God and Being," 1.

25. "The Old Law was given by the good God, Who is the Father of Our Lord Jesus Christ." Ia-IIae q. 98.2. In *ad Hebraeos* 1.1.19, Aquinas says Paul's words about how God spoke in "times of past" refers to the Old Testament, and that such divine speech rules out

Rival Versions of Christ's Fulfillment of the Law

in the context of his treatment of the interrelationship between Law and humankind's return to God as "destiny and goal" in the *Prima Secundae*.[26] It is within this overarching context of God's instruction of humankind through law in general that the first discussion of the ceremonial law appears in his treatise on law.[27]

The Old Law is only one form of law in the treatise on law.[28] However, even a cursory reading of the treatise makes clear that Aquinas exerts an enormous effort to explicate its details with great care. The discussion on the Old Law is comprised of a total of forty-six articles. Indeed, the number of articles on the Old Law exceeds the number of articles on eternal law, natural law, human law, and New Law, combined.[29] As noted by several scholars,

---

the view of the Manicheans: "By this he shows against the Manichaeans that the author of the Old and the New Testaments is the same." See also *Hic est Liber*, where Aquinas says the Old Law and the New Law bring life to humankind yet mediate that life in two ways. His view of the relation between the Old and New Law is held together by John 1:17: "Both of these" writes Aquinas, "are touched on in John 1:17: 'For the Law was given through Moses; grace and truth came through Jesus Christ.'" See *Hic est liber*, 2.

26. Chenu, *Aquinas and His Role in Theology*, 137. The *Prima Secundae* treats broadly of human actions in order to "know which ones lead us to happiness and which ones prevent our attaining it." Ia-IIae q. 6 Prol. The entire structure of the *Summa theologiae* reflects this broad theological vision of salvation history: the emanation of creatures from God and made in God's image in the *Prima Pars*; the return of creatures made in God's image in the *Prima Secundae* and *Secunda Secundae*; and the union of creation with Christ in the *Tertia Pars*.

27. Torrell, *Aquinas's Summa*, 33.

28. The treatise on law includes a discussion of four laws: 1) the eternal law, which is God's own wisdom or reason; 2) the natural law, which is the participation of creatures in eternal law; 3) the human law, which aids in specifying the natural law and establishes friendship among humankind; and 4) the divine Law, which establishes friendship between humankind and God. Aquinas divides divine Law into new and old, with the old coming through Moses to Israel, and new coming through Christ to both Israel and Church. Ia-IIae q. 91. See also Torrell, *Aquinas's Summa*, 34.

29. The other forms of law contain an average of three questions with four articles each. Aquinas devotes eight questions with a total of forty-six articles to the Old Law. My count of the articles in the treatise on law in the *Summa theologiae* is as follows: The eternal law contains three questions (q. 90–92), with a total of *twelve articles* distributed among the questions (q. 90.1–4; q. 91.1–6; q. 92.1–2). The natural law contains one question (q. 94) with a total of *six articles* distributed among the questions (94.1–6). The human law contains three questions (q. 95–97) with a total of *fourteen articles* distributed among the questions (q. 95.1–4; q. 96.1–6; q. 97.1–4). The Old Law contains eight questions (q. 98–105) with a *total of forty-six articles* distributed among the questions (q. 98.1–6; q. 99.1–6; q. 100.1–12; q. 101.1–4; q. 102.1–6; q. 103.1–4; q. 104.1–4; q. 105.1–4). The New Law contains three questions (q. 106–108) with a total of *twelve articles* distributed among the questions (q. 106.1–4; q. 107.1–4; q. 108.1–4).

the articles dealing with the ceremonial law in particular are some of the longest in the entire *Summa*.[30] The length of the articles on the ceremonial law suggests that Aquinas takes the history and purpose of the Jewish rites seriously.[31] As Jean-Pierre Torrell has observed, Aquinas examines the Law of Moses "in minute detail."[32] And yet, the length of the articles found in the Old Law may also indicate, as Michael Wyschogrod pointed out years ago, that Aquinas faced a degree of difficulty in his analysis of the Old Law: "The number of pages he devotes to the problem of the Old Law (over 150 in the *Blackfriars* edition) may signal a greater turbulence than appears on the surface."[33] In Ia-IIae q. 99 Aquinas undertakes a detailed treatment of the diverse precepts of the Old Law, which he divides into moral, ceremonial,

---

30. Hood, *Aquinas and the Jews*, 40; Wyschogrod, "A Jewish Reading," 126; Edward Synan, "Some Medieval Perceptions on Jewish Law," 120; Coolman points out that Ia-IIae q. 102.3 ad. 5 runs for more than 8,000 words. Coolman, "Christological Torah," 5.

31. A comparison of Aquinas and Kant on the significance of Jewish practices suggests there may be greater theological significance to Aquinas's efforts to ground Jewish rites in historical and theological ends in the treatise on law than has been realized. Kant saw the particularities of Jewish faith as a corruption of Christianity's universal nature, which was, in his view, rational religion. The idea that only one people would worship God seems to Kant unreasonable and against the true nature of the religion of reason. Immanuel Kant, *Religion within the Boundaries of Mere Reason*, 114. Kendall Soulen observes that, for Kant, "Christianity falls short of moral religion just insofar as it retains rudiments of Jewish belief, while it approximates to true religion just insofar as it breaks in principle with the Israelite dimension of traditional Christian faith. The true service of religion in the Christian church, therefore, consists in expelling the vestiges of Judaism from the body of Christian divinity. The task begun by the abolition of circumcision, the mark of Jewish flesh, must be completed by the abolition of the Hebrew Scriptures, the mark of the Jewish spirit." Soulen, *The God of Israel*, 57–68. As I show below, Aquinas resists the spiritualization of Judaism at its source, "the abolition of circumcision," when, in the Romans commentary, he argues for the permanent theological value of Jewish practice after the passion of Christ.

32. Torrell, *Aquinas's Summa*, 34. He also states that the treatise on the Old Law "deserves to be known better."

33. Wyschogrod, "A Jewish Reading of St. Thomas Aquinas," 126. Bourke and Littledale (the editors of the *Blackfriars* edition) of the volume on the Old Law, comment that the length of the articles shows that Aquinas "had to strain the characteristic 'article' structure almost to the bursting point." Unfortunately, however, they seem to attribute this difficulty to an inherent flaw in the Hebrew Bible: "[Aquinas] has, in fact, to some extent fallen victim to the intransigent untidiness of the Old Testament, which, as more recent scholars have increasingly come to recognize, is not so much a book as a bundle of traditions, heterogeneous in age, provenance and subject matter, which has been accumulated over many troubled centuries." Bourke and Littledale, introduction to Thomas Aquinas, *Summa Theologiae*, xxvi.

and judicial precepts. He takes up the discussion of the ceremonial law in Ia-IIae q. 101–3.

The *Cessatio Legalium* as a Crucial Concept in Twelfth-Century Accounts of Fulfillment

A more complete picture of Aquinas's notion of Christ's fulfillment and cessation of the Law in the treatise on law comes into view with the help of Chenu's historical treatment of twelfth-century medieval theological views of the relationship between the new and the old covenants.[34]

According to Chenu, the twelfth-century theological world understood fulfillment of the Old Law within a dialectic between the two poles: 1) continuity with the Old Law and 2) break with the Old Law.[35] Chenu explains that this century experienced an increasingly positive attention to figures in the old covenant and did not treat it as a bygone and defunct stage. Rather, theologians sought to elaborate upon how it might illuminate various aspects of Christendom.[36] It was thought that the new lies enveloped in the old and thus typological exploration of the old abounded.[37] Chenu explains that for these theologians, "History was thought to unfold as a divine plan and it contained stages whose continuity and breaks one had to observe with equal attention."[38] Attending to the two poles of what Chenu refers to as the "textual continuum" was "intrinsic to the progress of the economy of salvation, a progress that anticipated its final course through prefigurations of the future."[39] Continuity with biblical history

---

34. Chenu, "The Old Testament."

35. Ibid., 160.

36. Just a few of the examples Chenu offers are prophets as figures for the monastic life and old testament kings as ideas for the Christian prince. The true model of political society was furnished by the old testament: "It was clearly in the Old Testament that the crusade, that distinctive enterprise of all Christendom, found its inspiration, its basis, its rules, and all the ambiguities concerning worldly messianism that form a usual part of the imagery of prophetic books. The 'Lord of hosts' became not only the mystical but the earthly triumphant conqueror in that holy war." Ibid., 147; 150–1; 158.

37. Chenu: "More than the lifting of particular figures and ideas from the Old Testament, which the theology of the great masters balanced with texts from the New, was a whole manner of presenting arguments, a whole turn of style and thought, a whole cast of mind that revealed this envelopment of the New Testament in the Old—*Novum in veteri latet* (the New lies enveloped in the Old)." Ibid., 158.

38. Ibid., 160.

39. Ibid.

was encapsulated in Christ's words "I have not come to destroy the Law." And yet breaks with this same biblical history were encapsulated in Christ's words "but I say to you."[40]

However, increased attention to the old covenant was also accompanied by an awareness of progress. Among twelfth-century theologians there remained a "sufficient awareness" of what Chenu refers to as the "irreversible progress" of the new dispensation. Exemplifying this progress, according to Chenu, was the *cessatio legalium* (cessation of the Law) tradition that characterized the notion of fulfillment of Israel's Law. Chenu observes that fulfillment and cessation was expressed by a particularly common analogy of the Church displacing the synagogue:

> Men of the Middle Ages recognized and proclaimed the *cessatio legalium* (cessation of the Law). In contrast to the figure of Ecclesia with her open and radiant countenance stood the figure of *Synagoga* portrayed as a conquered queen, her crown fallen, her face veiled or her eyes blindfolded. This allegory popularized in art a theme found in polemics against the Jews; namely that the fulfillment offered by the New Covenant displaced the dead letter of the Law . . . as Gratian phrased it: "Under the Old Law many things were permitted which today have been abolished by the perfection of grace."[41]

The teaching on the *cessatio legalium* was, as Richard Schenk has pointed out, "almost universally affirmed by medieval Christian authors."[42]

Schenk points out that this teaching can be traced to the much-discussed controversy between Jerome and Augustine.[43] Schenk observes that the dispute between Augustine and Jerome on the cessation of the ritual law was, "a principal theological focus that fascinated and preoccupied medieval authors."[44] Indeed, "after the inclusion of the controversy by Peter Lombard in his Sentences," observes Schenk, "no Catholic theologian until Trent could easily pass over the questions framed by the patristic debate about the relationship of Christianity and Judaism."[45]

40. Ibid.
41. Ibid., 159.
42. Schenk, "Views of the Two Covenants," 895.
43. Ibid. The teaching can also be traced to Augustine's *Against Faustus* as well. Augustine mentions that these laws cease after the passion several times.
44. Schenk, "Views of the Two Covenants," 910.
45. Ibid.

Rival Versions of Christ's Fulfillment of the Law

Aquinas was very much aware of the teaching on the cessation of the Law as is evidenced by his own inclusion of a detailed description of the debate between Jerome and Augustine in both the Galatians commentary and the treatise on law in the *Prima Secundae*. Aquinas situates the debate precisely within his discussion of the duration of the ceremonial law and against the backdrop of Christ's fulfillment of the old sacraments in the context of salvation history.

Aquinas's Teaching on the Cessation of the Law in Ia-IIae q. 103

Aquinas's inclusion of the debate between Jerome and Augustine appears Ia-IIae q. 103. However, before examining question 103, it is necessary to highlight a theme that is especially prominent in articles 3 and 4, where Aquinas states that the ceremonial law is dead and deadly. Taking notice of the theme is important because it appears again in the Romans commentary, but Aquinas handles it differently.

Aquinas draws upon the debate between Jerome and Augustine to reconcile the apparent tension between biblical support for two contradictory ideas: the idea that the ceremonial law is permanent and the idea that the ceremonial law is impermanent or temporal. For Aquinas, the fact that the good God of Israel commanded the Law, and that Christ and the apostles observed this Law indicates the permanence of the Law.

On the other hand, he understands Paul to have taught that the Law as has no value after Christ and that it renders the justifying power of the passion void. Aquinas also understands the apostles to have affirmed this teaching at the Jerusalem conference. These texts indicate the impermanence of the ceremonial law.

These two pictures of the theological status of the ceremonial law after Christ appear in stated objections and in Aquinas's replies Ia-IIae q. 103.2–4. Texts that support the permanence of the Law are consistently cited in the objections. Texts that support cessation of the Law are consistently cited in Aquinas's replies.[46] Throughout question 103, Aquinas defends the

---

46. I do not mean to imply that these "two pictures" of the status of the ceremonial law after Christ represent an anomaly in Aquinas's thought which is usually an airtight system. Indeed, the scholastic method consisted of addressing precisely such apparent tensions that may arise from a reading of the sacred page. The method also included finding solutions to these tensions by appealing to authorities. "Whenever conflicting statements appeared, either because of some apparent contradiction in the text of Scripture or in the comment of some ecclesiastical authority, the arguments from both sides would be

claim that the ceremonial law is impermanent against biblical texts cited in the objections that suggest its permanence.[47]

In the second article of question 103, Aquinas addresses "Whether, at the time of the Law, the ceremonies of the Old Law had any power of justification?" Aquinas begins his argument (in the *sed contra*) with Paul as the primary authority, and synthesizes two Galatians texts: Galatians 3:21, "For if there had been a Law given which could give life, verily justice should have been by the Law"; and Galatians 2:21, "For if justice be by the Law, then Christ died in vain."[48] Aquinas synthesizes these texts into one Pauline axiom: "If there had been a Law given which could justify, Christ died in vain, i.e., without cause." In his reply, Aquinas answers that the ceremonial law had no power to cleanse from sin because expiation from sin comes only through Christ's Incarnation and passion, which had not yet taken place. The old sacraments, explains Aquinas, did not have "a power flowing from Christ already incarnate and crucified, such as the sacraments of the New Law contain."[49] Next, Aquinas cites Hebrews 10:4 to explain that the old sacraments were not efficacious as the new: "it was impossible that with the blood of oxen and goats sin should be taken away." He cites Galatians 4:9 to reinforce the point that these sacraments, in and of themselves, were "weak and needy elements." Aquinas closes by adding the caveat he repeats throughout his treatment on the Old Law: that these old sacraments were not as efficacious as the new does not mean they were not good. Before Christ, observance of the ceremonies could bring justification because the rites served as "a sort of profession, inasmuch as they foreshadowed Christ." After Christ, these ceremonies expire.

As Aquinas moves along, it becomes clear that Paul's letter to the Galatians is the primary authority that Aquinas cites to say the Law has now ceased after Christ. And, though Aquinas does not mention Augustine

---

debated briefly and a solution found." Weisheipl, *Friar Thomas D'Aquino*, 116–17.

47. The first question does not pertain to the end of the Law as much as the other three because it answers "Whether the precepts were in existence 'before the law,'" to which Aquinas answers that though some ceremonies existed they were not legal ceremonies established by Mosaic legislation but rather prompted by a heavenly instinct. Because the legal ceremonies are designated for divine worship this question addresses the apparent problem that worship (ceremonies) existed before Moses received the Law (i.e. some leaders were gifted with the spirit of prophecy).

48. Torrell explains that, "Usually, the *sed contra* is an 'authority,' such as Scripture or one of the Fathers of the Church. Torrell, *Aquinas's Summa*, 67.

49. Ia-IIae q. 103.2.

Rival Versions of Christ's Fulfillment of the Law

as an authority in Ia-IIae q. 103.2–3, the idea that the rites served as a sort of profession is assumed in the background of Aquinas's replies and finally surfaces in an explicit way when he explains how the rites become deadly after the passion of Christ in Ia-IIae q. 103.4.

In Ia-IIae q. 103.3, Aquinas addresses "Whether the ceremonies of the Old Law ceased at the coming of Christ?"[50] In the *sed contra*, Aquinas once again appeals to Paul as his authority for the reply. He begins with two citations from Paul, each of which emphasizes what I argued in chapter four (concerning the Hebrews commentary) was the theme of Aquinas's view of the teaching in Hebrews: "the shadow of the law's night."[51] Aquinas cites Colossians 2:16–17: "Let no man . . . judge you in meat or in drink, or in respect of festival day, or of the new moon, or of the sabbaths, which are a shadow of things to come." He then appeals to Hebrews 8:13, which states that because the new things come, the old decay and then end: "In saying a new (testament), he hath made the former old: and that which decayeth and groweth old, is near its end."[52] The ceremonies had to cease at the advent of the new sacraments because these new sacraments are now "the means of obtaining heavenly goods." The new sacraments are no longer things to come (as they were in the state of the Old Law), but these new sacraments are actually the things now present in the state of the New Law.

The first objection (Ia-IIae q. 103.3 ad. 1) that Aquinas lists against this explanation of the cessation of the Law is that it seems the ceremonial law in the Old Testament is permanent or "said to be forever" (citing Baruch 4:1). Here, as in the commentaries on Paul, Aquinas is aware of the biblical texts that indicate the ceremonial law is permanent. He even grounds the objection in an Old Testament text. His reply to this objection relies upon the division of the permanent aspect of the Law (moral law) from the impermanent (ceremonial and judicial). Aquinas takes the standard medieval view and argues that the old law is said to be eternal simply and absolutely (*in aeternum simpliciter et absolute*) only in regard to moral precepts, it lasts for ever in respect of the reality which those ceremonies foreshadowed."[53]

---

50. Ia-IIae q. 103.3.

51. "The time of the New Testament is called the day," Aquinas states, "because it repels the shadow of the Law's night." *Ad Heb.* 3.2.173.

52. Ia-IIae q. 103.3.

53. Ia-IIae q. 103.3 ad. 1. Aquinas also draws upon his interpretation of a few texts from the Gospels: John 19:30, where Christ says "it is finished" and Matthew 27:51 where the temple is rent.

The second objection (Ia-IIae q. 103.3 ad. 2) is that Law must be permanent because Christ observed the ceremonial law himself. In ad. 2 it is clear that Aquinas is aware of Christ's observance of the legal ceremonies. Aquinas responds to the objection by claiming that Christ's observance was before the passion: "Hence, before Christ's passion, while Christ was preaching and working miracles, the Law and the Gospel were concurrent, since the mystery of Christ had already begun, but was not as yet consummated. And for this reason Our Lord, before His passion, commanded the leper to observe the legal ceremonies."[54]

In Aquinas's view, the stronger objection to the idea of the cessation of the Law is that the apostles' observed the ceremonies, which he discusses in Ia-IIae q. 103.4: "Whether since Christ's passion the Legal Ceremonies Can be Observed without Committing Mortal Sin?" That the apostles' observed the Law even after the "mystery of Christ . . . was consummated" seems to problematize Aquinas's above reply for why Christ observed the Law. Aquinas attempts to answer the objection by appealing to Augustine in ad. 1. Before citing the debate between Jerome and Augustine, Aquinas's reply begins by claiming Paul's letter to the Galatians as his authority, revealing that the letter is the primary authority for his defense of the cessation of the Law: "The Apostle says (Gal 5:2): 'If you be circumcised, Christ shall profit you nothing.'"

Aquinas then attempts to attach Augustine and Jerome's premise that the ceremonial law is a mortal sin to what Aquinas views as the Pauline idea of Christ being unprofitable to those who observe circumcision: "nothing save mortal sin hinders us from receiving Christ's fruit. Therefore since Christ's passion it is a mortal sin to be circumcised, or to observe the other legal ceremonies."[55] For Aquinas, Galatians 5:2 serves as a marker for Paul's apparent teaching that the observance of circumcision after the passion makes the grace of Christ void. It is no longer beneficial at this particular time: "the Apostle's statement in Gal. 5:2 that *if you receive circumcision, Christ will be no advantage to you* refers to the era after grace . . . ."[56] Only mortal sin can void Christ's grace. Therefore, Paul's teaching is taken to mean that observance of circumcision is a mortal sin.

54. Ia-IIae q. 103.3 ad. 2.

55. Ia-IIae q. 102.4.

56. Aquinas makes this comment about Galatians 5:2 in the Romans commentary. *Ad Rom.* 2.4.238.

Rival Versions of Christ's Fulfillment of the Law

Aquinas views Paul's teaching that circumcision brings no advantage to one in the era after grace and uses this claim to support the Augustinian argument that the old sacraments are now false professions. After the middle period expires, the observance of the ceremonial law functions as a false profession. The Augustinian rationale is as follows: All ceremonies are professions of faith. Professions of faith are made in deeds and words. If such professions in word or deed are false professions, then the one making such a profession sins mortally. Since Christ *has* already come, it is false to declare that he *will* come. Therefore, the one observing a sacrament *for* declaring he will come (prefiguring Christ's passion), makes a false profession and sins mortally. Aquinas's reply is as follows:

> Now, though our faith in Christ is the same as that of the fathers of old; yet, since they came before Christ, whereas we come after Him, the same faith is expressed in different words, by us and by them. For by them it was said: Behold a virgin shall conceive and bear a son, where the verbs are in the future tense: whereas we express the same by means of verbs in the past tense, and say that she conceived and bore. In like manner the ceremonies of the Old Law betokened Christ as having yet to be born and to suffer: whereas our sacraments signify Him as already born and having suffered. Consequently, just as it would be a mortal sin now for anyone, in making a profession of faith, to say that Christ is yet to be born, which the fathers of old said devoutly and truthfully; so too it would be a mortal sin now to observe those ceremonies which the fathers of old fulfilled with devotion and fidelity. Such is the teaching of Augustine....[57]

Aquinas adopts Augustine's teaching from *Against Faustus* on the idea that a sacrament is a false profession of faith and synthesizes it with Galatians 5:2.[58] He then records the debate between Jerome and Augustine on when the cessation of the Law took place. The main point of disagreement be-

---

57. Ia-IIae q. 103.4.

58. Aquinas cites Augustine's *Against Faustus* 19:16: "It is no longer promised that He shall be born, shall suffer and rise again, truths of which their sacraments were a kind of image: but it is declared that He is already born, has suffered and risen again; of which our sacraments, in which Christians share, are the actual representation." Augustine writes, in 19.11: "The very intention of the observances was to prefigure Christ. Now that Christ has come, instead of its being strange or absurd that what was done to prefigure His advent should not be done any more, it is perfectly right and reasonable. The typical observances intended to prefigure the coming of Christ would be observed still, had they not been fulfilled by the coming of Christ."

tween these Fathers was the motive and purpose for the Jewish apostles' observance of the legal ceremonies after the passion. According to Aquinas, the objection runs as follows:

> It would seem that since Christ's passion the legal ceremonies can be observed without committing mortal sin. For we must not believe that the apostles committed mortal sin after receiving the Holy Ghost: since by his fullness they were *endued with power from on high* (Luke 24:49). But the apostles observed the legal ceremonies after the coming of the Holy Ghost: for it is stated (Acts 16:3) that Paul circumcised Timothy: and (Acts 21:26) that Paul, at the advice of James, took the men, and . . . being purified with them, entered into the temple, giving notice of the accomplishment of the days of purification, until an oblation should be offered for everyone of them. Therefore the legal ceremonies can be observed since the passion of Christ without committing mortal sin.[59]

Aquinas's summary of the controversy between Jerome and Augustine takes up the majority of the article. In Ia-IIae q. 103.4 ad. 1 he cites Augustine's Epistle 82 and then sides with Augustine's solution to the problem of distinguishing three periods, or the *tria tempora* doctrine: The Holy Spirit allowed Jews to observe the rites immediately after the passion, in the middle period, but not after the promulgation of the gospel. The rites become dead and deadly after this time.[60]

---

59. Ia-IIae q. 103.4 *obj.* 1.

60. Ia-IIae q. 103.4 ad. 1: "On this point there seems to have been a difference of opinion between Jerome and Augustine. For Jerome (*Super Galat.* 2, 11, seqq.) distinguished two periods of time. One was the time previous to Christ's passion, during which the legal ceremonies were neither dead, since they were obligatory, and did expiate in their own fashion; nor deadly, because it was not sinful to observe them. But immediately after Christ's passion they began to be not only dead, so as no longer to be either effectual or binding; but also deadly, so that whoever observed them was guilty of mortal sin. Hence he maintained that after the passion the apostles never observed the legal ceremonies in real earnest; but only by a kind of pious pretense, lest, to wit, they should scandalize the Jews and hinder their conversion. This pretense, however, is to be understood, not as though they did not in reality perform those actions, but in the sense that they performed them without the mind to observe the ceremonies of the Law: thus a man might cut away his foreskin for health's sake, not with the intention of observing legal circumcision. But since it seems unbecoming that the apostles, in order to avoid scandal, should have hidden things pertaining to the truth of life and doctrine, and that they should have made use of pretense, in things pertaining to the salvation of the faithful; therefore, Augustine (Epist. 82) more fittingly distinguished three periods of time. One was the time that preceded the passion of Christ, during which the legal ceremonies were neither deadly nor dead: another period was after the publication of the gospel, during which the legal

Rival Versions of Christ's Fulfillment of the Law

I will not rehearse the differences in Augustine and Jerome's views since this was done in chapter 6.[61] What is most important for my purposes here is to point out two things. First, Aquinas adopts the Augustinian *tria tempora* doctrine in the treatise on law to explain Christ's fulfillment of the Law as a fulfillment that also brings about a cessation of the ceremonial law, as well as its becoming deadly. Second, Aquinas relies on Paul's teaching on the Law in Galatians, which he understands to dovetail with Augustine's view of the old sacraments in *Against Faustus* and Epistle 82.

Therefore, in the treatise on law, Aquinas appeals to Paul's teaching as the primary biblical authority in his argument that the Jewish rites are fulfilled and cease after the passion. But Aquinas does not, as Levering argues, appeal to the more positive texts in Romans.[62] He relies upon Paul's letter to the Galatians to support his claim. Indeed, as I show below, Aquinas's argument for the cessation of the Law in the *Summa theologiae* is based on an interpretation of Galatians 5:2 that differs greatly from Aquinas's handling of that same verse in *Ad Rom.* 3.1.247.

---

ceremonies are both dead and deadly. The third is a middle period, viz. from the passion of Christ until the publication of the gospel, during which the legal ceremonies were dead indeed, because they had neither effect nor binding force; but were not deadly, because it was lawful for the Jewish converts to Christianity to observe them, provided they did not put their trust in them so as to hold them to be necessary unto salvation, as though faith in Christ could not justify without the legal observances. On the other hand, there was no reason why those who were converted from heathendom to Christianity should observe them. Hence Paul circumcised Timothy, who was born of a Jewish mother; but was unwilling to circumcise Titus, who was of heathen nationality.

The reason why the Holy Ghost did not wish the converted Jews to be debarred at once from observing the legal ceremonies, while converted heathens were forbidden to observe the rites of heathendom, was in order to show that there is a difference between these rites. For heathenish ceremonial was rejected as absolutely unlawful, and as prohibited by God for all time; whereas the legal ceremonial ceased as being fulfilled through Christ's passion, being instituted by God, as a figure of Christ."

61. See also *Ad Galatas* 2.3.86.

62. Cf. *Ad Rom.* 2.4.238; *Ad Rom.* 3.1.247. The first time he references Galatians 5:2 he interprets it according to the standard view. Circumcision was a benefit only in the past. The second time he references it he actually presents it as an objection to the claim that circumcision is an advantage as outward Judaism. He then follows that affirmation with an extended explication on the prerogatives and advantages of outward Judaism.

3. RIVAL VERSIONS OF FULFILLMENT: THE ECONOMIC SUPERSESSIONISM IN AQUINAS'S THEOLOGY IN TENSION WITH POST-SUPERSESSIONIST RESOURCES

Aquinas's view of Paul's teaching on the ceremonial law in Ia-IIae 103.2–4 shares economically supersessionist views of Christ's fulfillment of Jewish Law similar to those in the commentaries on Hebrews and Galatians. And although the Ephesians commentary also shares certain economically supersessionist elements found in Hebrews, Galatians, and the *Summa theologiae*, the Ephesians commentary contains an important post-supersessionist resource. Moreover, the Romans commentary provides a post-supersessionist resource based in Romans 3:1–2 that actually undermines the logic of the economic supersessionist views in all of these places.

Fulfilled, Destroyed, and Deadly: The Economic Supersessionism in Aquinas's *Summa theologiae* and Commentaries on Hebrews and Galatians

Aquinas's position on the cessation of the ceremonial law in the *Summa theologiae* explains the logic of Augustine's teaching with brevity and precision. He synthesizes Augustine's views with Paul's teaching on the "superfluous sacrament" from Galatians. Indeed, it is this view of Paul's teaching on the Law that Aquinas thinks dovetails with Augustine's teaching on the *tria tempora* and the idea that the Law is dead and deadly in the third era. Aquinas extends Augustine's thought on the cessation of the Law in the *Prima Secundae* by buttressing these Augustinian doctrines with his reading of Paul's letters to the Galatians and Hebrews. In this sense, one can say that Aquinas's reading of Paul does not overcome Augustinian supersessionism, as Boguslawski holds, but actually strengthens it.

Recall that Aquinas expresses a view of fulfillment in the Hebrews and Galatians lectures that could be referred to as "fulfilled, destroyed, and deadly." In this traditional form of fulfillment of the ceremonies, the Law is "destroyed" by both Christ and Paul; declared superfluous by the apostles at the Jerusalem conference; and thereafter it becomes deadly to anyone who observes it in the era after grace. The observance of the Law in the era of grace is an offense to Christ's passion and it must be renounced. Anyone who observes the rites after the passion is guilty of mortal sin. Aquinas teaches that circumcision is no longer of value since to say otherwise threatens to evacuate the gospel. Therefore, Aquinas's view of the fulfillment and cessation of the ceremonial law in the treatise on law directly corresponds to the "fulfilled, destroyed, and deadly" view of fulfillment in Galatians and Hebrews. Both visions of fulfillment are economically supersessionist.[63]

Jean-Pierre Torrell's description of the Law after it is fulfilled is representative of Aquinas's view of the ceremonial law after Christ in the treatise on law, and in the commentaries on Hebrews and Galatians. Torrell thinks Aquinas relativizes the value of the Law because God is not content with this teaching. Torrell remarks that although Aquinas's treatment of the Old Law in the *Summa theologiae* is a "magnificent apologia for the law," he "radically relativizes" the Law:

> While Thomas highlights the great educative value of the law for personal freedom and stresses its necessary role in service to the common good, he also radically relativizes it, since its usefulness is only pedagogical and disappears once its service is completed. God is not content with instructing us from the exterior by law.[64]

Torrell's language about the radical relativization and corresponding disappearance of the law resembles Isaac's language of "fulfilled and expired." The treatise on law and the commentaries on Hebrews and Galatians make clear that Aquinas understands Paul to teach that the old sacraments have been relativized and replaced by the new sacraments. If one considers these texts as representative of Aquinas's view of Paul's teaching on the ceremonial law, his theology can be described as economically supersessionist.

Fulfilled and Destroyed: Economic Supersessionism in Tension with Post-Supersessionist Resources in the Ephesians *Commentary*

Nevertheless, Aquinas does not consistently hold to the teaching that the ceremonial law is fulfilled, destroyed, and deadly after the passion of Christ. In the Ephesians commentary, Aquinas teaches the Law is dead,

---

63. This is not to say that Romans does not shape Aquinas's view of the fulfillment of the Law. Aquinas draws upon the notion that the Law is good but imperfect in several places throughout his discussion of the Old Law. However, when Aquinas teaches that the Law is fulfilled and then becomes dead and deadly he does not appeal to texts in Romans or Matthew 5:17. Romans is not the primary Pauline source of Aquinas's view of the cessation of the Law in the *Summa theologiae*.

64. Torrell, *Aquinas's Summa*, 34.

or destroyed by Christ, but he does not say it is deadly. Moreover, in the Ephesians commentary Aquinas defines the election of Israel as a promise of God and a "sacrament" of the society of saints. For this reason, the commentary can be considered as a step away from theme so prominent in the tradition of the *cessatio legalium* that emphasizes that Law is not an aspect of the promise but is an impermanent and carnal command.

However, in the Ephesians commentary, these positive resources exist alongside and in tension with economically supersessionist views of the ceremonial law and Israel. Ephesians shares certain economically supersessionist elements found in Hebrews, Galatians, and the *Summa theologiae*. First, Aquinas's view of Paul's teaching in Ephesians is similar to Hebrews and Galatians commentaries in that it describes Christ's destruction of the ceremonial law. Second, in the Ephesians commentary, Aquinas describes the promise of the special election of Israel, the *societas sanctorum*, as a thing of the past. The body of Christ has inherited the promise.

Fulfilled and Upheld:
Post-supersessionist Resources in Aquinas's Romans Commentary

Aquinas understands the permanent value of the ceremonial law to turn on whether Paul teaches that circumcision is "superfluous" (Gal 5:2) or "advantageous" (Rom 3:1–2) to the Jewish people in the era after grace. Indeed, Aquinas's attention to this question and his answer in the Romans commentary calls into question the *cessatio legalium* tradition and departs in significant ways from the "fulfilled, destroyed, and deadly" view of the *Summa theologiae*.

In the Romans commentary, Aquinas's teaching that Christ fulfilled the ceremonial law does not also render the Law void, destroyed, or deadly. However, the absence of this teaching is not what is most significant about his view of the ceremonial law in the Romans commentary. Rather, what is most significant is what Aquinas does say about the theological value of circumcision even after the passion. In his Romans commentary, Aquinas places Jewish rites on a higher theological ground than he does in the treatise on law and the other Pauline commentaries. Even as Aquinas insists upon the priority of the Christological prefiguring function of the Jewish rites before Christ, he also defends their literal meaning with a different

Rival Versions of Christ's Fulfillment of the Law

theological argument than he used in the *Prima Secundae*.⁶⁵ As I argued in chapter 5, Aquinas anchors the literal meaning of the Jewish rites in the authority of Paul's teaching on God's faithfulness to the Jewish people. In particular, their election and prerogatives is anchored in the claim that God does not lie. This high view of the theological status of the Jewish rites after Christ is most clearly evident in his handling of the question of "outward" Judaism in *Ad Romanos* 2–3. It is in his defense of "outward" Judaism, which he takes to mean circumcision, that Aquinas undermines the *cessatio legalium* tradition and resists the relativizing force of Galatians 5:2, which he thinks teaches that circumcision is superfluous.

Recall that in *Ad Romanos* 2.4, Aquinas discusses the idea of the "inward Jew" and the "external Jew." At first, Aquinas says that circumcision profits *only* if the Law, i.e., the moral precepts, are observed. This keeping of the moral law is defined as "inward Judaism." An outward Jew is one who only keeps the ceremonial law but neglects the moral law. Aquinas then explains that "he is truly a Jew who is one inwardly, i.e., whose heart is possessed by the precepts of the Law, which the Jews professed."⁶⁶ Since the inward character of Judaism, which again, is observing the moral precepts, is obtainable by both the Jew and the Gentile alike, inward Judaism "prevail over the outward."⁶⁷

However, after explaining this idea of the superiority of inward Judaism, Aquinas immediately follows with an objection from Paul in defense of the ongoing value of external Judaism, or the value of circumcision even after the passion of Christ.⁶⁸ Here, it becomes evident that Aquinas's

---

65. This may indicate some development in Aquinas's thought on the ceremonial Law from the *Prima Secundae* to the commentary on Romans, as well as the *Tertia Pars* of the *Summa*. It is possible that Aquinas's thought on the ceremonial shifts from a "fulfilled, destroyed, and deadly" view in the *Prima Secundae*, to a "fulfilled and upheld" view in the Romans commentary, which he edited himself in the last years of his life. Schenk argues that Aquinas strived to maintain the historical and literal integrity of the meaning of the Law, but increasingly emphasized its Christological meaning. Schenk even refers to this development as a "shift" and also uses the term "phase" to describe Aquinas's thought. The first phase emphasizes the twofold end of the ceremonies: literal and prefigurative. The second phase increasingly emphasizes the prefigurative with a fading interest in the literal end. Schenk, "Views of the Two Covenants," 911. However, Schenk rightly points out that the dates for the editions of Aquinas's works on Paul are still "unresolved."

66. *Ad Rom.* 2.4.244.

67. *Ad Rom.* 2.4.245.

68. Schenk holds that Aquinas's statement in *Ad Rom.* 2.4 concerning inward Judaism is evidence of a spiritualization of the older covenant as a covenant of faith in Christ in the manner he detects in the *Tertia Pars*. "Views of the Two Covenants," 911. He seems

awareness of what might be referred to as the difficulty of "two views of circumcision" after Christ ultimately prevents him from relativizing the theological value of "outward" Judaism or observance of the ceremonies.

Aquinas notices that Paul seems to say, on the one hand, that ceremonial law possesses a permanent theological value, and that the ceremonial law is, on the other hand, impermanent or superfluous after Christ.[69] It seems that Aquinas was preoccupied with the difficulty of two views of circumcision in Paul (as advantageous or as superfluous) in three places in his work: the Galatians commentary; the Romans commentary; and in Ia-IIae q. 103.2–4.

Recall that in the Galatians commentary, Aquinas raises a possible objection to the Pauline claim that "there is neither Jew nor Greek" in the era of grace by citing Romans 3:1–2: "What advantage then hath the Jew? Much in everyway."[70] Here it is clear that Aquinas views this verse from Romans as an objection to the view that circumcision no longer has status. In the *respondeo* Aquinas says that Jews and Greeks

> can be considered . . . according to the *state in which they were before faith*. In this way, the Jew *was greater* because of the benefits he derived from the law. In another way, according to the state of grace; and in this way, the Jew is not greater. And this is the sense in which it is taken here."[71]

Here, Aquinas is commenting directly upon the advantage of the Jews after the passion of Christ. He does not take the opportunity, as he does in the Romans commentary, to advance an argument that there is a value to

---

to miss Aquinas's attentiveness to Paul's objection to the idea of inward Judaism and his argument that the advantage of the Jew remains "Much in everyway."

69. Edward A. Synan is the only scholar I am aware of that has remarked on Aquinas's struggle with impermanent and permanent notions of the Law. Synan observed that the fact that the *Summa theologiae* represents Aquinas's mature thought combined with the extreme length of the articles on the Old Law reveal that a particular tension in the Law "preoccupied" Aquinas to the end of his life: "That the enigma of laws, announced by Holy Scripture to be *both permanent and passing,* preoccupied him to the end is visible in the extreme length of the Summa articles on the issue." Synan does not demonstrate his thesis regarding Aquinas's preoccupation with what might be referred to as the "permanence and impermanence of the ceremonial law" in Scripture. Synan mentions it briefly, and on the way to making the point that, at the end of the day, Aquinas's conscience would not permit him to defend the persistence of the Jewish ceremonial laws. Synan, "Some Medieval Perceptions of the Controversy on Jewish Law," 120–21.

70. *Ad Galat.* 3.9.186.

71. *Ad Galat.* 3.9.186. [Emphasis added]

Rival Versions of Christ's Fulfillment of the Law

circumcision based on the idea that God commanded it or that God chose the Jewish people as his elect people. Rather, he restricts Jewish advantage to something in the past or something that *was*: "Before the faith, the Jew was greater." Whereas, in the Romans commentary, the "Much in everyway" of Romans 3:2 compels Aquinas to argue at length for the Jews' advantage (*amplius*) even after grace, in the Galatians commentary, he concludes that the theological advantage to the Jew only existed before Christ's passion.

In the Romans commentary Aquinas once again sets two statements from Paul on circumcision against each other: one that seems to support the advantage of the Jew after grace, and another that supports the disadvantage of the Jew after grace. Aquinas discusses the more positive Pauline teaching on circumcision based in Romans 3:1–2—this is the same teaching Aquinas thinks supports the advantage of Jews *only in the past*, in the Galatians commentary. In the Romans commentary, however, Aquinas reads Romans 3:1–2 as referring to *the present advantage*. It becomes clear that Aquinas understands Paul's rhetorical question in Romans 3:1 "What advantage has the Jew?" and the answer in 3:2 "Much in everyway!" as an objection and a reply to a question. He rephrases Paul's question so that it more directly addresses the issue of the theological status of circumcision after Christ: "What advantage has the Jew? Or what is the value of circumcision, i.e. outward?"[72] Aquinas even translates Paul's rhetorical question into the form of a scholastic objection: "*It seems* from his previous teaching that there is no value." Aquinas then understands Paul to provide the answer: "Then when he says 'Much in everyway' he answers the objection."[73] "'Much in everyway!' refers first to Judaism's prerogative; and second, 'to the value of circumcision.'"[74] Here, Aquinas does not say that the value of circumcision was only in the past. Rather, he sees the Galatians 5:2 teaching that circumcision is superfluous after Christ as problematized by Paul's strong language in Romans 3:1. Indeed, it does not seem unreasonable to conclude that Aquinas understands the Romans 3:2 "Much in everyway!" to refute the traditional claim based in Galatians 5:2 that circumcision no longer has status. Aquinas says that when Paul exclaims "Much in everyway!" he answers the objection and affirms the permanent value of outward Judaism and circumcision.[75]

72. *Ad Rom.* 3.1.247.
73. *Ad Rom.* 3.1.248.
74. *Ad Rom.* 3.1.248.
75. *Ad Rom.* 3.1.248.

In addition to affirming circumcision as an advantage even after the passion of Christ, Aquinas makes two other positive claims about the theological status of the Law after Christ:

1) As I showed in chapter 5, Aquinas connects the value of circumcision in the era after grace to the prerogatives of Israel as promises of God.[76] He makes the theological argument that God's faithfulness would actually be compromised if the prerogatives of Israel were taken away or annulled. Aquinas therefore secures the permanent theological status of the Jewish rites after Christ as a matrix of prerogatives that cannot be taken away because they are wrapped up in the faithfulness of God's promises to the Jewish people: "For if the Jews' prerogative were abrogated on account of the unbelief of some, it would follow that man's unbelief would nullify God's faithfulness—which is an unacceptable conclusion."[77] Here, "outward" Judaism, or, to use Wyschogrod's term, "carnal" Judaism's prerogative is secured *in the era after grace* by the authority of Paul's affirmation of God's irrevocable promise to these elect people.

2) Aquinas claims the rites retain a figuring function as figures of present spiritual benefit. In making these moves, Aquinas avoids the relativizing of the Jewish rites that takes place in the treatise on law, and the commentaries on Galatians, Hebrews, and Ephesians.

When viewed in the context of the other commentaries and the *Summa theologiae*, the "Much in everyway!" not only represents a tension between a positive teaching in the Romans commentary, and the more negative view of the Jewish rites in the Galatians commentary and *Summa theologiae*. In the Romans commentary Aquinas thinks Paul actually defeats the objection that circumcision is superfluous—an objection Aquinas rephrases as "It seems circumcision has no value." Aquinas's view of the ceremonial law after the passion of Christ reflects the "shock of the present tense."[78] The present tense descriptions of Israel compel Aquinas to construct an argument for the theological value of circumcision that undermines a significant premise in the logic of the *cessatio legalium* tradition: the premise that circumcision has no value after Christ.

---

76. *Ad Rom.* 3.1.249.
77. *Ad Rom.* 3.1.253. [Emended]
78. Soulen, "They are Israelites."

9

Aquinas as Resource for Jewish-Christian Relations

THERE EXIST RIVAL VERSIONS of Christ's fulfillment of the ceremonial law in Aquinas's thought. This study shows that this tension is most pronounced when comparing, on the one hand, the teaching from the commentaries on Galatians and Hebrews, and the *Summa theologiae*, which states that the ceremonial law is dead and deadly after the passion of Christ, and, on the other hand, the teaching from Romans commentary, which states that the ceremonial law is a present spiritual benefit that retains a theological value as a prerogative of the Jewish people that cannot be declared superfluous without compromising the faithfulness of God.

In Hebrews and Galatians, Aquinas emphasizes the former view of fulfillment: the Law is described as fulfilled, destroyed, and deadly after Christ's passion. In the lectures on Romans and Ephesians, Law and covenant are melded together as prerogatives of the Jewish people. In Romans and Ephesians, Paul's emphasis on the goodness of God's plural covenants and promises to Israel. In the Ephesians commentary, Jewish Christians are even given a foundational place in Christ's Church as one of two "walls of the Temple."[1] Here, "Jewish Christians" are spoken of as part of the increase and growth of the Church with no mention of the Law becoming

---

1. *Ad Ephesios* 2.6.129.

deadly after the Augustinian middle period, or that the Church of the Jews was "not destined to endure."[2]

Moreover, in the Romans commentary, Aquinas defends the perpetuity of the prerogatives with an argument based on the theological claim that God is faithful to God's promises. Aquinas argues that to take away or remove the prerogatives of Israel, which includes Israel's covenant *and* Law, would actually nullify the faithfulness of God and call into question the theological claim that God does not lie. In the commentary on Romans, this theological defense of the prerogatives can be considered an argument against the *double sens* of fulfillment that causes the Law to expire and become dead since Aquinas affirms that the Law is a spiritual benefit for Jews.

Aquinas's thought is a significant resource for the new era of Jewish-Christian relations. First, the "fulfilled and upheld" view of the ceremonial law after Christ can serve as a resource for building mutual respect among Jews and Christians in the era after *Nostra Aetate*. Aquinas's view of circumcision in the Romans commentary affords a positive status to postbiblical Israel after the passion of Christ that can assist the Church in overcoming economic supersessionism. His affirmation and defense of the ceremonial law as "fulfilled and upheld" reinforces the teaching of *Nostra Aetate*, and strengthens the Vatican's teaching that the Jewish people remain dear to God and are a permanent reality.[3]

Indeed, Karl Thieme's affirmation and defense of the value of postbiblical Judaism share similarities with Aquinas's positive view of Jewish Law and election in the Romans commentary.[4] Both theologians share the belief that the Jewish people remain God's elect; that the Jewish people can be pleasing before God as Jews, despite unbelief in Christ. Therefore, Thieme's struggle with Nazism, which required overcoming the traditional Christian view that carnal Israel is a degenerate people, finds support in Aquinas's premodern attempt to make sense of difficulties in Paul on the theological status of the Jewish Law after Christ.

2. *Ad Galatas* 2.3.86.

3. That the Jews "remain dear to God" is a theme in the Church's teaching that first appeared in *Lumen Gentium* 16.

4. Connelly, *From Enemy to Brother*, 187. Thieme no doubt moves beyond Aquinas in many ways, especially in his affirmation of the need to defend the idea of Jewish participation in grace. Connelly, *From Enemy to Brother*, 230

Aquinas as Resource for Jewish-Christian Relations

Second, Aquinas provides a model of reading of Scripture that is open to the possibility of locating and repairing inconsistencies on the value of the ceremonial law after the passion of Christ.[5] Aquinas' attention to what Steven Fowl has called the "multifaceted literal sense" (the idea that the literal sense can refer to a number of realities) allows one to identify tensions in authoritative traditional readings of Scripture. An example is his concern in the *Summa theologiae* and the Pauline commentaries to take seriously texts that witness to the ceremonial law as perpetual and texts that seem to say the Law is obsolete after the passion.

Moreover, Aquinas is open not only to identifying tensions but challenging traditional authorities in order to find solutions to conflicting interpretations of Scripture.[6]

The *cessatio legalium* tradition has created a deep incoherence in the Christian tradition. It implies that God is now indifferent to Jews and was lying when God said that the covenant with the Jewish people would be forever. Additionally, the *cessatio legalium* tradition seems plagued by contradictory views of Paul's teaching on circumcision. Is circumcision advantageous (Rom 3:1–2) or superfluous (Gal 5:2) for the Jewish people in the era of grace? Aquinas attempts to resolve this difficulty in the Romans commentary in a rather remarkable way, by discovering a literal *ratio* for the continuing significance of Jews and Judaism in Paul's present tense affirmations of Israel.

Perhaps Aquinas's move represents a challenge to the traditional interpretation of Jewish Law that is not unlike his challenge to Aristotle's conception of happiness.[7] In the same way that Aquinas invoked "Aristotle against Aristotle,"[8] Aquinas seems to invoke a positive Pauline statement on the value of circumcision to overturn the negative Pauline statement that Jewish Law has no value after Christ. It seems Aquinas may have set

---

5. Steven Fowl, "Thomas Aquinas and the Multifaceted Literal Sense of Scripture."

6. This dialectic is not peculiar to Aquinas.

7. Aquinas claimed that Aristotle's criteria for happiness actually caused a difficulty for the Aristotelian view that such happiness is actually attainable. As Alasdair MacIntyre explains, Aquinas argued that since only a variety of imperfect happinesses can be had in human life, the happiness Aristotle identified, the ultimate good (of the human soul) must lie "in the relationship of the soul to something outside itself, and that . . . in no state in this created world can the type of good in question be found." Aquinas is able to overcome the apparent tension between the Augustinian and Aristotelian traditions through a careful and critical reading of Aristotle on Aristotle's own terms. McIntyre, *Three Rival Versions*, 137.

8. MacIntyre, *Three Rival Versions*, 137.

Paul's Romans 3:1–2 against Paul's Galatians 5:2 in order to resolve what he saw as a tension between an Augustinian interpretation of the status of Jewish practice of circumcision and the status attributed to that practice in the letter to the Romans.[9] In this way, Aquinas seems to reopen questions on the apostles' observance of the Law and whether the apostles assumed that the Law would continue for Jews and Jewish believers in Christ. It should be noted that the fact the Holy Spirit allowed the apostles to observe the Law in the apostolic period was, for Aquinas, the strongest argument against the *cessatio legalium* (Ia-IIae q. 103.4 ob. 1).

Isaac was probably not aware of the *cessatio legalium* tradition in medieval theology when he challenged the "fulfilled and expired" view of Christ's fulfillment of the Law. Nevertheless, his neglected "Proposition 9" is concerned with the same the basic concept.

"Proposition 9: Jesus was born and lived 'under the Law,' did he intend or announce its abrogation? Many writers hold that he did, but their statements exaggerate, distort, or contradict the most important passages in the gospels."[10] Isaac's attempt to challenge this concept was, at the end of the day, a challenge to the *cessatio legalium* tradition. Aquinas's reply to the objection that circumcision is of no value in the era after grace represents a rejection of a key premise in the logic of traditional fulfillment theologies that assume the *cessatio legalium* as normative after the passion of Christ. Therefore, aspects of Aquinas's theology not only support Thieme's positive vision of the Jews. Aquinas's Romans commentary seems to call into question the same idea that Isaac challenged: the claim that the Jewish law has expired after Christ.

Based on Aquinas's "fulfilled and upheld" view of the ceremonial law, I would argue that it is possible to answer "yes" to Wyschogrod's 1987 challenge to Thomistic studies as to whether or not the teaching on the *mortifera* character of the ceremonial law can be interpreted more benevolently.

Indeed, Wyschogrod and Aquinas seem to me to share more common ground than has yet been realized. They both express a profound awareness and concern with a theological claim deeply significant for

---

9. The teaching that Jewish Law is fulfilled and rendered obsolete by Christ, which is often associated with Hebrews and Galatians, remains a challenge for contemporary theological interpretation of Scripture even after the era of Thieme and Isaac. Indeed, Thieme's debate with Ernst Karl Winter over whether Paul's positive affirmation of Jewish law and election in Romans trumps Galatians and Hebrews seems to mirror aspects of the discussion over the question of supersessionism in Aquinas's theology.

10. Isaac, *Jesus and Israel*, 49.

Aquinas as Resource for Jewish-Christian Relations

post-supersessionist theology: the claim that God keeps God's promises. Commenting upon what is now an oft-quoted Pauline phrase, "The gifts and call of God are irrevocable" (Rom 11:29), Aquinas says that: "it should be noted that 'gift' is taken here for a promise made according to God's foreknowledge or predestination, and 'call' is taken for election." "Because both are so certain," explains Aquinas, "whatever God promises is as good as given and whomever He elects is somehow already called."[11]

Here, Aquinas's rejection of the idea that God's promise of the election of the Jewish people might be nullified is similar to Wyschogrod's reply to Karl Barth in a conversation concerning the transcendent nature of God's promises:

> On a sunny morning in August 1966 I visited theologian Karl Barth in his modest home on the Bruderholzallee in Basel. He had been told that I was a "Jewish Barthian," and this amused him to no end. We spoke about various things and at one point he said: "You Jews have the promise but not the fulfillment; we Christians have both the promise and fulfillment." Influenced by the banking atmosphere of Basel, I replied: "With human promises, one can have the promise but not the fulfillment. The one who promises can die, or change his mind, or not fulfill his promise for any number of reasons. But a promise of God is like money in the bank. If we have his promise, we have its fulfillment and if we do not have the fulfillment we do not have the promise." There was a period of silence and then he said, "You know, I never thought of it that way." I will never forget that meeting.[12]

In Aquinas's Romans commentary, God's promise to Israel is described as transcending human notions of promise. As Aquinas states in *Ad Romanos* 11.4.926, God's promise to the Jewish people is "as good as given."

In November of 2013 I had the opportunity to spend the afternoon with Michael Wyschogrod at his home in the Bronx. During one of our conversations, I shared with him that I had read his essay on Aquinas, and that it is possible to interpret Aquinas's view of the ceremonial law "more benevolently." I told him that in the commentary on Romans, Aquinas argues that if the prerogatives of the Jewish people were to be abrogated on account of Jewish unbelief in Christ it would be unfitting, and would call into question the faithfulness of God. Wyschogrod began to nod and said,

---

11. *Ad Rom.* 11.4.926.

12. Wyschogrod, "Why Was and Is the Theology of Karl Barth of Interest to a Jewish Theologian?" 211–24.

"I agree with that." "But," he said firmly, "it would not simply be 'unfitting.' It would be *unacceptable*." After our meeting, I realized that Wyschogrod had better expressed the sense of Aquinas's words in *Ad Rom.* 3.1.253 than I. For Wyschogrod and Aquinas, the idea that the prerogatives of Israel have been abolished because of unbelief in Christ would not simply be unfitting; it would be unacceptable because God does not lie.[13]

---

13. *Ad Rom.* 3.1.253: "For if the Jews' prerogative were abrogated (*praerogativa Iudaeorum tolleretur*) on account of the unbelief of some, it would follow that man's unbelief would nullify God's faithfulness—which is an unacceptable (*inconveniens*) conclusion." Although *inconveniens* is an adjective that can be translated "unfitting," Aquinas uses the term to refer to a statement (the theory that the prerogatives might be removed). In this context, it seems the term should carry more force: unreasonable, absurd. Deferrari, *A Lexicon of St. Thomas*, 533.

Bibliography

WORKS OF THOMAS AQUINAS

Expositio super Iob Ad Litteram. Vol. 26. Leonine. Rome: Ad Sanctae Sabinae, 1965.
Principium Fratris Thomae De Commendatione Et Partitione Sacrae Scripturae. Edited by R. A. Verardo. Marietti. Opuscula Theologica 1. Rome: Merietti, 1954.
Sancti Thomae Aquinatis, Doctoris Angelici, Ordinis Praedicatorum Opera Omnia: Ad Fidem Optimarum Editionum Accurate Recognita. 25 vols. Parmae: Typis Petri Fiaccadori, 1852.
Sancti Thomae Aquinatis Opera omnia. Edited by Robert Busa. Stuttgart-Bad Canstatt: Fromman-Holzboog, 1980.
Sancti Thomae de Aquino Opera omnia. Leonine edition. Rome, 1882–. Vols 4–11, *Summa Theologiae.*
Scriptum super libros Sententiarum. Vol. I–II, edited by P. Mandonnet; Vol. II–IV, edited by M. F. Moos. Paris: Sumptibus P. Lethielleux, 1929–47.
Super Epistolas S. Pauli Lectura. Vol. I–II, edited by Raphael Cai. Taurini: Marietti, 1952.
Super Evangelium S. Ioannis Lectura. Edited by Raphael Cai. Turin: Marietti, 1952.

MODERN TRANSLATIONS

Catena Aurea: Commentary on the Four Gospels Collected Out of the Works of the Fathers. Southampton, UK: Saint Austin, 1997.
Commentaries on Saint Paul's Letters. vol. 37–40. Edited by J. Mortensen and E. Alarcon and translated by Fabian Larcher and Matthew Lamb. Lander, WY: Aquinas Institute for the Study of Sacred Doctrine, 2012.
Commentary on Saint Paul's Epistle to the Ephesians. Translated and introduced by Matthew L. Lamb. Albany, NY: Magi, 1966.
Commentary on Saint Paul's Epistle to the Galatians. Translated and introduced by Fabian R. Larcher. Albany, NY: Magi, 1966.
Commentary on the Epistle to the Hebrews. Translated by Chrysostom Baer. South Bend, IN: St. Augustine's, 2006.

Bibliography

Commentary on the Gospel of John, Vol. 1–3, Translated by Fabian Larcher and James A. Weisheipl. Washington, DC: The Catholic University of America Press, 2010.

Commento al Corpus Paulinum (expositio et lectura super epistolas Pauli apostoli) vol. 1–3. Seconda Lettera ai corinzi-Lettera ai galati. ESD-Edizioni Studio Domenicano, 2006.

Commentary on Romans. Translated by Fabian Larcher OP and edited by Jeremy Holmes. Aquinas Center for Theological Renewal: Ave Maria University. Online: http://nvjournal.net/files/Aquinas_on_Romans.pdf.

On Love and Charity: Readings from the Commentary on the Sentences of Peter Lombard. Washington, DC: Catholic University of America Press, 2008.

"The letter to the Duchess of Brabant 'On the government of the Jews.'" In *Aquinas: Political Writings*, edited by R. W. Dyson, 233–38. Cambridge: Cambridge University Press, 2002.

Summa Theologica. Translated by Fathers of the English Dominican Province. 5 vols. New York: Benziger, 1948.

Summa Theologiae: Volume 29, The Old Law: 1a2ae. 98–105. Translated by David Bourke and Arthur Littledale; edited by Thomas Gilby. New York: Cambridge University Press, 1969.

The Literal Exposition on Job: A Scriptural Commentary Concerning Providence. Translated by Anthony Damico. An American Academy of Religion Book. Atlanta: Scholar's, 1989.

Thomas Aquinas: Selected Writings. Translated and edited by Ralph McInerny. New York: Penguin Classics, 1999.

GENERAL BIBLIOGRAPHY

Abrahams, I. "Thomas Aquinas and Judaism." *The Jewish Quarterly Review* 4.1 (1891) 158–61.

Aitken, James K. "Seelisberg Conference." In *A Dictionary of Jewish-Christian Relations*, edited by Edward Kessler and Neil Wenborn, 341–43. Cambridge: Cambridge University Press, 2008.

Ante-Nicene Christian Library. Translations of the Writings of the Fathers down to A.D. 325. Edinburgh: T. & T. Clark, 1867.

Augustine. *Against Faustus. Nicene and Post-Nicene Fathers*. Series I. Vol. 4. Grand Rapids, MI: Eerdmans, 1974.

———. *The City of God against the Pagans*. The Loeb Classical Library. Cambridge: Harvard University Press, 1957.

Baglow, Christopher T. *"Modus et Forma": A New Approach to the Exegesis of Saint Thomas Aquinas with an Application to the Lectura Super Epistolam Ad Ephesios*. Analecta Biblica 149. Roma: Pontificio Istituto biblico, 2002.

Baum, Gregory. *Is the New Testament Anti-Semitic?: A Re-examination of the New Testament*. Mahwah, NJ: Paulist, 1965.

Baur, Ferdinand Christian. *Paul the Apostle of Jesus Christ: His Life and Works, His Epistles and Teachings*. Peabody, MA: Hendrickson, 2003.

Becker, Adam H., and Annette Yoshiko Reed. *The Ways That Never Parted: Jews and Christians in Late Antiquity and the Early Middle Ages*. Minneapolis: Fortress, 2007.

Bieringer, Reimund, Didier Pollefeyt, and Frederique Vandecasteele-Vanneuville. *Anti-Judaism and the Fourth Gospel*. 1st ed. Louisville, KY: Westminster John Knox, 2001.

Bibliography

Billy, Dennis. "Grace and Natural Law in the Super Epistola Ad Romanos Lectura: A Study in Thomas' Commentary on Romans 2:14–16." *Studia Moralia* 26 (1988) 15–37.

Black, Clifton C. "St. Thomas' Commentary on the Johannine Prologue: Some Reflections on Its Character and Implications." *Catholic Biblical Quarterly* 48 (1986) 681–98.

Bloesch, Donald G. "All Israel Will be Saved: Supersessionism and the Biblical Witness." *Interpretation* 43 (1989) 130–42.

Boadt, Lawrence. "St. Thomas Aquinas and the Biblical Wisdom Tradition." *The Thomist* 49 (1985) 575–611.

Boguslawski, Steven C. "Review of *Modus Et Forma*: a New Approach to the Exegesis of Saint Thomas Aquinas with an Application to the Lectura Super Epistolam Ad Ephesios." *Thomist* 67.3 (2003) 499–503.

———. "Review of Aquinas and the Jews, by John Y. B. Hood." *Journal of Ecclesiastical History* 48.2 (1997) 346–47.

———. *Thomas Aquinas on the Jews: Insights into His Commentary on Romans 9–11*. Mahwah, NJ: Paulist, 2008.

Boyarin, Daniel. *Border Lines: The Partition of Judaeo-Christianity*. Philadelphia: University of Pennsylvania Press, 2006.

Boyle, John F. "'Division of the Text' with Particular Reference to the Commentaries of Saint Thomas Aquinas." In *With Reverence for the Word: Medieval Scriptural Exegesis in Judaism, Christianity, and Islam*, edited by Jane Dammen McAuliffe, Barry D. Walfish, and Joseph W. Goering, 276–83. New York: Oxford University Press, 2010.

Boys, Mary C. *Has God Only One Blessing?: Judaism as a Source of Christian Self-Understanding*. Mahwah, NJ: Paulist, 2000.

Braine, David. "Aquinas, God and Being." In *Analytical Thomism: Traditions in Dialogue*, edited by Craig Paterson and Matthew S. Pugh, 1–24. Farnham, UK: Ashgate, 2006.

Broadie, Alexander. "Medieval Jewry through the Eyes of Aquinas." In *Aquinas and Problems of His Time*, edited by G. Verbeke and D. Verhelst, 57–68. New York: Cornell University Press, 1976.

Brockway, Allan, Paul Van Buren, Rolf Rendtorff, and Simon Schoon. *The Theology of the Churches and the Jewish People: Statements by the World Council of Churches and Its Member Churches*. Geneva: World Council of Churches, 1988.

Calvin, John. *A Harmony of the Gospels: Matthew, Mark, and Luke*, Vol. 1, edited by David W. Torrance and Thomas F. Torrance. Translated by A. W. Morrison. Grand Rapids: Eerdmans, 1980.

Cameron, George G. "Guttmann's Verhaltniss Des Thomas Von Aquino." In *The Critical Review of Theological & Philosophical Literature*, edited by S. D. F. Salmon, 185–88. Edinburgh: T. & T. Clark, 1892.

Cessario, Romanus. *The Godly Image: Christ and Salvation in Catholic Thought from St. Anselm to Aquinas*. Petersham, MA: St. Bede's, 1990.

Chazan, Robert. "Christian-Jewish Interactions over the Ages." In *Christianity in Jewish Terms*, edited by Tikva Frymer-Kensky et al., 7–24. New York: Basic, 2002.

Chazan, Robert. *Daggers of Faith: Thirteenth-Century Christian Missionizing and Jewish Response*. Berkeley: University of California Press, 1989.

Chenu, Marie-Dominique. *Aquinas and His Role in Theology*. Illustrated ed. Collegeville, MN: Liturgical, 2002.

———. "La Théologie De La Loi Ancienne Selon Saint Thomas." *Revue Thomiste* 16 (1961) 485–97.

Bibliography

———. "The Old Testament in Twelfth-Century Theology." In *Nature, Man, and Society in the Twelfth Century: Essays on New Theological Perspectives in the Latin West*, edited by Jerome Taylor and Lester K. Little, 146–61. Chicago: University Of Chicago Press, 1997.

Childs, Brevard S. *Biblical Theology of the Old and New Testaments: Theological Reflection on the Christian Bible*. Minneapolis: Augsburg Fortress, 1993.

Cohen, Jeremy. *Christ Killers: The Jews and the Passion from the Bible to the Big Screen*. Oxford: Oxford University Press, 2007.

———. *The Friars and the Jews: Evolution of Medieval Anti-Judaism*. New York: Cornell University Press, 1984.

———. *Living Letters of the Law: Ideas of the Jew in Medieval Christianity*. Berkeley: University of California Press, 1999.

Connelly, John. *From Enemy to Brother: The Revolution in Catholic Teaching on the Jews, 1933–1965*. Cambridge: Harvard University Press, 2012.

Coolman, Holly Taylor. "Christological Torah." *Studies in Christian-Jewish Relations* 5, no. 1 (2010): 1–12.

Croner, Helga B. *More Stepping Stones to Jewish-Christian Relations: An Unabridged Collection of Christian Documents, 1975–1983*. New York: Paulist, 1985.

———. *Stepping Stones to Further Jewish-Christian Relations*. No loc: Stimulus, 1977.

Cuellar, Miguel Ponce. *La Naturaleza De La Iglesia Segun Santo Tomas: Estudio Del Tema En El Comentario Al "Corpus Paulinum."* Coleccion Teologica. Navarra, Spain: Ediciones Universidad de Navarra, 1979.

Dales, C. Richard, and Edward B. King. *Robert Grosseteste: De Cessatione Legalium*. London: Oxford University Press, 1986.

Dalin, David G., and Matthew Levering, eds. *John Paul II and the Jewish People: A Jewish-Christian Dialogue*. Lanham, MD: Rowman & Littlefield, 2008.

Daly, Mary. "The Notion of Justification in the Commentary of St. Thomas Aquinas on the Epistle to the Romans." South Bend, IN: University of Notre Dame, 1971.

Dauphinais, Michael, and Matthew Levering. *Reading John with St. Thomas Aquinas: Theological Exegesis and Speculative Theology*. Reprint. Washington, DC: Catholic University of America Press, 2010.

Davies, Brian. *The Thought of Thomas Aquinas*. Oxford: Oxford University Press, 1993.

Deferrari, Roy J. *A Latin-English Dictionary of St. Thomas Aquinas, Based on The Summa Theologica and Selected Passages of His Other Writings*. Boston: St. Paul Editions, 1986.

———. *A Lexicon of St. Thomas Aquinas Based on the Summa Theologica and Selected Passages of His Other Works*. Washington, DC: Catholic University of America Press, 1948.

Denifle, Heinrich. "Quel livre servait de base à l'enseignement des maîtres en théologie dans l'Université de Paris?" *Revue Thomiste* 2 (1984) 129–61.

Deploige, S. S. *Thomas Et La Question Juive*. Paris: Libraire B. Bloud, 1897.

Di Noia, Joseph. "Christ Brings Freedom from Sin and Death: The Commentary of St. Thomas Aquinas on Romans 5:12–21." In *Saint Thomas's Interpretation on Saint Paul's Doctrines*, 60–75. Proceedings of the IX Plenary Session. Vatican City: The Pontifical Academy of St. Thomas Aquinas, 2009.

Diprose, Ronald E. *Israel in the Development of Christian Thought*. Rome: Istituto Biblico Evangelico Italiano, 2003.

Bibliography

Donaldson, Terence L. "Supersessionism in Early Christianity." Paper presented as the Presidential Address at the Canadian Society of Biblical Studies Annual Meeting, Carleton University, Ottawa, Ontario, 2009.

Dubois, Marcel-Jacques. "Thomas Aquinas on the Place of the Jews in the Divine Plan." *Immanuel* 24–25 (1990) 241–66.

Elders, Leo. *Saint Thomas's Interpretation on Saint Paul's Doctrines*. Proceedings of the IX Plenary Session. Vatican City: The Pontifical Academy of St. Thomas Aquinas, 2009.

Englund, Steven, John D. Levenson, Donald Senior, and John Connelly. "Getting Past Supersessionism." *Commonweal* 141, no. 4 (February 21, 2014): 13–26.

Farmer, William R. *Anti-Judaism and the Gospels*. 1st ed. Valley Forge, PA: Trinity, 1999.

Fisher, Eugene. "The Evolution of a Tradition: From Nostra Aetate to the 'Notes.'" In *Fifteen Years of Catholic-Jewish Dialogue 1970–1985: Selected Papers*, 241–54. Rome: Libreria editrice vaticana, 1988.

Fowl, Stephen E., ed. "Selections from Thomas Aquinas's Commentary on Romans." In *The Theological Interpretation of Scripture: Classic and Contemporary Readings*, 320–37. Blackwell Readings in Modern Theology. Cambridge, MA: Blackwell, 1997.

———. *The Theological Interpretation of Scripture: Classic and Contemporary Readings*. 1st ed. Oxford: Wiley-Blackwell, 1997.

———. "Thomas Aquinas and the Multifaceted Literal Sense of Scripture." Paper presented at the SBL Annual Meeting, Christian Theology and the Bible Section: The Literal Sense of Scripture according to Various Interpreters, Chicago, November 17, 2012.

Fredriksen, Paula. *Augustine and the Jews: A Christian Defense of Jews and Judaism*. New York: Doubleday, 2008.

———. "The Birth of Christianity and the Origins of Christian Anti-Judaism." In *Jesus, Judaism, and Christian Anti-Judaism: Reading the New Testament After the Holocaust*, edited by Paula Fredriksen and Adele Reinhartz, 8–30. Louisville, KY: Westminster John Knox, 2002.

Friedman, Lee M. *Robert Grosseteste and the Jews*. Cambridge: Harvard University Press, 1934.

Frymer-Kensky, Tikva, et al., eds. *Christianity In Jewish Terms*. New York: Basic, 2002.

Gager, John G. *The Origins of Anti-Semitism: Attitudes toward Judaism in Pagan and Christian Antiquity*. New York: Oxford University Press, 1985.

Gayraud, H. "L'antisemitisme De S. Thomas d'Aquin." Paris: n.p., 1896.

Gorday, Peter J. "Jews and Gentiles, Galatians 2:11–14, and Reading Israel in Romans: The Patristic Debate." In *Engaging Augustine on Romans: Self, Context, and Theology in Interpretation*, edited by Daniel Patte and Eugene TeSelle, 199–236. New York: Continuum, 2002.

Grosseteste, Robert. *De Cessatione Legalium*. Edited by Richard C. Dales and Edward B. King. London: Published for the British Academy by the Oxford University Press, 1986.

Guttmann, Jacob. "Das Verhältnis Des Thomas Von Aquino Zum Judenthum Und Zur Judischen Litteratur." In *Collected Papers of Jacob Guttmann: An Original Anthology*, edited by Steven T. Katz, 13–60. New York: Arno, 1980.

Hall, Pamela M. *Narrative and the Natural Law: An Interpretation of Thomistic Ethics*. South Bend, IN: University of Notre Dame Press, 1999.

———. "The Old Law and the New Law." In *The Ethics of Aquinas*, edited by Stephen J. Pope, 194–206. Washington, DC: Georgetown University Press, 2002.

Bibliography

Hann, Robert R. "Supersessionism, Engraftment, and Jewish-Christian Dialogue: Reflections on the Presbyterian Statement on Jewish-Christian Relations." *Journal of Ecumencial Studies* 27 (1990) 327–42.

Harink, Douglas. *Paul among the Postliberals: Pauline Theology beyond Christendom and Modernity*. Grand Rapids: Brazos, 2003.

Healy, Nicholas M. *Thomas Aquinas: Theologian of the Christian Life*. Aldershot, UK: Ashgate, 2003.

Hibbs, Thomas. "Divine Irony and the Natural Law: Speculation and Edification in Aquinas." *International Philosophical Quarterly* 30 (1990) 419–29.

Hofer, Andrew. "The Circumcision of the Lord: Saving Mystery." STL thesis, Pontifical Faculty of the Immaculate Conception of the Dominican House of Studies, Washington, DC, 2003.

———. "The Circumcision of the Lord: Saving Mystery After Modern Oblivion." *Nova Et Vetera* 3.2 (2005) 259–78.

Hood, John Y. B. *Aquinas and the Jews*. Philadelphia: University of Pennsylvania Press, 1995.

Hütter, Reinhard. "In Hope He Believed against Hope (Romans 4:18). Faith and Hope, Two Pauline Motifs as Interpreted by Aquinas: An Approach to the Encyclial Letter of Pope Benedict XVI, *Spe Salvi*." In *Saint Thomas's Interpretation on Saint Paul's Doctrines*, 39–59. Proceedings of the IX Plenary Session. Vatican City: The Pontifical Academy of St. Thomas Aquinas, 2009.

Isaac, Jules. *Has Anti-Semitism Roots in Christianity?* Translated by Parkes Dorothy and Parkes James. 1st ed. New York: National Conference of Christians and Jews, 1962.

———. *Jesus and Israel*. New York: Holt, Rinehart and Winston, 1971.

———. *Jésus et Israël*. Paris: Michel, 1948.

———. *L'enseignement du mépris*. Paris: Fasquelle, 1962.

———. *The Teaching of Contempt: Christian Roots of Anti-Semitism*. Translated by Weaver Helen. 1st ed. New York: Holt, Rinehart and Winston, 1964.

Jenson, Robert W. "Toward a Christian Theology of Judaism." In *Jews and Christians: People of God*, edited by Carl E. Braaten and Robert W. Jenson, 1–13. Grand Rapids: Eerdmans, 2003.

John Paul II and the Jewish People: A Jewish-Christian Dialogue. Lanham, MD: Rowman & Littlefield, 2008.

Kant, Immanuel. *Religion within the Boundaries of Mere Reason*. Cambridge: Cambridge University Press, 1999.

Keating, Daniel A. "1 and 2 Corinthians: The Sacraments and their Ministers." In *Aquinas on Scripture: An Introduction to His Biblical Commentaries*, edited by John Yocum and Daniel Keating, 126–36. London: T. & T. Clark, 2005

Kerr, Fergus. "Thomas Aquinas." In *The Medieval Theologians: An Introduction to Theology in the Medieval Period*, edited by G. R. Evans, 201–20. 1st ed. Oxford: Wiley-Blackwell, 2001.

———. *Thomas Aquinas: A Very Short Introduction*. 1st ed. Oxford: Oxford University Press, 2009.

Kessler, Edward, and Neil Wenborn. *A Dictionary of Jewish-Christian Relations*. Cambridge: Cambridge University Press, 2008.

Kinzer, Mark S. *Postmissionary Messianic Judaism: Redefining Christian Engagement with the Jewish People*. Grand Rapids: Brazos, 2005.

Bibliography

Koch, Cardinal Kurt. "Building on Nostra Aetate: 50 Years of Christian-Jewish Dialogue." John Paul II Center for Interreligious Dialogue, Angelicum University, Rome, May 2012. Online: http://jcrelations.net/Building_on__Nostra_Aetate.3813.0.html?L=0.

Knasas, John F. X. "Aquinas on Heretics and 'Jews.'" *Soter: Religijos Mokslo Zurnalas* 14.42 (2004) 165–74.

Levering, Matthew. "Aquinas." In *The Blackwell Companion to Paul*, edited by Stephen Westerholm, 361–74. Oxford: Wiley-Blackwell, 2011.

———. *Christ's Fulfillment of Torah and Temple: Salvation according to Thomas Aquinas.* South Bend, IN: University of Notre Dame Press, 2002.

———. *Jewish-Christian Dialogue and the Life of Wisdom: Engagements with the Theology of David Novak.* New York: Continuum, 2010.

———. "Ordering Wisdom: Aquinas, the Old Testament, and Sacra Doctrina." In *Ressourcement Thomism: Sacred Doctrine, the Sacraments, and the Moral Life: Essays in Honor of Romanus Cessario, O.P.*, edited by Reinhard Hütter and Matthew Levering, 80–91. Washington, DC: Catholic University of America Press, 2010.

———. *Scripture and Metaphysics: Aquinas and the Renewal of Trinitarian Theology.* Oxford: Wiley-Blackwell, 2004.

Liebeschutz, Hanz. "Judaism and Jewry in the Social Doctrine of Thomas Aquinas." *Journal of Jewish Studies* 13 (1961) 57–81.

Lindbeck, George. "The Story-Shaped Church: Critical Exegesis and Theological Interpretation." In *Scriptural Authority and Narrative Interpretation*, edited by Garrett Green, 161–78. Reprint. Eugene, OR: Wipf & Stock, 2001.

Littell, Franklin H. *The Crucifixion of the Jews.* Macon, GA: Mercer University Press, 2000.

Lubac, Henri de. *Medieval Exegesis: The Four Senses of Scripture*: Vols. 1–3. Grand Rapids: Eerdmans, 1998.

Mailloux, B. S. *Thomas Et Les Juifs.* Montreal: l'Oeuvre de Presse Dominicaine, 1935.

Marshall, Bruce. "Christ and the Cultures: The Jewish People and Christian Theology." In *The Cambridge Companion to Christian Doctrine*, edited by Colin E. Gunton, 81–100. Cambridge: Cambridge University Press, 1997.

———. "Elder Brothers: John Paul II's Teaching on the Jewish People as a Question to the Church." In *John Paul II and the Jewish People: A Christian-Jewish Dialogue*, edited by Dalin David and Matthew Levering, 113–29. New York: Rowman & Littlefield, 2007.

———. "Postscript and Prospect." *Nova Et Vetera* 7.2 (2009) 523–24.

———. "*Quasi in Figura*: A Brief Reflection on Jewish Election, after Thomas Aquinas." *Nova Et Vetera* 7.2 (2009) 523–28.

Moyaert, M., and D. Pollefeyt. "Israel and the Church: Fulfillment beyond Supersessionism." In *Never Revoked: Nostra Aetate as Ongoing Challenge for Jewish-Christian Dialogue*, edited by M. Moyaert and D. Pollefeyt, 165–75. Leuven: Peeters, 2010.

Nanos, Mark D. *The Irony of Galatians: Paul's Letter in First-Century Context.* Minneapolis: Fortress, 2002.

———. "Peter's Hypocrisy (Gal. 2:11–21) in the Light of Paul's Anxiety (Rom. 7)." In *The Mystery of Romans: The Jewish Context of Paul's Letters*, 337–71. Minneapolis: Fortress, 1996.

Neuhaus, Richard John. *American Babylon: Notes of a Christian Exile.* New York: Basic, 2009.

Neusner, Jacob. *Judaism: The Basics.* London: Routledge, 2006.

Novak, David. *Talking with Christians: Musings of a Jewish Theologian.* Grand Rapids: Eerdmans, 2005.

Bibliography

Ochs, Peter. *Another Reformation: Postliberal Christianity and the Jews*. Grand Rapids: Baker Academic, 2011.

Oesterreicher, John M., ed. *The New Encounter: Between Christians and Jews*. New York: Philosophical Library, 1986.

Paterson, Craig, and Matthew S. Pugh. *Analytical Thomism: Traditions in Dialogue*. Farnham, UK: Ashgate, 2006.

Pawlikowski, John T. "Antisemitism." In *A Dictionary of Jewish-Christian Relations*, edited by Edward Kessler and Neil Wenborn, 22. Cambridge: Cambridge University Press, 2008

Perrier, Emmanuel. "The Election of Israel Today: Supersessionism, Post-supersessionism, and Fulfillment." *Nova Et Vetera* 7.2 (2009) 485–503.

Persson, Per Erik. *Sacra Doctrina: Reason and Revelation in Aquinas*. Philadelphia: Fortress, 1970.

Pesch, Otto Hermann. "Paul as Professor of Theology: The Image of the Apostle in St. Thomas's Theology." *The Thomist* 38 (1974) 584–605.

Plant, Stephen. "Jules Isaac." In *A Dictionary of Jewish-Christian Relations*, edited by Edward Kessler and Neil Wenborn, 214. New York: Cambridge University Press, 2008.

Rogers, Eugene F. *Thomas Aquinas and Karl Barth: Sacred Doctrine and the Natural Knowledge of God*. South Bend, IN: University of Notre Dame Press, 1999.

Robberechts, Edouard. "Introduction to the Life and Work of Jules Isaac." Presentation at the International Conference of the International Council of Christians and Jews and the Interuniversity Institute of Jewish Studies & Culture, Aix-en-Provence, June 30, 2013. Online: http://www.iccj.org/redaktion/upload_pdf/201307121332010.Sunday-Opening-Edouard-Robberechts.pdf.

Ruether, Rosemary Radford. *Faith and Fratricide*. Reprint. Eugene, OR: Wipf & Stock, 1996.

Ryan, Thomas. "The Love of Learning and the Desire for God in Thomas Aquinas's Commentary on Romans." In *Medieval Readings of Romans*, edited by William S. Campbell et al., 110–14. London: T. & T. Clark, 2007.

Sandmel, Samuel. *Anti-Semitism in the New Testament?* Minneapolis: Fortress, 1978.

Schenk, Richard. "Covenant Initiation: Thomas Aquinas and Robert Kilwardby on the Sacrament of Circumcision." In *Ordo Sapientiae Et Amoris: Image Et Message De Saint Thomas d'Aquin À Travers Les Récentes Études Historiques, Herméneutiques Et Doctrinales: Hommage Au Professeur Jean-Pierre Torrell OP À L'occasion De Son 65e Anniversaire*, edited by Carlos-Josaphat Pinto de Oliveira, 555–93. Fribourg, Switzerland: Editions universitaires, 1993.

———. "Views of the Two Covenants in Medieval Theology." *Nova Et Vetera* 4.4 (2006) 891–916.

Sherman, Franklin, ed. *Bridges—Documents of the Christian-Jewish Dialogue: Vol 1—The Road to Reconciliation*. Mahwah, NJ: Paulist, 2011.

Siker, Jeffrey S. *Disinheriting the Jews: Abraham in Early Christian Controversy*. Louisville, KY: Westminster John Knox, 1991.

Smalley, Beryl. *The Gospels in the Schools, c. 1100—c. 1280*. London: Hambledon, 1985.

———. *The Study of the Bible in the Middle Ages*. South Bend, IN: University of Notre Dame Press, 1964.

———. "William of Auvergne, John of La Rochelle and St. Thomas Aquinas on the Old Law." In *Studies in Medieval Thought and Learning from Abelard to Wyclif*, 11–71. London: Hambledon, 1981.

Smiga, George M. *Pain and Polemic: Anti-Judaism in the Gospels*. Mahwah, NJ: Paulist, 1992.

Soulen, R. Kendall. *The God of Israel and Christian Theology*. Minneapolis: Fortress, 1996.

———. "Israel and the Church." In *Christianity in Jewish Terms*, edited by Tikva Frymer-Kensky et al., 167–74. Boulder, CO: Basic, 2002.

———. "Replacement Theology." In *A Dictionary of Jewish-Christian Relations*, edited by Edward Kessler and Neil Wenborn, 375. Cambridge: Cambridge University Press, 2008.

———. "Supersessionism." In *A Dictionary of Jewish-Christian Relations*, edited by Edward Kessler and Neil Wenborn, 413–14. Cambridge: Cambridge University Press, 2008.

———. "'They Are Israelites': The Priority of the Present Tense for Jewish-Christian Relations." In *Between Gospel and Election: Explorations in the Interpretation of Romans 9–11*, edited by Florian Wilk, 1–8. Tübingen: Mohr Siebeck, 2010.

Spicq, Ceslas, "Saint Thomas d'Aquin Exegete." In *Dictionnaire de Theologie Catholique*, vol. 15, edited by A. Vacant, E. Mangenot and E. Amann, col. 694–738. Paris: Libraire Letouzey et Ane, 1946.

Stothert, R. *Reply to Faustus the Manichaean*. Nicene and Post-Nicene Fathers, 155–345. Series I. Vol. 4 Grand Rapids: Eerdmans, 1974.

Stump, Eleonore. "Biblical Commentary and Philosophy." In *The Cambridge Companion to Aquinas*, edited by Norman Kretzmann and Eleonore Stump, 252–68. Cambridge: Cambridge University Press, 1993.

Swierzawski, Waclaw. "Faith and Worship in the Pauline Commentaries of St. Thomas Aquinas." *Divus Thomas* 75 (1972) 389–412.

———. "God and the Mystery of His Wisdom in the Pauline Commentaries of St. Thomas Aquinas." *Divus Thomas* 74 (1971) 466–500.

Synan, Edward. "Some Medieval Perceptions of the Controversy on Jewish Law." In *Understanding Scripture: Explorations of Jewish and Christian Traditions of Interpretation*, edited by Michael Wyschogrod and Clemens Thoma, 102–24. Mahwah, NJ: Paulist, 1987.

Torrell, Jean-Pierre. *Aquinas's Summa: Background, Structure, and Reception*. Washington, DC: Catholic University of America Press, 2005.

———. "Ecclesia Iudaeorum—Quelques Jugements Positifs De Saint Thomas d'Aquin à L'égard Des Juifs Et Du Judaism." In *Les Philosophies Morales Et Politiques Au Moyen Âge*, vol. 3, edited by B. Carlos Bazán et al., 3:1732–41. Ottawa: Legas, 1995.

———. *Saint Thomas Aquinas, Vol. 1. The Person and His Work*. Revised. Washington, DC: Catholic University of America Press, 2005.

Torrell, Jean-Pierre, and D. Bouthillier. "Quand Saint Thomas Méditait Sur Le Prophète Isaïe." *Revue Thomiste* 90 (1990) 5–47.

Tugwell, Simon. *Albert and Thomas: Selected Writings*. Mahwah, NJ: Paulist, 1988.

Valkenberg, Pim, and Henk Schoot. "Thomas Aquinas and Judaism." In *Aquinas in Dialogue: Thomas for the Twenty-First Century*, edited by Jim Fodor and Frederick Christian Bauerschmidt, 47–66. Oxford: Wiley-Blackwell, 2004.

Bibliography

Valkenberg, Wilhelmus G. B. M. *Words of the Living God: Place and Function of Holy Scripture in the Theology of St. Thomas Aquinas*. Thomas Instituut Te Utrecht. Leuven: Peeters, 2000.

Van der Ploeg, J. "The Place of Holy Scripture in the Theology of St. Thomas." *The Thomist* 10 (1947) 398–422.

Verbeke, G., and D. Verhelst. *Aquinas and Problems of His Time*. Leuven: Leuven University Press, 1976.

Vlach, Michael. *The Church as a Replacement of Israel*. New York: Lang, 2009.

Wawrykow, Joseph, and Thomas Prügl. "Thomas Aquinas as Interpreter of Scripture." In *The Theology Of Thomas Aquinas*, edited by Rik Van Nieuwenhove, 386–415. South Bend, IN: University of Notre Dame Press, 2005.

Weigel, George. *Witness to Hope: The Biography of Pope John Paul II*. New York: Harper Perennial, 2005.

Weisheipl, James A. *Friar Thomas D'Aquino: His Life, Thought, and Work*. 1st ed. New York: Doubleday, 1974.

Westerholm, Stephen, ed. *The Blackwell Companion to Paul*. Oxford: Wiley-Blackwell, 2011.

White, Carolinne. *The Correspondence (394–419), between Jerome and Augustine of Hippo*. Lewiston, NY: Mellen, 1990.

Williams, A. Lukyn. *Adversus Judaeos: A Bird's-Eye View of Christian Apologiae until the Renaissance*. Cambridge: Cambridge University Press, 2012.

Williamson, Clark M. *A Guest in the House of Israel: Post-Holocaust Church Theology*. Louisville, KY: Presbyterian Publishing Corporation, 1993.

Wilson, Stephen G. *Anti-Judaism in Early Christianity*. Waterloo, Ontario: Wilfrid Laurier University Press, 1986.

Woodward, Michael Scott, trans. *The Glossa Ordinaria on Romans*. Kalamazoo, MI: Western Michigan University Press, 2011.

Wyschogrod, Michael. "A Jewish Reading of St. Thomas Aquinas." In *Understanding Scripture: Explorations of Jewish and Christian Traditions of Interpretation*, edited by Clemens Thoma and Michael Wyschogrod, 125–40. Mahwah, NJ: Paulist, 1987.

———. *The Body of Faith: God and the People Israel*. New York: Rowman & Littlefield, 2000.

———. "Response to the Respondents." *Modern Theology* 11.2 (1995) 229–41.

Wyschogrod, Michael, and R. Kendall Soulen. *Abraham's Promise: Judaism and Jewish-Christian Relations*. Grand Rapids: Eerdmans, 2004.

Yocum, John P., and Daniel A. Keating. *Aquinas on Scripture: An Introduction to His Biblical Commentaries*. London: T. & T. Clark, 2005.

Yoder, John Howard. *Jewish-Christian Schism Revisited*. Edited by Michael G. Cartwright and Peter Ochs. Harrisonburg, VA: Herald, 2008.

www.ingramcontent.com/pod-product-compliance
Lightning Source LLC
Chambersburg PA
CBHW070325230426
43663CB00011B/2218